WHATSHISNAME

The Life and Death of Charles Hawtrey

By
Wes Butters

First published in 2010 by
Tomahawk Press
PO Box 1236
Sheffield S11 7XU
England

www.tomahawkpress.com

ISBN 13: 978-0-9557670-7-4

Proofread by Kenneth Bishton - kenbishton@talktalk.net

Edited by Bruce Sachs

Designed by Tree Frog Communication 01245 445377

Printed in the EU by Gutenberg Press Limited

For Maisie
In my life I love you more

CONTENTS

Acknowledgments .... vi–ix
Prologue .... x–xvi
Cast of Characters .... xvii–xxi

1. The Death of Charles Hawtrey 23–44
2. A Star is Born 45–60
3. Conti's 61–73
4. Hero Worship 74–86
5. The Makeup Behind the Mask 87–101
6. Desperate Times 102–128
7. On the Up 129–146
8. Carry On Charlie 147–168
9. Death in Hounslow 169–195
10. Drink! Drink! Drink! 196–215
11. The Deal Years 216–236
12. Heaven Knows I'm Miserable Now 237–244

Afterword by Peter Rogers (1914–2009) 245

Appendices:
Notes 248–257
Theatre 258–260
Filmography 260–278
TV and Radio 279–287
Bibliography 288–290

Joy Leonard, Hawtrey's closest female friend, unveils his blue commemorative plaque on 117 Middle Street, Deal, 1998.

ACKNOWLEDGMENTS

This book is the result of a naïve idea by an 18-year-old university student. Faced with a summer break of six months he decided to write a book, thinking it would fill the gap nicely. Now, having turned 30, he can freely admit his initial estimate was ever so slightly out.

Over the years, wherever I've ended up with my radio work, I've moved with me the box of notes and taped interviews which I collated that August back in 1997. The plan was always one day to write that book. Then, just last year, on a roll after completing *Kenneth Williams Unseen*, I dragged it down from the attic and finally got cracking.

With this biography, because it has taken so long, it's difficult to know whom to thank first. I shall begin, therefore, by thanking the one constant character, Charles Hawtrey. As with most biographers, I like to imagine my subject's guiding presence throughout the writing process. I've met Hawtrey's friends and family, held his personal possessions and looked at his private photographs. I've dreamt about him, drank in his local pubs and stood in his house. I've felt and, to some extent, lived his inner turmoil myself (when we know so strongly what we want from life, we can only be left disappointed: it never goes to plan). Everyone interviewed for this book knew him, which made me the odd one out. I sometimes wish we could have met but am reminded of Perry Como, shortly before his death, meeting a lifelong fan who asked his hero what he remembered about recording his early songs. "I don't remember anything. Fuck off," the legendary crooner is said to have croaked.

Joy Leonard, Aubrey Phillips and Bernard Walsh, his closest friends, had for years resisted interviews. They put their trust in me and broke their silence. I shall never forget their friendship, especially with Joy. Her recent sudden death upset me greatly and I was exceptionally proud to play a part at her funeral. She will be missed.

I am indebted to Louise Dillon and Catrina Margette, whose collection of interviews for their proposed biography was graciously donated. Patrick Newley was forever on hand to paint a picture of the times, as was Steve

Taylor, who gave me invaluable information relating to Hawtrey's mother and family background. So did Hawtrey's remaining relations, John and Maureen Hartree, and Carole Ellison.

In his respective hometowns, Hounslow and Deal, I found masses of material and welcoming assistance. Eddie Menday, Hounslow's local historian, helped me track down Hawtrey's childhood friends Joan Hanson, Sid Filbrey, Violet Humphries and Doris Pocock. In hindsight, I am amazed at my teenage fearlessness, approaching complete strangers in the Deal streets and shops, which secured many off-the-cuff interviews during my original pilgrimage in '97: Elizabeth Bainbridge, Barry Bullock, Chris Burrows, Chris Clear, Nancy Dawson, Ray Dennis, Marcus Gidman, Marlene Hargrave, Basil Kidd, Fire Fighter Knight, Bryn Hawkins, David Reid, Dennis Senior, Peter and Barbara Stephens, Lucy Windsor and Joan Woodley.

I am extremely grateful to Evelyn Griffiths, for an enjoyable day spent listening to her gramophone recordings with Hawtrey, and Denis Wright. I thank Peter Byrne and Cynthia Hayes, both generous and kindly hosts, for their memories of Conti's, while Peggy Cummins gave a unique account of her time working for Hawtrey at the Q Theatre. His early professional life was also coloured by Brad Ashton, Francis Matthews, Frank Williams and Ernest Maxin, followed by *Carry On*ers Richard O'Callaghan and Barbara Windsor, the late Peter Rogers, his assistant Audrey Skinner, and scriptwriter Norman Hudis (all providing new information on the somewhat saturated topic of *Carry On*). It was interesting, if not sad, to hear anecdotes told by Ronnè Coyles, Paul Denver, Dave Peters and Spencer K. Gibbons, relating to Hawtrey's later work in the theatre, and Martin Jenkins' description of his last radio shows. On the other hand, my conversations and iPhone exchanges with Don Boyd, regarding his last film made around the same time, painted him in a much different, happier light. Lastly, without Peter Willis and his remarkably vivid account, there would be no insight into Hawtrey's bleak and ill-attended funeral.

I have used extensive material held by the BBC's Written Archive at Caversham (Charles Hawtrey RCONT files), Granada Television in Manchester, and the Raymond Mander and Joe Mitchenson Theatre Collection, London. Special thanks, therefore, go to those organisations and in particular Louise North and James Codd, Adrian Figgess, and Richard Mangan. I am pleased to acknowledge Richard Dyer, who has allowed me to quote from his work, the British Film Institute (including Dave McCall, the man who discovered the picture of Hawtrey and Errol Flynn), Sue Briggs and Beth Easton at the East Kent Mercury, Mike Brewis of South West Film and Television Archive, and Guy Marshall and Guy Bedminster at Hounslow Library Local Studies.

To Ronald Grant and Martin Humphries of the Cinema Museum, London, I repay their eleventh hour contributions by donating Hawtrey's personal possessions. For use of their personal archives, I am fraternally yours Robert Cope, Steve Ellison, Kevin Langford, Nick Lewis, Graham Rinaldi and David Wyatt. Alan Coles deserves a special mention and a few Drambuies in The Ship Inn for sending me umpteen DVDs and many of the rare photographs you now own in this book. For her reassuring help and support, love and thanks must go to Letitia Cowan. And, at Tomahawk Press, I would like to salute proof reader Ken Bishton, designer Steve Kirkham and publisher Bruce Sachs.

Finally, I refer to my subject simply as Hawtrey. While this may read odd to some readers, it was a conscious decision; formality and respect is what he always wanted.

Wes Butters
The Royal Hotel, Deal
February 2010

PROLOGUE

There are a lot of very funny Charlies. Chaplin and Drake, for instance. And, of course, Hawtrey. Charles Hawtrey? I don't blame you for asking. For Charlie is, I suppose, one of the most famous Mr What's-his-names in British films. On Sunday afternoon, viewers can see him as one of Will Hay's pupils in **Good Morning Boys***. Later, somewhere, somebody will probably say: "Very funny movie. They had old, er, you know … the bloke in the* **Carry Ons***." And somebody else will click his fingers and say: "Yeah, I know who you mean. The one who used to be in* **The Army Game***? He's been about, hasn't he?" Indeed he has …*

The Sun, 16 August 1972

Holidaying families fill the auditorium. Just £1.50 has bought them a ticket to see a legendary funny man in the flesh. It's May 1976, the height of spring, but they're about to watch a pantomime. It's the Wyvern Theatre, Swindon, but it feels like the opening night of a huge West End show. As the lights dim, the stage manager presses 'play' on the cassette machine and a hissy muzak recording of 'Over the Rainbow' blasts out of the speaker system. It's actually a production of *Snow White and the Seven Dwarfs* but, thanks to cunning copyright dodges like this, the entire budget is no more than £500. Half of that has gone to the star. The rustling of sweet wrappers and excited murmurs continue through the opening number. He'll appear at any moment, utter his catchphrase and make them all laugh, just as he has done in countless *Carry On* films. The mums and dads will laugh at his double entendres, nudging each other and exchanging looks, whilst the kids will not understand what's making their parents laugh so much; he's funny looking and says funny things but the smut will evade their innocent minds. Finally the moment arrives: "Where's Muddles?" asks Martha, the dame. From stage right he enters. The place erupts with laughter and applause. It's really him! He looks older, somewhat paler and dishevelled than in the films, but it's him! He walks towards Martha and Snow White, his steps purposeful and determined, yet at the same time slightly wobbly and hesitant. The adulation simmers as the expectation begins to boil. They know what's coming. Just two words and they can laugh again. On the stage it's a different story. White moves a few steps stage left. Martha holds his breath. The waft of stale booze and Listerine has turned the atmosphere musty and the embarrassment that will follow is enough to break character. In the event, the stage manager is poised to press 'play' again. "Oh, hell-ooo!" The catchphrase is delivered to rapturous applause and hoots of laughter. Upon its dying down, Martha takes his cue: "Oh, Muddles! What's going to happen?" Silence. Muddles is looking into the bright white of the spotlight. He can't see the audience, but he can hear them, laughing. "Oh, hell-oooo!" White interjects: "Muddles, do you know what's going to happen?" Pointless. Laughter is what he wants. He knows he can flick it on by simply saying "Oh, hello". So he says it again. This time, the sound isn't as loud. In fact, the giggles are turning into mumbles. It doesn't make sense. "Oh, hell-oooooo!" he shouts, desperately. Martha gives a wink backstage and grabs one arm: "Oh come on, Muddles! Let's go and find the wicked witch!" The pause button is lifted and the spools in the cassette tape begin to turn.[1]

It was clear to anyone who knew him at this point, in the mid-seventies, that even though he was breathing, Charles Hawtrey had been dead for years.

Before his stage entrances suggested something was amiss, audiences anticipated his presence like they would one of the world's most famous movie stars, which, in his own peculiar way, he was. Thanks to those *Carry On* films his face was recognisable from Los Angeles[2] to Luton, Adelaide to Amsterdam. He was as far from Brando as his character Pint-Pot was to Don Vito Corleone. Yet he was, and remains, one of the cinema's greatest icons.

When, in November 1998, I organised the unveiling of a blue commemorative plaque on the front of his final home, I had the foresight to break from tradition and insist the design include a photograph of his face. It seemed the obvious thing to do in his case: "Charles Hawtrey 1914–1988 - Film, Theatre, Radio and Television Actor Lived Here", punctuated above by a publicity still sent to me by the *Carry On* office at Pinewood Studios. I knew I had made the right call when two young boys, cycling up to the house on their BMXs, stopped to see the building's new addition. "Who's that then?" the younger boy asked his friend. "It's that bloke outta the *Carry Ons*, innit?" he said, before they moved off and left me to smile knowingly to myself. If it weren't for the picture the plaque wouldn't have meant anything to them.[3]

Nameless or not, the public's love for Hawtrey lives on. His influence is felt in every camp and weedy character in film and television. And, though his life and work have been timidly examined in lectures, documentaries and, to this point, a slim 93-page biography, all have done little to shed light on his prolific work and achievements, keeping instead to the well-known topics of Will Hay, *Carry On*, Alcohol and Death (in that order).

It's Hawtrey's fault, of course. By the end of his life he'd become such a "sad pain in the arse"[4] that the acting establishment wanted to sweep his remains under the thickest shag pile carpet. Interviews were denied, letters to agents went unanswered, or their replies were negatively blunt (Liz Fraser: "I know of your proposed biography, but I do not want to talk about him"). This unanimous reaction may have led other biographers to think it was a dead end but, to me, it raised more questions. Just what had Hawtrey done to anger so many people? Why was his life story so neglected, when each of his contemporaries had enjoyed the releases of biographies and autobiographies?

Throughout the coming decade the jigsaw of his life was assembled with pieces acquired from all corners of the world. Each more intriguing than the last. The consensus had always been that Kenneth Williams was the overall tortured soul of the *Carry On* series, but with this new information that supposition was gradually being proved wrong.

Whereas Williams's turmoil emanated from his suppressed sexuality, it was a failed career, an embarrassing family background and the dependence and sudden death of his mother that scarred Charles Hawtrey's soul to its very core. His *entire* life was jinxed. His *entire* life was ruined — in his own words. For all the comparisons one can make, Hawtrey and Williams were emotionally adverse. Calvinistic Williams purged himself of sexual thoughts and encounters by "scrubbing the walls or cleaning the windows, even if it was three in the morning."[5] Hawtrey, meanwhile, enjoyed indulging in *"flagrante delicto* with a 16-year-old boy" whilst his house burnt down around him.[6] Whilst later in life both loved their mothers and alcohol in equal measure, Williams had more to offer the audience than just his *Carry On* routine of flared nostrils and screams of "Oooh, matron!" Hawtrey wasn't as multi-faceted. When Williams made his way down Great Portland Street to record an erudite performance on Radio 4's *Just a Minute*, Hawtrey was very probably "staggering down Deal High Street, half-cut, swearing at the taxi-drivers and smashing pub windows."[7]

An inebriated Williams was a show-off, loud and brave, not afraid of taking on the intelligentsia with his knowledge of history, the arts and the English language. It wasn't that Hawtrey didn't have the talent; he was obviously suffering from mental illness, as had the maternal side of his family. A lifetime's knocks had helped carve him into a Walter Mitty character, living off the fat of personal triumphs that meant the world to him, but which had never set the real world on fire. In his later years the distinction between real-life and delusion became blurred and lost; he would speak aloud to his dead mother, sometimes arguing with her. He became reclusive, tormented and embittered. He wouldn't eat for days, "sending out taxis to fetch supplies of booze and scraps of food."[8]

Yet when the time came to call it a day, Kenneth Williams hurriedly penned his final diary entry and necked a handful of barbiturates, while Hawtrey chose to see through his much slower suicide, which, again, throws up more questions. How had the man who played the "chuckling and happy" Charlie Muggins – my own favourite character – in *Carry On Camping*, ended up miserable and alone, wanting to die?[9]

CARRY ON CAMPING

8   INT.   THE STORE   DAY

The DEPARTMENT MANAGER comes out of an office door at the rear and starts across the showroom. As he approaches one of the tents he comes to a stop. We see that the tent is shaking rather alarmingly, and hear a GIRL's shrill giggle come from inside. Then her protesting voice …

GIRL: No, no, sir, you mustn't do that … no, really …!

More giggling. The MANAGER, a stuffy pompous character, raises his eyebrows and goes nearer.

GIRL: No, no, please, sir! If you keep on doing that you'll … oh!

This as the tent collapses with a rattle of tent poles. The MANAGER glares down at the two figures threshing about under the canvas, then pulls it off them to expose CHARLIE MUGGINS and a rather flustered GIRL ASSISTANT. CHARLIE looks up at the MANAGER, chuckling happily.

CHARLIE: Oh hullo.

MANAGER: Miss Dobbin! What is the meaning of this?

DOBBIN: I'm sorry, Mr. Short, but the gentleman kept fiddling with things.

CHARLIE: That's right. You see, I've been dying to know what it was like inside a tent.

MANAGER: I see. All right, Miss Dobbin, I'll attend to this customer.

The GIRL ASSISTANT scuttles off gratefully.

CHARLIE: Nice girl. She was just telling me how to stick the pole up.

MANAGER: Quite. You're interested in purchasing equipment, sir?

CHARLIE: Oh yes rather. I've been dying to try camping and, as I've never done it before, I thought I'd go to the very best place for advice.

MANAGER: (smugly) Quite so, sir. So you came here.

CHARLIE: Yes. The best place was closed.

MANAGER: (coldly) I can assure you that we can supply absolutely everything essential for a really successful camping holiday.

CHARLIE: Oh good, because I need everything.

MANAGER: Are you going alone, sir?

CHARLIE: Oh yes. Why – do you supply that too? How wonderful!

MANAGER: (sighs) This way please, sir.

And leads CHARLIE off towards his office.

Charles Hawtrey is among the last members of the *Carry On* team to be biographically analysed, but I would argue the most interesting. Moving through the fortieth and fiftieth anniversaries of the *Carry On* films, countless biographies, radio and television documentaries and dramatisations of the lives of Williams, Sid James, Hattie Jacques, and the rest, Hawtrey's been right under our noses all along, untapped and undiscovered. He's so familiar, yet until this moment we knew nothing of his story.

CAST OF CHARACTERS

Brad Ashton (b.1931) A scriptwriter for Dick Emery, Tommy Cooper, and David Frost, he was also Groucho Marx's head writer for a brief time in the mid-60s. He considers his first assignment, Hawtrey's ITV series *Best of Friends*, as "toughening up training that got me through the thirty-odd years of my career that followed."

Don Boyd (b.1948) The Scottish director of *The Princess and the Pea*, a short film that was to be Hawtrey's last. While continuing to champion and produce independent British film, Boyd is now a visiting professor of Film Studies at Exeter University and a Governor of the London Film School

Peter Byrne (b.1928) Having started out at the same stage school, Bryne's career went on to cross paths with Hawtrey's on numerous occasions, culminating in the direction of his final stage role in *Jack and the Beanstalk*, Christmas 1979.

Judy Campbell (1916-2004) Her premiere of the song 'A Nightingale Sang in Berkeley Square', with Hawtrey accompanying on piano, was in the 1940 revue show *New Faces*. Vera Lynn, Nat King Cole and Rod Stewart are among those to have covered it since.

Roy Castle (1932-1994) Playing Captain Keene in *Carry On … Up the Khyber*, the popular entertainer was struck by Hawtrey's idiosyncratic behaviour off the set.

Peggy Cummins (b.1925) A Welsh-born actress Hawtrey had cast in his first theatrical production in 1945. She left for Hollywood soon after, appearing in six films, and garnering added attention for dating billionaire Howard Hughes.

Ronnè Coyles (b.1930) He is still an active pantomime dame, some 42 years after starring with Hawtrey in *Jack and the Beanstalk* at the Victoria Theatre, Salford.

Paul Denver (b.1940) Another performer from the stable of producer Aubrey Phillips, Denver served as Hawtrey's straight-man in *Carry On Holiday Startime*, a summer show at the Gaiety Theatre, Rhyl, in 1970.

Jack Douglas (1927–2008) Douglas's insight into Hawtrey's psyche was rather astute, despite never actually working with him; by the time his *Carry On* roles had progressed from short cameos, Hawtrey had left the series. In all, Douglas appeared in the final eight *Carry On* films, as well as numerous television specials and stage shows.

Richard Dyer (b.1945) Currently the Professor of Film Studies at King's College, London, Dyer was a lecturer at Warwick University when, a year after Hawtrey's death, he celebrated his life at the National Film Theatre, as part of a gay and lesbian cinema retrospective.

Carole Ellison (b.1943) Her step-aunt was Rosina Hartree, Hawtrey's sister-in-law. Although she never met him, Ellison was one of the handful of mourners at his funeral.

Spencer K. Gibbons (b.1952) After winning the TV talent show *New Faces*, he was given the lead role in Peter Byrne's *Jack and the Beanstalk* at the Wyvern Theatre, Swindon. Hawtrey took an immediate dislike to him and Gibbons still regards it as a "totally disappointing" experience.

Marcus Gidman (b.1936) The Station Commander of Deal Fire Station arrived on the scene first when Hawtrey's home went up in flames in 1984.

Evelyn Griffiths (b.1919) In 1930 she won a competition to find Wales' leading child soprano and was sent to London to record a handful of duets with Hawtrey, who represented England. She lives in Bridgend.

John Hartree (b.1935) His father was William John Edwin Hartree, Hawtrey's older brother. He emigrated to Australia with his wife Maureen and was joined in 1971 by his parents.

Cynthia Hayes (b.1916) A child actress, she became a "Conti chick" in 1927 and appeared with Hawtrey in shows including *Where The Rainbow Ends* at the Holborn Empire in 1928, and *A Midsummer's Night Dream* at Drury Lane in 1930.

Roy Hudd OBE (b.1936) To date, courtesy of YouTube, 140,000 people have watched Hudd's interview with an intoxicated Hawtrey on Anglia

Television's *Movie Memories*, directed by John Booker. Below the video the comments left by viewers include: "Charlie, pissed as a lord!" and "Oh! Charles! Bent as a corkscrew, of course. Such a great actor and such a sad end."

Norman Hudis (b.1923) American producers lured Hudis away from Britain after writing the first six *Carry On* films and thirty-nine episodes of *Our House* for ABC Television. He has lived in California ever since, though returns regularly to appear at *Carry On* events.

Martin Jenkins (b.1939) Founding Artistic Director of the Everyman Theatre in Liverpool, he joined the BBC in 1966 and rose to become Chief Producer in Radio Drama. He still produces radio plays for the independent sector and lectures on the American university circuit.

Bryan Johnson (1926-1995) A Shakespearean actor with Sir Donald Wolfit's company before representing Great Britain at the 1960 Eurovision Song Contest, his song, 'Looking High, High, High', came second.

Basil Kidd (1923-2008) A photographer for the East Kent Mercury, it was Kidd's lens that greeted Hawtrey as he was rescued naked from the fire.

Joy Leonard (d.2010) As an entertainer herself, living in Deal, Leonard befriended Hawtrey in the early 1970s. In November 1998 she unveiled a blue plaque at his former home at 117 Middle Street.

Brian Matthew (b.1928) Veteran BBC broadcaster, whose interview with Hawtrey in November 1980 was the only in-depth look at his life, continues to broadcast on BBC Radio 2 in the early Saturday morning slot.

Francis Matthews (b.1927) A frequent face in Hammer horror films, and later the voice of TV's *Captain Scarlet*, Matthews worked with Hawtrey on *The Army Game*'s movie spin-off, *I Only Arsked*, and believes him to have been suffering from "psychological problems".

Ernest Maxin (b.1923) Best known as the man who choreographed and directed the classic *Morecambe and Wise* shows for the BBC. Two of Maxin's earliest television engagements were producing *Our House* and *Best of Friends*, in which Hawtrey starred.

Michael Medwin OBE (b.1923) With Norman Rossington (1928-1999), Medwin played alongside Hawtrey in the Granada Television series *The Army Game* and also turned up in the *Carry On* series.

Peggy Mount OBE (1915-2001) An English actress of stage and screen, primarily cast as a 'battle-axe' or bullish matriarch. On working with Hawtrey at the Palladium in *A Night of A Thousand Stars*, she commented: "His timing was absolutely perfect. [It was] one of my most memorable performances."

Patrick Newley (1955-2009) One time press agent to writers Quentin Crisp and Robert Maugham, Newley secured a sizeable advance for Hawtrey's autobiography, having agreed to help 'ghost write' it. Because of Hawtrey's erratic nature, not a single word was ever written and the project was eventually shelved.

Richard O'Callaghan (b.1940) For nearly two decades his mother, the late actress Patricia Hayes, acted with Hawtrey in *Norman and Henry Bones* on BBC radio's Children's Hour. Eventually, Hawtrey and O'Callaghan worked together in *Carry On Loving* and *Carry On at Your Convenience*.

Aubrey Phillips (b.1933) An actor/producer/manager for over 50 years, his pantomimes continue to play, primarily in the North West of England. Phillips suggests he was quite possibly the closest male friend Hawtrey had: "I mean I had him around my neck for fucking twelve bloody years, knew the man inside out."

Doris Pocock (b.1919) Together with Violet Humphries and Joan Hanson, she was a childhood friend in Hounslow, often invited to his backyard shows. She has the unique distinction of being pictured with Hawtrey in the only surviving candid photograph from this period.

Peter Rogers (1914-2009) Although he produced over one hundred films since 1949, "Mr. Carry On" was happy to accept that his thirty-one part series would be his only significant legacy. Refusing to retire, he continued to work from his office at Pinewood Studios, replying to fan mail and planning for the next *Carry On* movie, until his death at 95.

Joan Sims (1930-2001) A year after embarking on her 19 *Carry On* appearances, all of which coincided with Hawtrey's, the pair featured in the ABC Television series *Our House*. She was the only member of the *Carry On* team with whom Hawtrey would keep in regular contact.

Gerald Thomas (1920-1993) Thomas's partnership with Peter Rogers resulted in the most successful series of comedy films in the history of British cinema. As director of the *Carry On* films, he was able to lay claim to have been the only person present for every shot ever filmed.

Bernard Walsh (d.2010) A 'high-end' estate agent, his weekend retreat in Deal inspired Hawtrey to move to the south coast. Despite his boredom with Hawtrey's drinking, Walsh remained one of his loyal friends, single-handedly organising his private affairs, and deflecting press interest and lucrative offers for his own personal story once Hawtrey had died.

Frank Williams (b.1931) Over a decade before he began playing the Reverend in *Dad's Army*, Williams was Captain Pocket in *The Army Game* and *I Only Arsked!* He can often be spotted dining along the High Street in Edgware, where he has lived for most of his life.

Peter Willis The only journalist savvy enough to discover the location of Hawtrey's top-secret funeral, he has since become the Daily Mirror's Associate Editor.

Barbara Windsor MBE (b.1937) The last surviving regular female member, Windsor has always maintained that Hawtrey was her favourite actor of all the *Carry On* team.

Joan Woodley (b. 1916) Both Woodley and Hawtrey were members of the Children's Hounslow Operatic and Dramatic Society, circa 1926. After the war she recalled spotting him on the tube, learning his lines.

CHAPTER ONE

THE DEATH OF CHARLES HAWTREY

*A chance of "going back to try again" —
such simple words, yet so full of
encouragement and infinite kindness. I
have tried but doubt very much if I have
done any better than before.*[1]

Sir Charles Hawtrey, **The Truth At Last**

It's truly ironic that one of Charles Hawtrey's earliest engagements was in the 1931 production of *Peter Pan*, at the London Palladium. For, although the next 57 years saw him grow old, he, like Pan, always remained a boy. Everything about Hawtrey, physically and mentally, was a throwback to childhood: his Harry Potter style glasses, puny physique, and an intense infatuation with "dear mama".

His was a life built upon such paradoxes, "ruined" by an increasing bewilderment, desperation even, that his many prestigious accomplishments, traversing all areas of the arts, hadn't garnered the kind of reverence he felt destined for. Fleeting acquaintanceships, with Laurence Olivier, Errol Flynn, Charles Laughton and others, only served to measure his own success and reputation within the acting establishment which, to his dismay, were miles apart from theirs. Instead, he found himself belonging to that select group of comics who quite simply *look* funny, with audiences and casting-directors preferring to laugh *at* him, as opposed to laughing *with* him. Eric Morecambe and Tommy Cooper utilised this innate tribute to great effect. Hawtrey resented it.

As Gyles Brandreth surmised of Kenneth Williams, "Because, of course, the great comic-actor wants to be the great serious actor. The grass is always greener."[2] And this difference between comic and comic-actor is where Hawtrey's own frustration began, fuelled by his ever-youthful appearance and a voice that sounded as though it was constantly trying to break.

Back in 1933 he was, proclaimed a crude newspaper advertisement, a "Teacher of Modern Dancing, Winging, Buck and Musical Comedy."[3] Moreover, he could astound observers with his self-taught virtuoso routine called 'The Storm' by simultaneously tap dancing and playing the piano. So when the doctors delivered their verdict in 1988, he will have chosen to recall his fancy footwork rather than any of those "world famous" *Carry On* roles that, in comparison, showcased "bugger all".

"Mr. Hawtrey, we have to amputate your legs or you will die," came the medical bombshell, which should have been half-expected since the last few decades had witnessed a non-stop consumption of cigarettes and alcohol, as well as teenage rent boys and Royal Marines bandsmen from the local barracks. Even a heart attack in 1981, resulting in numerous health complaints, including difficulty with his legs, had done nothing to curb his recklessness.

But the experts' grave recommendation was in vain. At 74 years old, Charles Hawtrey was through carrying on.

"In that case I shall die with my boots on," he retorted, à la Wilde, whilst lighting up a fag and then refusing to discuss the matter further.[4] It had taken an age, but now, at last, the "bespectacled, spindle-shanked, dotty and weedy eccentric"[5] could give a firm two-finger salute to the world that had snubbed his real talents in favour of his typecast alter ego, the one who had to flounce across stage and screen chirping, "Oh, hello!"

No one was interested in his two directorial movie efforts of the 1940s or his impressive array of theatrical productions around London and its West End. Few recalled his radio work in programmes such as *Just William* and *Norman and Henry Bones – The Boy Detectives* (in which he played the juvenile lead for almost two decades), or his other schoolboy roles in the Will Hay comedies (by then he was in his mid-twenties). Even less knew him as England's one time leading boy soprano, recording gramophone records for Regal and Columbia at the age of 15, and starring in a handful of silent films from eight. And being

Shunned, the star who gets no laughs as a sad drunk

FOLLOWING the tragic and lonely death of Kenneth Williams, The People can reveal how one of his Carry-On colleagues has become a sad, eccentric hermit.

Manic Charles Hawtrey — once one of Britain's best-loved comedians — is now an embittered, broken man.

Sniggers

The zany antics that once brought happy laughs from millions of fans, now bring only embarrassed sniggers from pub drinkers.

These days falsetto-voiced Hawtrey's only public performance is lying on bar-room floors like a dead "the son of the light-comedy actor-manager, Sir Charles Hawtrey, who won his knighthood for services to the theatre",[6] didn't mean much, either. (Not that he was anything of the kind — his father was actually a motor mechanic.)

The trouble was *everyone* remembered *Carry On*: thirty films[7] that had become Britain's biggest film series thanks to its stable of legendary regulars, although its octogenarian producer would argue otherwise.

Peter Rogers: 'When it came to casting, Gerald [Thomas, the director] and I made it quite clear to every artiste, whatever their status, that the star of the film was *Carry On*. Everybody's name came under the title. We never compromised on this principle. You could have changed the cast every time and they still would have been accepted. As long as it was called *Carry On*, nobody cared. Certainly the *Carry Ons* didn't rely on Charles Hawtrey, in no way!'[8]

Rogers frequently refused to concede that the cast, and Hawtrey in particular, helped contribute to the success of his franchise. But one could never agree with his opinion after sitting through the box office flop *Carry On England* with newcomers Patrick Mower and Judy Geeson, say. Or indeed the 1992 ill-fated comeback, *Carry On Columbus*, wherein the original team was replaced by the likes of Alexei Sayle, Julian Clary and Rik Mayall, and which was met with similar financial failure. (Unperturbed, "Carry On London Limited" have, since 2003, promised another adventure, with each sporadic press release naming different line-ups of ex-soap actors and top-heavy models. As of 2010, nothing has been filmed.)[9]

There's an obvious argument for attributing some success to the period in which the series was made: a post-war Britain that wanted a good old laugh and a happy, colourful film. But let's not be naïve or too analytical. The original "*Carry On* clan" of Sid James, Kenneth Williams, Hawtrey, Hattie Jacques, Joan Sims, Kenneth Connor and Bernard Bresslaw was of such good stock that the very foundations of the series were built upon their inclusion. Take them away and it just isn't a *Carry On*, as their contemporaries and later titles undoubtedly prove.

In terms of career growth for its performers, however, it was ruthlessly cannibalistic: the more successful the series became, the more the characters became caricatures and, as a consequence, the less other producers, predominantly in serious drama, were inclined to cast actors best-known for leering over Barbara Windsor's breasts or trying to seduce Kenneth Williams in a one-man tent. Or being a weedy and camp, cartoon-

☆ ☆ ☆ ☆   THE SUN, Thursday, September 29, 1988   **13**

STAR WHO HAS TO CARRY ON BOOZING

like pixie, mincing about the screen with a birdcage, drenched in pea soup or dressed as "Lady Puddleton". Which is exactly what went wrong with Hawtrey, as well as the others: helplessly having to do them to ensure regular incomes. In Hawtrey's case this was £2000 per film, £3000 less than Williams and James, who were the highest paid.

Publicly at least he wasn't one to bite the hand that fed him and at the height of his *Carry On* fame Hawtrey was reliably pleasant about the series.

Charles Hawtrey: 'Let's face it, the *Carry On* films just aren't like ordinary films. They're an institution, a corner of comedy that will be forever England! [They] haven't made me rich, but they've given me a world-wide identity.'[10]

He wasn't being modest. A simple calculation values his *entire Carry On* income at £46,000. Similarly, in August 1987, a year before his death, as part of *The Sun* newspaper's celebrations for the forthcoming 30th anniversary of the first *Carry On* film, Hawtrey continued to skirt around his true feelings and remain loyal to the brand.

Charles Hawtrey: 'They were quite an ordeal for me. I only weighed 8st. 8lb. yet I was given a lot of the danger work. I still do some stage work. But I'm quite happy living by the sea.'[11]

Carry On star must lose both legs or die

By PAUL HOOPER and TRACEY KANDOHLA

CARRY ON star Charles Hawtrey was given the grim choice last night: Have your legs amputated or die. But the 72-year-old funnyman REFUSED the life-saving surgery.

Doctors revived bachelor Hawtrey after his heart stopped seven days ago — then they discovered he needed the operation because of a serious artery condition.

The comic who made millions laugh as the bespectacled wimp in 23 Carry On films is facing his ordeal alone.

No family or film colleagues have been to see him in Buckland Hospital, Dover, Kent.

But The Sun yesterday took a big bouquet to his bedside in a small side ward.

Flowers

The desperately weak actor whispered: "Thank you. You are the only people who have visited me.

"The flowers have brightened up my day. I

THE BOOZER—Pages 12 & 13

am a very sick man. I don't know exactly what's wrong with me.

"But I won't be going anywhere for quite a long time yet."

Hawtrey — who starred with big names like Kenneth Williams, Sid James and Barbara Windsor — had become a recluse in recent years.

His doctor said: "Mr

Hawtrey was in a very serious condition when he came in. He is still poorly, although there has been improvement.

Pain

"Your flowers have really perked him up. It was very kind of you to bother.

"He is in a lot of pain and needs his legs amputation Continued on Page 13

The "stage work" had, in fact, dried up almost a decade earlier and the "happy" life by the sea was shattered in 1984 when his three-storey smuggler's cottage was set alight by a 16-year-old rent boy determined to scare the old man into paying him. Instead, the mainly wooden building quickly turned into a blazing inferno and Hawtrey, sans toupée (et vêtements), was rescued from the second floor window. If it weren't for Fire Fighter Bullock's swift use of helmet, the morning's papers would have immortalised more of Hawtrey than just his baldhead (which exists anyway, having been accidentally captured in a promotional shot of Hawtrey reclining in a field and wearing loose-fitting shorts, in *Carry On Camping*.)

By 1988 an exposé in *The People* newspaper revealed Hawtrey had become "a sad, eccentric hermit … [whose] only public performance is lying on bar-room floors like a dead fly, arms and legs in the air. Nowhere near as outgoing as he appears on the screen. The direct opposite to his fun-loving character in the *Carry On* films"[12], though, really, that wasn't entirely accurate. True, he hated being approached for autographs by children too young to know who he was ("Piss off, little boy!"), he hated the familiarity with which people would shout out "Carry On Charlie!" and, above all, he hated being confused with other members of the *Carry On* team ("I suppose you think I'm fucking Barbara Windsor?").

Bernard Walsh: 'But if they approached him in a nice manner and said, "Excuse me, Mr. Hawtrey, I've enjoyed your work so much, you're so funny, congratulations …" that sort of thing, he'd love them, he was very polite back.'[13]

LOSE LEGS OR DIE

Continued from Page One

tated because of the narrowing of the arteries.

"But he has refused the operation."

Nurses also revealed that Hawtrey has tried to contact a friend in Australia to break the bleak news but failed.

The lonely star, who battled for years against a massive booze problem, hid away at his terraced home in Deal, Kent.

Hapless Hawtrey had to flee naked when fire swept through the three-storey house four years ago.

He was trapped on the smoke-filled first floor.

Firemen wearing breathing gear plucked him to safety after neighbours spotted him without a stitch on, screaming for help from his window.

Neighbour

After the blaze the star had to face embarrassing questions about his private life.

For a lad in his 20s also had to be rescued from the blazing building.

A neighbour said: "Hawtrey was naked but the young lad had his trousers on.

"He was shouting for help and there was smoke and flames everywhere.

"All Hawtrey said as the firemen reached him was, 'But I've got no clothes on.' He didn't panic."

The star refused medical attention on that occasion, too. Despite suffering burns, he would not even go to hospital.

"I regard myself as self-healing," he said after the incident.

One friend of the actor said yesterday: "I saw Charles three weeks ago and he was barely recognisable.

"He rarely leaves his home and even sends a taxi to do some of his shopping for him."

Hawtrey ... blaze victim

Well, of course he would be; that's exactly what he craved. But annoyingly it wasn't the norm. When he staggered into the last Deal pub he hadn't been barred from, The Royal Hotel, on the seafront, one evening in late September 1988, he had fortuitously collapsed in a "drunken stupor" and shattered his femur. Fortuitous because, once he'd been blue-lighted to Buckland Hospital, Dover, they'd discovered the peripheral vascular disease that was rapidly allowing gangrene to set in to his legs. It also explained why his heart had suddenly and unexpectedly stopped beating and paramedics had had to revive him. A swift transfemoral (above the knee) amputation to both legs might just prevent septicaemia.

This was enough to convince Hawtrey that the years of harboured bitterness about his unfulfilled life and career should be acknowledged publicly — and fast. Alan Watkins, again representing *The Sun*, was granted one final audience for a more substantial article ultimately entitled "Carry On Boozing".

Charles Hawtrey: 'What do you know about it? It was not your career that was ruined. They used me and dumped me. I could have been as famous as Sid James. What did he have that I didn't? The only reason I did them was that I needed regular money, like all actors. But after I had done about seven or eight I realised that I was typecast forever and would never get proper work because of these films. I then decided that if that was to be my fate I ought to get more substantial parts. But the whole *Carry On* thing was very bitchy and people did all sorts of private deals with the film company. Only Kenneth Williams was honest about it. He hated the way the films were made. We went on location just *once* in the entire series and that was only as far as Snowdon. *Carry on up the Jungle* was shot in a fucking greenhouse with clips of charging elephants cut in afterwards. I was quite deliberately frozen out of the top roles. I could have played them but I never got the chance. Kenneth Williams and Babs were good friends. The rest of them shit all over me. But they managed to get what they wanted out of it: I got bugger all and, at the end, was shit on very badly. I was told I was too old after the *Carry On Camping* film. But the real reason was that they found a couple of rising stars who would do it for less money. So they just dumped me. I did a lot of work for them – a lot more stunts than anyone else in the films. I took risks.' [14]

Although Hawtrey wouldn't have cared for the Tamla Motown artist Smokey Robinson (he favoured classical works and Broadway musicals) it does seem a somewhat apt juncture to recall the lyrics of his number one hit:

> *Just like Pagliacci did*
> *I try to keep my surface hid*
> *Smiling in the crowd I try*
> *But in a lonely room I cry*
> *The tears of a clown*

Granted, it's a cliché, but even the saddest clowns that spring to mind had their moments of major recognition: Milligan, Howerd, Williams, to name just three. Their career highs were the stuff of dreams for Hawtrey. And they each managed to bounce back from their lows. In reality he wasn't "frozen out" (he stubbornly refused to be in them) or told he was "too old" after *Carry On Camping* (his last appearance was in *Carry On Abroad* three years later). He wasn't "shit on very badly", nor had Peter Rogers found "a couple of rising stars who would do it for less money". Tragically, his acid-tongued and erroneous life-story read like the bitter ramblings of a deluded old man.

It did nothing to endear him to the acting world he had persistently sought approval from. The next day, in response, his former colleagues attending Kenneth Williams' memorial service at the Actors' Church in Covent Garden were keen to have their say, eager to deflect blame and accusations. [15]

Barbara Windsor: 'I am terribly sad over what's happened but he is a very elusive, quiet man. I haven't seen him for 14 years – the last time we made a *Carry On* special.'

Kenneth Connor: 'I have seen the story about Charles's illness, but I don't want to read it. I am sickened by the news. We have just been to bury one and we have another one on the way. We have not neglected him. It has been a great year for the Grim Reaper.'

Liz Fraser: 'No one has been interested in him lately. It is not always easy to get in touch, and it takes two to tango.'

Fraser's cutting dismissal is in stark contrast to the compassionate and perceptive message supposedly sent from the heavens to a psychic hired by *The Sun* for the article which was headed "It's So Sad!"

Sid James (speaking through medium Charles Loundon): 'You'll love it up 'ere mate.It's a right old Carry On. And far from thinking your talent

IT'S SO SAD!

By MANDY ALLOTT and ANGELA DAVIES

CARRY On stars yesterday denied abandoning ailing Charles Hawtrey.

The comedy film veterans said Hawtrey, 72, had become a recluse at his home in Deal, Kent.

And they insisted they did **NOT** know he was facing death from an artery condition after refusing to have both his legs amputated.

The weedy comedian's movie mates sent him good luck messages as they attended the memorial service for Kenneth Williams.

BARBARA WINDSOR

Hawtrey . . . elusive man

said: "I am terribly sad over what's happened but he is a very elusive, quiet man.

"I haven't seen him for 14 years — the last time we made a Carry On special.

LIZ FRASER said: "No

one has been interested in him lately. It is not always easy to get in touch, and it takes two to tango."

And **KENNETH CONNOR** said: "I have seen the story about Charles's illness, but I don't want to read it. I am sickened by the news.

"We have just been to bury one and we have another one on the way. We have not neglected him. It has been a great year for the Grim Reaper."

Hawtrey, of Deal, Kent, has an artery condition and has already suffered a heart attack.

was wasted you will see how genuinely loved you were and how revered you will still be as one of our comic giants.'[16]

Hawtrey was a fortnight from finding out if he would indeed "love it up 'ere". The show business writer Patrick Newley, who once came close in getting Hawtrey to write his autobiography, thought back to their final encounter.

Patrick Newley: We sent cards and everything to him whilst he was in hospital. A lot of people did. It got round the business very quickly and he was inundated with cards and flowers, which was amazing. It showed that people cared. He was loved by the people on screen. Bryan Johnson gave me a number to call him. I rang up, but he was rather grumpy and a bit shirty so I said, "If you need anything give me a call." But he never did.'[17]

Even though the contents of *The Sun*'s first piece were sensationalist and morbidly curious, Hawtrey got to be front-page news, extending to a further two pages inside. His deadly decline was bringing him the fame and adulation he had always yearned. The public were generous with their affectionate get-well messages and gifts, and the entertainment industry, which he believed had cast him aside, was on the face of it being complimentary and full of praise in the press.

Charles Hawtrey: 'Thank you. You are the only people who have visited me. I am a very sick man. I don't know exactly what's wrong with me. But I won't be going anywhere for quite a long time yet.'[18]

On the contrary, he knew exactly what was wrong with him because the doctors had graphically described the horrific consequence of all that heavy drinking and smoking, especially after his earlier health problems had first set alarm bells ringing and they'd advised him to stop.[19] Now time had been called. As Roger Lewis, in his own biographical study of the man, drolly noted, "Hawtrey had been legless often enough in his life not to want to go the whole hog."[20]

Chris Clear: 'It was in The Antwerpe [pub] and he was very, very drunk. He was asleep on the side there and a lot of people were spitting on him. And I woke him up — they was [sic] literally spitting on him

... and I woke him up, put him in the car and took him home. That's the only time I ever met him. The next thing, I read about him in *The Mercury* saying he'd rather die than have his legs cut off, and I thought, "Well, fair play ... You're supposed to be a raving iron-hoof."[21] You know what I mean?'[22]

Bernard Walsh: 'I was the first person he called to tell about his legs. He said, "What will I do now with my bicycle clips?" And I thought, "Oh God, what on earth do I say?" I said, "Charles, it's up to you but if they've advised you to have your legs cut off, you should have them cut off." But he changed the subject immediately. He didn't want to know all about that.'[23]

Walsh was an estate agent to the stars. Working from his townhouse office in Belgravia he had also come to befriend several of his clients including Laurence Olivier and his wife Vivien Leigh. Bizarrely, Hawtrey and the illustrious couple knew one another, having met at a bus stop on the way to Pinewood and co-starred as siblings in a 1937 show respectively, but it was Joan Sims who recommended Walsh when Hawtrey wanted to move to Deal on the Kent coast. Subsequently, the pair had become close friends and some 19 years later, knowing he'd never return, Hawtrey's four-bedroom house, which Walsh had initially helped to procure, was put back on the market. A previously unseen letter from a confidential cache of surviving papers explains.

25 October 1988

Dear Charles,

I am so pleased that you have agreed to move into Winthorpe Lodge, which has been highly recommended by people at Deal Hospital, and I think you will be comfortable there. I confirm that I gave the proprietor, Mrs. Hyde, your cheque for the sum of £800, to cover the first four weeks of your stay.

Dolly and Jim are doing an excellent job of cleaning No. 117 and making it ready for prospective purchasers to view. I have now, as agreed with you yesterday, put the house on the market, inviting offers in the region of £135,000 for the Freehold. This is a little on the high side but houses in Middle Street, with the advantage of a garage, rarely come on the market. I have enlisted, as sub-agent, the help of Mrs Pamela Long, who now owns the

firm Bright and Bright, through whom we originally found the house,
which, I see from my records, you purchased in November 1969.

With kind regards,

Bernard Walsh

Dolly and Jim must have been brave souls. One of the firemen
involved in the '84 fire rescue describes the cellar as being "shin-deep in
empty wine bottles"[24], whilst Walsh himself recalls it as "damp and
smelly … smelling of cats."[25]

Sadly, the sanguine expectations in Walsh's letter, a mere two days
before Hawtrey's death, were not realised.

Bernard Walsh: 'He eventually went into [Winthorpe Lodge], where he
wasn't happy … where he died. He found that the woman was watching
him all the time. He didn't like that place at all. I went down to see him
there. His solicitor [Christopher Richardson] asked me to take a will down
with me to get him to sign it because he was leaving everything to
various charities[26]. I wasn't mentioned, I insisted on not being. "You've
got to try and find out whether he wants to be cremated or buried or
what," his solicitor said to me. I said I'd try but I didn't think I could. I
said, "Charles, it's here, I'm leaving it here. If you want to sign it, you
sign it and send it back. It's all in an envelope all ready to send back. I
want nothing more to do with this. It's out of my control." And I heard
no more, except that he hadn't signed it and hadn't sent it back. He just
wasn't interested. But all the solicitor wanted to know was what his
wishes were: does he want to be buried or cremated? And he wouldn't
even discuss it! I went to see him in the nursing home three times and he
was just sitting there, clutching his legs. Didn't speak. Didn't say a word,
'til then: "Oh, Bernard I'm not being very attentive, am I?" and then he'd
drop off again.'[27]

It's odd to think of the man who had so much fun in hospitals — *Carry
On Nurse, Doctor, Again Doctor* and *Matron* — coming to loathe the nurses
at his deathbed. Ahead of the scrutinising "woman" at Winthorpe Lodge
was Nurse Watson at Buckland Hospital. Rather than getting the
autograph she requested, she is said to have had a vase and a few choice
expletives hurled at her instead.[28] The other nurses told the newspapers

CHARLES HAWTREY DEAD

Hawtrey ... tragic

By MICHAEL BURKE

● CARRY ON star Charles Hawtrey died alone and in misery yesterday . . . from booze, fags and a broken heart.

● The 72-year-old funnyman — a heavy smoker and a chronic alcoholic for more than 25 years— weighed less than SIX STONE after ignoring all pleas to start eating.

● His only close friend Bernard Walsh said last night: "He just wouldn't look after himself enough to stay alive. But I don't think he realised he had such little time left."

about Hawtrey's futile attempts to locate "a friend in Australia to break the bleak news".[29] In actual fact he was trying to track down his estranged 82-year-old brother Jack who, years before, like their father William, had jumped ship and left the oedipal relationship to flourish between his mother and younger sibling.

How sad it is that after years of deliberate non-communication, Hawtrey wanted, yet failed, to say goodbye.

Aubrey Phillips: 'He rang me a few times while he was there and said he wasn't very well. Obviously he was very sober each time he rang. Then he rang me late at night and said he hadn't been well all day, but he still sounded all right — that was the first time he really told me what was wrong with him. He said, "I've just been reading a book, dear boy. I think I can get my veins taken out and pig's veins put in. I'm going to have a word with the surgeon tomorrow." But the following morning he was dead.'[30]

Phillips, Hawtrey's theatrical manager and friend during the late 1960s and throughout the 1970s, was devastated when a local priest, Father Leonard, called to tell him the news. One of the Archbishop of Canterbury's personal assistants, Leonard was the only person Hawtrey would allow into his private room. According to the priest Hawtrey was well aware of his imminent death.

SAD TORMENT OF THE CARRY ON WIMP

By MICHAEL BURKE

CRACKPOT Carry On comic Charles Hawtrey was a bitter man when he died yesterday.

The skinny, bespectacled, squeaky-voiced wimp of the screen reckoned he was a FLOP in real life, too.

Days without food .. nights full of drink

Hawtrey . . . as comic cop

Father Leonard: 'All the time he kept saying he didn't want anybody to see him in the state he was in. Although he sounded perhaps all right on the phone, he really didn't look well at all. He looked dreadful. He didn't want anyone to see him. He made me swear that nobody would be allowed into the hospital to see him and that no one would be allowed at his funeral.'[31]

Aubrey Phillips: 'Charles and I had met Father Leonard in a Dover pub. This was in the days when pubs shut at ten o'clock, so when we came out Charles said, "We must have more drink, more drink, more drink!" We went to an Italian restaurant that Father Leonard knew and chatted up the owners into giving us some bottles of plonk. Then it was off back to the vicarage to get pissed, sitting in big armchairs. I don't remember the night going through or the morning coming in. I know we ended up drinking Communion wine, because when we woke up in the morning all our lips were red.'[32]

Charles Hawtrey passed away on Thursday 27 October 1988. For a man who had died alone, believing fame had unfairly eluded him, the following morning's press coverage was impressive. Headlines celebrated "Hawtrey The Brave"[33] and applauded the "Sad Star Who Kept All of Us Laughing",[34] with entire pages, front pages, TV and radio news bulletins each paying tribute to the *Carry On* star in granny specs".[35]

Terry Scott: 'I don't think Charles realised how much we all loved him. He was a recluse towards the end of his life. I think he was a very sad and lonely man. I know he seemed to think no one cared, but because he guarded his privacy so fiercely we didn't feel we could suddenly storm into his life. That didn't mean we didn't care. The only thing we knew about Charles's private life was that he had a cat. We knew this because he was always cadging free fish for it. But none of us had seen the pet or knew where he lived.'[36]

Barbara Windsor: 'It [was] such a terrible shock so soon after Kenny's death. Charlie was a very funny man who was my favourite character in the all the *Carry On* films. Everyone got on well with Charlie, he was always such good company. But when he stopped making the films he just disappeared from sight.'[37]

Frankie Howerd: 'Charles didn't want to see anyone because he was so ill. I didn't realise it was this bad. [He was] the greatest Carry Onner. He was the one star the filmmakers always wanted in the *Carry On* films. He appeared in more than any other actor and was superb at what he did.'[38]

Howerd is forgetting Kenneth Williams and his record 26 *Carry On* appearances, compared to Hawtrey's 23.[39] Still, it was a glowing tribute from the man who, Hawtrey proclaimed, had him to thank for an

CARRY-ON STAR HAWTREY DIES

Lonely comic refused an op to save his life

Hawtrey ... recluse.

Carry On Hawtrey dies at 72

By RICHARD WALLACE

RECLUSIVE Carry On star Charles Hawtrey died yesterday at 72.

His death was the second blow this year to Britain's most enduring comedy style. Co-star Kenneth Williams died from an overdose of sleeping pills just six months ago.

Hawtrey went into hospital near his home at Deal, Kent, last month after a heart attack. Doctors discovered a serious artery condition but he refused an operation, and moved to a private nursing home where he died in his sleep yesterday.

Last night his co-star Barbara Wind-

COMEDY COLLEAGUES
MOURN ANOTHER LOSS

sor said: 'It's a terrible shock so soon after Kenny's death. Charlie was a very funny man who was my favourite character in all the Carry On films.'

Since giving up acting 16 years ago, Hawtrey — real name George Hartree — lived the life of a recluse.

Miss Windsor added: 'Everyone got on well with Charlie, he was always such good company. But when he stopped making the films he just disappeared from sight.' Hawtrey's close friend Bernard Walsh said the star had been overwhelmed with get-well messages and gifts when news of his illness leaked out.

'Charles couldn't really bear being the centre of attention,' he said. 'He hated being recognised but everyone assumed he was approachable.

'Unfortunately, some tended to greet

him like a long lost friend and he would get annoyed.'

Hawtrey, once dubbed 'the most famous whatsisname in British films', starred in 23 out of the 28 Carry On pictures. Weighing just 8st 8lb he was always cast as the puny wimp who fought back with a biting putdown.

Born in Hounslow, West London, he studied at the Italia Conti school, making his stage debut in The Windmill Man in 1925. He made 250 films and starred in the Will Hay comedies as a wayward schoolboy. He was also a playwright and composer.

For over 40 years he lived with his mother and, in 1984, had to be rescued by firemen from his burning home.

CARRY-ON CHARLES IS BURIED IN SECRET

Alone to the end

Sun EXCLUSIVE

With love . . . a message from Barbara Windsor

Touching tribute . . . from Frankie Howerd

Pictures by HARRY PAGE

Hawtrey . .made millions laugh

CARRY On star Charles Hawtrey was laid to rest yesterday in the way that he lived — a loner with NONE of his showbiz friends present.

The funnyman, who made millions laugh as Britain's most famous wimp, wanted fellow stars to stay away from the no-frills funeral.

Relatives obliged — by going to the extreme of **SWITCHING** the crematorium twice, **LYING** repeatedly about the date, **ORDERING** funeral directors to stay mum and **KEEPING** his name off the crematorium's list of funerals.

Carry On pals Barbara Windsor, Bernard Bresslaw, Frankie Howerd, Joan Simms and June Whitfield respected Hawtrey's wishes by sending small bouquets with brief messages.

But many other stars had no idea the funeral was taking place.

Just nine family and friends turned up for the **EIGHT**-minute service at Mortlake Crematorium, West London — miles

By PETER WILLIS

from his home in Deal, Kent. The 72-year-old bachelor died last week after refusing life-saving surgery to amputate both legs.

Admire

Curate Phillip Warner told the congregation: "Charles was in public life, but he didn't want to become public property.

We must admire him for resisting this."

The star — who died a bitter man believing others had cheated him out of becoming a star — will have no headstone or marker to show he had lived . . . except for his 23 hilarious Carry On films.

Carry On director Gerald Thomas, representing the comedy team, said: "If he'd really had his wish he'd have been the only person at the funeral."

introduction to Peter Rogers, a meeting which had led to two *Carry On* roles and a Christmas television special.

And, following on from Barbara Windsor's comment, perhaps Williams' probable suicide six months earlier *did* have some kind of an impact on Hawtrey's mental frame of mind. Reported one newspaper: "Neighbours said that since Kenneth Williams' death Hawtrey has not left his home. He is said to have taken his pal's demise very badly."[40]

Bernard Walsh: 'He adored Joan, he adored Barbara and he adored Hattie. He didn't like Kenneth. It was a difficult ... They were friends but all the time Kenneth was promoting Kenneth ... Kenneth could be very, very bitchy. Kenneth just had to be the star of the show and that conflicted with Charles.'[41]

In significant contrast to the nationals, *The East Kent Mercury*, Hawtrey's local paper, contained scant mention of his passing. Its six-sentence piece was tucked away on page three and simply headed "*Carry On* Star is Dead." "Mr. Hawtrey," it read, "was one of the town's best known, yet least known characters. In Deal he preferred his anonymity.'[42]

This, he had made certain, would extend into death, too.

Carole Ellison: 'I knew it was secret where the funeral was to be held. I can only remember there being a few of us: my cousin John, Uncle Jack, my mother and me, Bernard Walsh, the director of the *Carry Ons* and someone connected with my Uncle. My mother had had the newspapers keep ringing her up, so I'd said, jokingly, "I'm going to ring *The Sun* up and see how much I can get to tell them where it is."'[43]

Bernard Walsh: 'He was cremated under his own name: Charles [sic] Hartree. It was early in the morning on Wednesday 3 November. It was a bright day but very sad. Very quick. Charles just wanted everything to be quick and over and done with. He was taken to Mortlake Crematorium in West London and cremated, and that's all it was. A simple service. A very nice vicar was at the church, he said a simple prayer, sung one hymn and that was that.'[44]

Again, Walsh's private papers, locked away for the past two decades, are a marvellous source of information. The Confirmation of Funeral Arrangements, for example, shows a detailed breakdown of the costs incurred:

Removal of the deceased	£156.00
Coffin selected	£280.00
Professional Services and Administrative Overheads	£240.00
Hearse	£65.00
Limousine (one)	£60.00
Crematorium Fees	£75.00
Church Fees	£0
Minister's Fee	£0
Doctor's Fees for Cremation Certificates	£50.00
Newspaper Notices	£0
Other items (floral tributes)	TBA

Curate Phillip Warner (to the nine members of the congregation): 'Charles was in public life, but he didn't want to become public property. We must admire him for resisting this.'[45]

Peter Willis: 'I've never come across such a small send-off for such a massive British star. There were no other stars there and, essentially, the feeling was that he was such a loner who kept himself to himself. I'm sure Barbara Windsor and people like that would have attended if they had been wanted there. It seemed to be a shame but it's what he would have wanted. Having been arranged by the few friends he'd got, I just sensed from the number of people in attendance that he must have been a very private man. I've certainly never attended a funeral on such a small scale. I remember they were keeping it very, very quiet. They clearly didn't want many people there. There wasn't even a notice on the board saying it was taking place. There was no sign of it when I arrived there and I was convinced it wasn't going to happen. Initially I thought I had been given some wrong information.'[46]

Willis, yet another *Sun* journalist, and his photographer Harry Page, were lucky to be there; more of Hawtrey's final wishes included changes of date, time and venue. Moreover, the funeral directors, J. H. Kenyon Ltd, were sworn to secrecy and ordered to keep Hawtrey's name off the list of funerals. It's a wonder the floral tributes reached the service, too. "With all our love, Stephen and Barbara Windsor" and "For Charles with admiration and happy memories, Frankie Howerd" read the cards of condolence, with others from Bernard Bresslaw, Joan Sims and June Whitfield.[47]

Peter Willis: 'A friend would come and take the cards away from the flowers when my photographer came round. Then suddenly the hearse pulled up and it took place. I thought it was very sad for somebody who had achieved so much in his life, had been so successful — being admired and respected by millions of people — that there wasn't a send-off for him that reflected that.'[48]

Gerald Thomas: 'If he'd have had his wish he'd have been the only person at the funeral.'[49]

Eight minutes later it was all over.
In its succinct obituary, the *Doncaster Star* captured Hawtrey's

innermost thought far better than any other: "Despite his success in comedy he never fulfilled his own expectations of stardom."[50] It could have been his epitaph — had there been a gravestone, which there wasn't. His ashes were scattered at the base of a rose tree in the rose garden (plot 50C) by Jack Hartree and the 'Superintendent of Mortlake Crematorium', a move sanctioned by Bernard Walsh.

Bernard Walsh: 'Afterwards I was waiting to get into the car with his brother, this big old man, Jack, and this nephew — they'd come hot foot from Australia when they heard he'd died — and Jack said to me, "I hope people are not saying we've come over here to see what we can get." But because Charles left no will they got the lot. Years before, this nephew, John, rang his doorbell and said, "Charles I'm your nephew from Australia." "Go away!" Charles said and he wouldn't let him in, even though he was hammering away at the door. When he called back, later that day, Charles refused to even open the door to him ... pretended he wasn't there!'[51]

Carole Ellison: 'My cousin [John Hartree] had a man clear the house out down in Deal, but he brought back some boxes and said to my mother, "Will you look after these things?" Which we did, in our cellar for years, but when my Aunt came over from Australia I asked her if she still wanted them and she said, "No. Get rid of them". So we did — most of it — down the dump. I shouldn't have got rid of it really, but at the time we thought, "What will we ever need these for?" There were masses of musical scores that he'd written, a letter from Margaret Thatcher after he'd written to her and she'd replied ... Now, of course, I feel so foolish for getting rid of it all! I'm surprised I kept the bits I did ...'[52]

But those remaining items that did evade Carole Ellison's clearout, still manage to give us an obvious sense of Hawtrey's worldly possessions, and his deep love of music:

- Two vinyl recordings of Prokofiev's *Peter and The Wolf, Op. 67*
- Two phonograph recordings of Evelyn Griffiths and Master Charles Hawtrey
- An album of Foxtrots by Benny Goodman's Sextet
- An album of the second movement of Litolff's *Concerto Symphonique No. 4*

- Sheet music for 'The Loveliness of You' (from the 1937 musical film *You Can't Have Everything* starring Alice Faye and the Ritz Brothers), 'For Me and My Gal' (as sung by Judy Garland in the 1942 musical) and Steve Allen's best seller, 'This Could Be The Start of Something' (altered by Hawtrey's own hand to a lower key)
- A poster for *Snow White and The Seven Dwarfs* at the Basildon Arts Centre, Christmas 1974
- A miniature hymnbook, c.1903
- Hawtrey's baptism card
- An invitation from Italia Conti for "Tea and Music", August 1935
- A couple of photographs, one depicting an army squadron, the other Jack Hartree in younger years
- 39 postcards, the majority from 1904 – 1912

The eventual sale of Hawtrey's house in June 1989 raised, a letter from Jack Hartree to Bernard Walsh reveals, £120,000. Combined with other equity it gave an estate total of £163,165 (£164,929 gross).[53] Its most recent owners, Peter and Barbara Stephens, claimed the place is haunted by the ghosts of Hawtrey and his cat, which may explain the reason it went back on the market some four years later at £129,500 and again in 2001, at a reduced price of £199,000, when the Stephens' themselves were finally driven out by the paranormal activity.

Peter Stephens: 'I was locked in the cellar with the key on the other side! But then, he had that as a little "playroom", apparently.'[54]

Barbara Stephens: 'Our cat "Champagne Charlie", which we named after him, was always scared stiff and once, when we came back from France with a few crates of wine, we left them in the cellar, came up here and heard a crash, so we went back down … and there they all were, all the bottles out of their boxes, all stood up in lovely neat rows!'[55]

It is interesting to hypothesise over what might have transpired had Hawtrey agreed to a double amputation (something Arthur Askey had optimistically chosen in 1982, but died soon after). Kenneth Eastaugh, in his 1978 *The Carry-On Book*, believed he was set for a comeback in the never filmed *Carry On Again Nurse*, scheduled for production the following year,[56] while Aubrey Phillips says, prior to that, Peter Rogers had tried many more times to persuade Hawtrey to return. If this was

BRIGHT & BRIGHT
ESTB. OVER 50 YEARS

ESTATE AGENTS & VALUERS
Management, Mortgage & Property Services
Managing Director: Mrs P. E. LONG

29 VICTORIA ROAD,
DEAL, KENT CT14 7AS.
TEL: 0304 374071

117, MIDDLE STREET, DEAL, KENT.

F1124

A substantial period HOUSE situated in the charming Conservation area of Deal, only yards from the seafront and close to the town centre with all its amenities. The property offers spacious accommodation on three floors and has several period features including two attractive fireplaces and exposed beams. There are four good size bedrooms and two bathrooms, as well as a separate sitting room and dining room. An unusual feature of this property is the distinct advantage of a large garage with access from Farrier Street.

The property does requires some modernisation and redecoration but there is definite scope to provide a comfortable large family home of character.

Estate agent's property sheet from 1989, a year after Hawtrey had died and his brother had requested the sale of the house.

the case, one can also assume that *Carry On Columbus* would have afforded Hawtrey a cameo part, even if it meant wheeling himself on to the deck of the Santa Maria.

The day after he died, the film critic Gilbert Adair, writing in *The Times*, revealed that during the making of a *Carry On* film, Hawtrey had attempted, for some unknown reason, "to offer consolation to a young woman faced with the immemorial choice between death and a fate worse than death." "Oh, pooh!" he told her, "I don't know about death, but I've tried the other thing and it's not nearly as bad as they make out."[57]

He must have been at the Drambuie again. Hawtrey's life wasn't just bad, it was disastrous. He knew it and rebelled against it. The obituary writers were entitled to use adjectives such as "embittered", "broken", "sad" and "soured", because he was. But it wasn't his fault that he'd lived and died that way.

Hope is what *really* killed Charles Hawtrey, after an entire lifetime of goading and teasing him. It wasn't the knock-backs because of typecasting, the endless stream of begging letters to TV and radio producers that, more often than not, led to nothing or the cheap out-of-season pantomimes he ultimately had to do. It was the hope that one day the spotlight would come to illuminate him in his own right. That having achieved his destiny, and basking in the adulation of his peers, he would be acclaimed as one of the greatest talents of his generation.

Joy Leonard: 'But it wouldn't have been him, without the legs. No, no he couldn't have managed that. He couldn't have tackled that at all, to be minus his legs. And, I could understand it. He'd rather be dead.'[58]

And so we find ourselves, again, noticing how ironic it all was. Because, in the end, the "best known wimp in show business"[59] turned out to be the bravest "thin wet hen in granny specs";[60] an appearance that had been born over 70 years before, in a distinctly average terraced house in Hounslow, West London.

CHAPTER TWO
A STAR IS BORN

My career started back in the Ice Age.[1]

Charles Hawtrey, 1973

harles Hawtrey was born George Frederick Joffre Hartree into a world very different from that of the man whose name he assumed. His namesake, the son of a distinguished Reverend, was born into privilege and educated at Eton and Oxford. A celebrated stage actor, comedian, director and producer/manager, he was knighted by King George V in 1922. By comparison, George Hartree lived in a rented house in West London with his parents William and Alice (née Crow), William John Junior ("Jack", Hawtrey's 9-year-old brother) and a lodger named Victor Fleetwood. His education was at the local Grove Road and Spring Grove Grammar schools. He got his first taste of the limelight by "putting on plays in the back garden of our house"[2] and cannily charging other children to watch.

Conversely, and rather endearingly, Sir Hawtrey and Master Hartree had at least *some* similarities. Both were talented boy sopranos, Sir H had mentored Noël Coward and Hartree had replaced him (in the plays *Peter Pan* and *Where the Rainbow Ends*, the latter produced by Sir Hawtrey) and both entered into business with the famed drama teacher Italia Conti.

The assortment of fragile century-old postcards stored by Carole Ellison since his death trace Hawtrey's parents back to Aston Fields, Northfield and Redditch in the West Midlands. The maternal side of his family originated there, his mother born in Redditch in 1882.

Raphael Tuck and Sons' "REAL PHOTOGRAPH" Postcard. No. 19

MR. CHARLES HAWTREY   Photo by Ellis and Walery.

from Emmie

Sir Charles Hawtrey. (No relation.)

But the Hartree family had, in the mid-1870s, relocated to the region from Somerset, where a variation on the county's village names of East and West Harptree undoubtedly gave birth to his father's ancestral surname.

Once settled, William's father, John Hartree Senior, had ended up working in the engine sheds at the Great Western Railway's workshops in Leamington Spa. His son, born in Birmingham in 1884, was soon put to work as a "finisher" in a bicycle factory in the same town.

John Hartree: 'My grandfather, William, eventually became an auto engineer with the Austin Motor Company [founded in Northfield in 1905] and was a main player in the development of the famous Austin 7 [in production from 1922 –1939] which he took on tour to Europe as well as driving it up and down the steps of Clovelly Village, Devon.'[3]

When the Austin Motor Company expanded, the family, consisting of William, Alice and their 4-year-old son Jack, moved to 217 Cromwell Road, Hounslow, in the summer of 1910. It would remain the Hartrees' home for the next 59 years.

The most intriguing and revelatory aspect of those surviving postcards is the many references to Alice's unspecified illness, particularly by her mother and brother Frank. They were, perhaps, a noteworthy sign of things to come.

[To William Hartree] Good morning. Alice had tea with us on Sunday. She seems alright now. Mama. (9 March 1904)

Dear Sis, I hope you are feeling better with your head and have had a very merry Xmas and I hope you will have one of the brightest New Years, with prosperity and wealth. (29 December 1905)

Dear Alice, I hope you are better. I have been sent up here in Lincolnshire till Monday and then I got to go back to Long Acre. I don't know when I shall come back. How is Jack going? I hope you are better. Will. (25 July 1908)

My Dear Sis, I trust these lines will find you better … Love to self and Jackie. (13 April 1909)

My Dear Sister, Hope you are alright. You are going through the mill a little … (3 October 1917)

William and Alice Hartree.

The reconstruction of the 'flaming handbag' in Terry Johnson's television drama *Cor Blimey* (adapted from his stage show *Cleo, Camping, Emmanuelle and Dick*) and various references through the years by Hawtrey's fellow *Carry On* cast members, have made famous Alice Hartree's bouts of dementia-induced behaviour. They recalled, amongst other embarrassing scenes, "The whole of the corridor in front of the [sound] stage covered in toilet paper that she'd thrown around."[4] Naturally, with hindsight comes the strong suspicion that its genesis is therefore contained within these postcards, though her strained mental health is understandable when one learns of her own difficult background.

Following her father's death in 1887, Alice's mother, Mary Crow, couldn't cope with raising seven children single-handedly ("She has tried for the last year to keep them all at home but finds it impossible"[5]). Eighteen months later, Mary, whom the Vicar of Redditch described as an "honest, hardworking, respectable woman who has striven hard to maintain her family under difficulties",[6] admitted her 9-year-old daughter Alice into the Royal Albert Orphan Asylum, Worcester, where she stayed until February 1896 ("taken out by her mother who had found employment for her in a needle factory"[7]). Alice's 7-year-old sister Kate was also admitted a year after her, and didn't leave for eight years.

The postcards illuminate, too, signs of desperation in Alice and William's marriage in the years before Hawtrey was born, when William's specialised work meant long periods away from both his wife and their young son Jack. A simple timeline suggests that Alice would have been nearly four months pregnant when the couple married on 25 October 1905 at Aston's registry office, which may indicate a marriage built on duty, rather than mutual love. And, to pretend he was the more senior of the two, in an era when such things mattered, the certificate shows Alice had shed three years from her age, bringing her inline with her new husband, both of whom were now 25.

To, Mr. Hartree, c/o Mrs Gentry, 1 Portman Street Mews, Portman Square London.
Why do you not write? Write soon or we shall send a bomb! Alice is watching every post for a letter. Love [Alice's mother] (4 August 1907)

Dearest, you don't know how I miss you dear. I can't sleep at night without you. Believe me to remain broken hearted. (25 May 1909)

To, Master Jack Hartree, 187 Bristol Road, Northfield, Nr. Birmingham.
How would you like to be here by the sea, love from Dad x (Brighton, 26 November 1909)

We are just going to Land's End. Weather lovely. Having nice time. Will xx (Penzance, 21 March 1910)

D[earest].A[lice]. Have had a rough time since I came back. Am going back to London Friday, Will (Bury St Edmonds, 7 April 1910)

Am off back to London today. Rather cold down here. Love to all. Will x (Brighton, 10 April 1910)

Expect I am staying here another week. Stop at Redditch longer if you like. Will send some money tonight. Hope all are well. Will (Seaford, 20 September 1910)

D.A. I arrived here safe, jolly tired and worked all Monday. I am returning Thursday. Arrive Heston about 7.30pm. It seems funny up here. It is daylight up till 10pm. I've not had such a bad job. Fairly easy and the gout so very good and easy. Will xxx (Broughty Ferry, 12 July 1911)

Staying here for lunch. Going to Biarritz and then onto Spain, Will (Pau, France, 1912)

It's mere speculation, but isn't it worth supposing Alice thought another baby would bring them together? Enter Hawtrey, not difficult to imagine since he always looked juvenile anyway, born on 30 November 1914 and baptised on 29 October 1916 at Saint Stephen's Church, Hounslow. The bond between the baby and its mother was intense from the outset. The only input William had in his early life was in choosing his son's middle name Joffre. This was in honour of Joseph Jacques Césaire Joffre, the French Commander-in-Chief who, by regrouping retreating allied armies and defeating the Germans at the first Battle of the Marne three months before Hawtrey's arrival, had become a popular war hero. Though quite why the gesture was made is unknown.

Joy Leonard, the closest female companion Hawtrey would come to have in Deal, vividly remembered this lifelong infatuation between mother and son, and his curious pet-name for her.

Joy Leonard: 'When he'd had a lot to drink he used to get maudlin, about "Kitty". I shall never forget when he once said to me, "I didn't like my father, didn't like him at all. He didn't like me."

So I said, "Well, that was his loss, matey."

"My mother had an affair with either Rolls or Royce," he told me. "I'm hoping I'm his son. Oh, Joy, please tell me I'm a bastard. Please, you'll make me so happy."

I said, "Charles, you're a bastard!"

"Thank you darling, thank you. That's made me happy. I'm certainly not my father's son. I'm the bastard!"

I said, "That's right, you are!"'[8]

Such audacious claims were not uncommon for Hawtrey in later years. In entertaining this first one, for what it's worth, we learn that Charles Stewart Rolls, to give him his full name, was killed in a flying accident in 1910, thereby ruling him out of any paternity pool. His partner, fifty year old Sir Frederick Henry Royce, on the other hand, was very much alive when Hawtrey's conception would have taken place, and had even separated from his wife Minnie two years earlier in 1912. Furthermore, not only did they share the name Frederick but, later in life, Hawtrey suffered the same hair loss as his hoped for father. Sensationalist conjecture? Maybe so. Though it is the type of evidence that Hawtrey would have surely noted and approved of himself.

By revealing the so-called family secret to her impressionable and ambitious son, Alice Hartree fed Hawtrey's growing sense of being different. He started to regard Jack as a step-brother and, as a consequence, the family began to pair off: Hawtrey and Alice versus Jack and William.

But there may have been some truth to her disclosure.

Maureen Hartree, Jack Hartree's daughter-in-law, says he always believed the reason they didn't get on was because Hawtrey was of a different father: "They weren't a bit alike. Chalk and cheese. They were

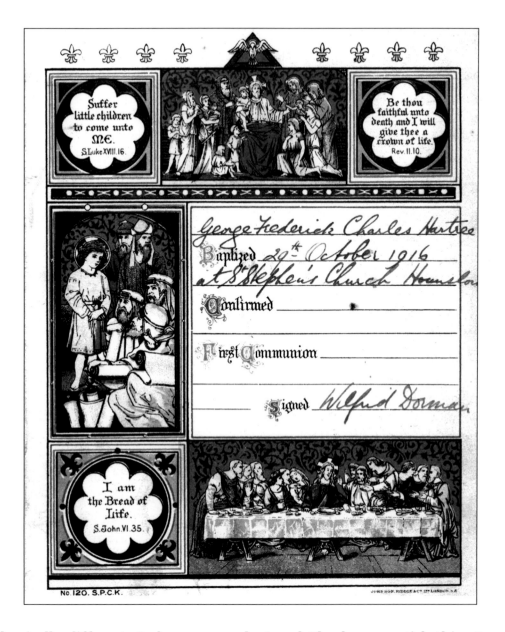

Suffer little children to come unto ME.
S. Luke XVIII. 16.

Be thou faithful unto death and I will give thee a crown of life.
Rev. II. 10.

George Frederick Charles Hartree
Baptized 29th October 1916
at St Stephen's Church, Hounslow
Confirmed _____
First Communion _____
Signed Wilfred Dorman

I am the Bread of Life.
S. John VI. 35.

No. 120. S.P.C.K.   JOHNSON, RIDDLE & Co. 12a LONDON. S.E.

physically different. Jack was corpulent and Charles was stick thin. Even my husband has the Hartree belly!'[9]

John Hartree: 'We're not quite sure of who his father was. I'll make no bones about that. If you look at the photographic evidence, there's no resemblance between Charles and the rest of the male Hartree family. But those things happened in those years.'[10]

Clearly, it would explain a lot if this were true.

Nevertheless, the entire set-up smacks of 'Little Hans', Freud's analysis of a 5-year-old boy that formed the basis for his most famous theory: the

'Oedipus Complex'. "It is the fate of all of us," Freud mused, "to direct our first sexual impulse towards our mother and our first hatred and our first murderous wish against our father."[11]

Hawtrey's hatred never progressed to love, or even to indifference, either for his father or his brother. He was overwhelmingly in love with Alice, and she with him, which left the other two out in the cold.

Doris Pocock: 'Jack never seemed to be there, very often, I don't know why it was … There was some little mystery about that.'[12]

Joy Leonard: 'He showed me a letter from him once. I was so surprised, I said, "I didn't realise you had a brother, Charles?" "Oh, yes but we don't get on. I don't like him because I'm a bastard. My father was Rolls-Royce! So I don't look upon him as my brother. My dear mama — Kitty — I was her favourite. My brother was the favourite of the one who's *supposed* to have been my father." He adored his mother. His heart was one hundred per cent for Kitty.'[13]

Violet Humphries: 'She was thin, like him, and even her mannerisms he copied. Oh, very much like her — absolutely, mother's boy! But I never knew his father.'[14]

Doris Pocock: 'His mother was always very prim and proper. But she had a friend, who lived quite near, called Mrs Mason, and together they'd go out of an evening and have a nice social evening at a pub, coming home the worse for drink! I don't remember him ever having a father … I don't remember a father there at all.'[15]

Brian Matthew: Your family name wasn't Hawtrey, was it? Was your father's name Hartree?

Charles Hawtrey: Erm. [Pause]. Well, I hardly knew *him*.

Brian Matthew: Oh, really

Charles Hawtrey: Yes.

Brian Matthew: I see.[16]

Exit William Hartree.[17]

Above Left: Jack Hartree, his wife Rosina and their baby son John, in 1936. Above Right: The earliest-known image of George Hartree, with friend and neighbour Doris Pocock, c. 1921. Below: Alice Hartree with her grandson.

It's not a complete surprise to hear young "Georgie Hartree" was a "bit theatrical" at school. Sid Filbrey, who attended the same primary school, agrees with many of his former school pals that he was "just the same as he was in the *Carry On* films."[18] A description we have heard before, especially in reference to Kenneth Williams. Yet Hawtrey had initiative and was staging his first professional productions from an incredibly young age.

Violet Humphries: 'On Saturday afternoons he used to have plays in his back garden, dressing up in different costumes and we girls used to go. We thought it was great! About a couple of hours in his back garden, with him prancing about! He used to charge us 1p old money to see him act the fool. Of course the money he collected — he went to the pictures with it!'[19]

Joan Hanson: 'We sat on chairs in the back garden where he performed his show. I can remember his mother giving us a small glass of lemonade. The show lasted a very short while; a monologue, etc.'[20]

Doris Pocock: 'I remember George as a very thin, lanky boy, always rather strange, always acting a fool. He often had a group of us children in his shed at the bottom of his garden and gave displays. It was a rough old shed, more like a big chicken shed,[21] with a few raised boards at the end; I think the boards were put on some boxes of some kind. I used to slip into the back of the shed and see some of the girls dancing with him. I'd ask my mother for a coin and it was very grudgingly given. No seats or anything to sit on, I think we just stood around. He was assisted by Trixie Mason and her sister Peggy, two children of his mother's friend who lived down the road. At 1p a time we enjoyed the show! My mother would have to come and fetch me and take me home, I was so engrossed!'[22]

It is thanks to Doris Pocock that the only candid photograph of George Hartree has survived. Here is Hawtrey, circa 1921, pictured with her amongst the rhubarb on the allotments behind their homes; Pocock, wearing curls and a bow, smiles to herself, looking at something in her hands and clasping a stuffed toy under her arm, Hawtrey holds one of the floppy hats he probably used in his shows. Dressed in a torn jumper, he leans, self-assured, into frame, aware of the camera, showing us how beautiful he is as a child — even with pointy ears.

Speaking to the *Radio Times* in 1952, he revealed that after paying his cast a few pennies in wages, he would finish up with a personal profit of three pence or so. By his own estimation, Hawtrey was 7 years old.

The following year he made his first film appearance, in 1922's *Tell Your Children*.

Charles Hawtrey: 'I can remember very little about it except that it was all about waifs and strays … and I was both! I was a waif and a stray. [It featured another] little boy and a little girl; we were without parents and I looked after the sister that was crippled, and the young brother. I got five shillings a day, which of course was a fortune! I was told not to look at the camera, but you could hear it whirring, and was told what to do as the camera turned.'[23]

In a televised interview with Roy Hudd in December 1980, Hawtrey reminisced further, though his drunken mumbling, which led to the half-hour footage being hacked down to just four minutes, made little sense.

Charles Hawtrey: I was 8 years old. In those days it was called the infant school, it's now called primary.

Roy Hudd: So you mean you were in films actually *before* the Will Hay films?

Charles Hawtrey: Oh, silent![24]

The slurred conversation then cuts, abruptly, and incongruously, to Hawtrey at his best: the scene in *Carry On Constable* where he enters, full of life, carrying his birdcage and flowers, fully erect, joyfully greeting the audience with a chirpy "Hello!" and shamelessly stealing the scene from Sid James, Kenneth Williams, Kenneth Connor and Leslie Phillips. How pitiful it was, once the clip had ended, to cut back to modern-day Hawtrey, pie-eyed and garbled, wearing a hideous tie-dye green shirt and a toupee sliding about his head.

John Booker: 'When he arrived at the studios his reputation for liking a tipple had preceded him. Strict orders were given that he should not be given access to alcohol in the hospitality room until after the recording. I remember he was obsessed about his toupee — I don't know why as it looked most unrealistic in real life — and spent a very long time with the make-up girl until he was happy it looked OK. Unfortunately, he obviously brought his own drinks in

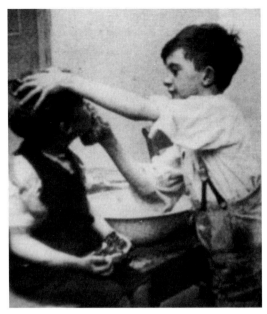

Left: George (right) as a "waif and stray" in a scene from his first film, 1922's *Tell Your Children*. Above: Roy Hudd's smile belies his real feelings after Hawtrey's intoxicated interview on *Movie Memories* in 1981.

his case and after he had requested to go and "rest" for an hour in his dressing room there was panic when it was realised he was well and truly sozzled. Roy Hudd did his best but it was a losing battle.'[25]

Anglia Television included the appearance in a book to accompany Hudd's series with a rare picture of Hawtrey, 60 years previous, in *Tell Your Children*.[26] But unlike director John Booker, it's an encounter Hudd himself would rather forget.

Roy Hudd: 'Indeed, I did interview, or rather attempt to interview, Charles on *Movie Memories*. Alas, he was then a very sad case indeed. So, rather than besmirch the man, I would rather not comment.'[27]

Directed by Donald Crisp,[28] *Tell Your Children* centred around "Two young people, a boy and a girl, just entering manhood and womanhood respectively, who fall in love and, following opposition from their parents, run away to get married."[29] What had set Hawtrey apart from the other wannabe child stars, apparently, was his ability to exaggerate certain mannerisms the stage experience gained in his father's pigeon coop had taught him and this was perfect for a silent film reliant on such visual techniques to explain the story. (As well as title cards designed by 23-year-old Alfred Hitchcock who was just starting out in the business.)

PC Timothy Gorse. Courtesy
Cinema Museum.

Another film called *This Freedom* swiftly followed in 1923 and starred Fay Compton, a classical English actress later to play Ophelia opposite both John Barrymore and John Gielgud's celebrated Hamlets. *Kinematograph Weekly*, in the only review that exists, indicates he may have played one of her children but it will forever remain a mystery; having been shot on nitrate stock, both *This Freedom* and *Tell Your Children* have long since perished, ruining our chance to witness the birth of Hawtrey's fifty-year film career.

According to the article, Compton's character wants to grow up "independent like a man, earning her own living." While she goes off to build her career, the children are left in the care of trained servants who stunt their morality and make them all "perverted", leaving the ambitious mother to realise the price she has paid for her freedom.[30]

Joan Woodley: 'He would have been about eleven or twelve years old when I joined the Hounslow Operatic and Dramatic Society as a dancer. The show I first remember being in was *Theodore or The Captive Princess* and Charles Hawtrey was the Lieutenant of the brigand band. He was the comic element of the show. We all called him Loopy. He got invited to parties where he did little tricks and played something he called "The Storm".'[31]

Cynthia Hayes: 'I can remember him playing the piano for a lesson we had once and he was tap dancing at the same time. That, I always thought, was incredible! He was standing up at the piano, playing and tap dancing! I was filled with admiration.'[32]

His piano playing was self-taught; he never had a single lesson. "The Storm" and other such piano improvisations could be heard being rehearsed on his "all white grand piano,"[33] at all hours, by Hawtrey's neighbours and passers-by on Cromwell Road. But no one seemed to mind. It's as though they considered *his* talents *their* success and, even though he would sprint through his early years with scores of successful stints on radio and film, Hawtrey would not consider moving away from Hounslow. He was a local lad through and through and his neighbours proudly looked upon him as being one of them. Indeed, when in May 1933 the "Hounslow Children's Operatic and Singing Class" was re-formed, Hawtrey himself arranged and taught the dances for a new version of *Theodore* and gave weekend concerts in support of the group. Wrote *The Middlesex Chronicle*: "It is interesting to note that Charles Hawtrey, the well-known wireless and film artiste, who arranged most of the dances, gave a highly successful performance in a previous *Theodore* as the Lieutenant. It might be said that his dramatic talent was discovered in this operetta."[34]

It was inevitable that his early forays in film and amateur dramatics, coupled with the determined push from his mother Alice, would lead Hawtrey to professional work in the theatre. From 27 December 1926, for six nights, he played a "Street Arab" in the "Children's Christmas Fairy Play", *The Windmill Man*, at the Hippodrome, Boscombe. Somewhere within this story of two royal children who break their toys, taken to Toyland and tried by a jury of dolls, Hawtrey sang a solo number, 'A Country Life for Me', which helped put his name in print for the first time. "Among the child actors, George Hartree, as Bert, is especially clever," read the *Bournemouth Times* on New Year's Day, 1927.[35]

When the production moved to Folkestone's Pleasure Gardens in late January, *The Stage* also commented: "Bert is capitally played by George Hartree."[36]

He later admitted that whatever money was made from this work, it was actually earned illegally.

Charles Hawtrey: 'I did jobs where you had to have an LCC [London County Council] Permit and the inspector would come round and ask the chaperone to see your permit. Well, I hadn't got one so the chaperone used to hide me in a wardrobe! I nearly suffocated but, anyway, it was worth it. In those *very* early days — do you remember Cine Cabaret? Cine Variety? Well, they were cinemas where they sold oranges, etc. and I was dressed in a sailor suit and a sailor hat and walked onto the stage and played an *enormous* grand piano, with the lid up, you see? And I did one or two flourishing chords and the lid fell down! And there was so much dust you couldn't see me, the audience *roared* with laughter! But I was unperturbed and sort of waved my arms around to get rid of the dust, sat down again and said, "I'm so sorry, I'll start again" and they were quiet, listening to me playing, so it went all right.'[37]

The following Christmas brought Hawtrey two more parts, those of "White Cat" and "Bootblack" in *Bluebell in Fairyland*, at the Scala Theatre in London. But waiting another whole year for his next casting didn't appeal. What George Frederick Joffre Hartree required now was someone to take him to the next level and find him regular work, a mentor, a teacher with a reputation for success. She would be his guide to achieving fame and its rewards.

She would also give him a new identity.

CHAPTER THREE
CONTI'S

I can remember, I can remember
The months of November and December
Were filled for me with peculiar joys
So different from those of other boys.
For other boys would be counting the days
Until end of term and holiday time;
But I was acting in Christmas plays[1]

Noël Coward, 'The Boy Actor'

In 1928, shortly after his 14th birthday, Alice Hartree took her son to Great Portland Street in central London to meet Italia Conti, a drama teacher whose "Academy of Dramatic Arts" was regarded the finest stage school in the country. Conti was every bit the stereotype of a domineering headmistress: no-nonsense, formidable and austere. She cut a thin, gangly figure, but deliberately exuded enough star quality of her own to bring a quiet hush to any room she would "sweep into, rather than enter."[2] Her voice was equally affected, more grandiose than grand, yet she had very effectively carved out a dominant and respected reputation within the acting world.

Peter Byrne: 'She had a place in Bournemouth [Evelyn Cottage, 127 Southbourne Overcliff Drive] and I understand that during the war she had the house painted red, white and blue, which could be seen way out to sea. So the Admiralty and security people came round and said, "You really must paint your house a different colour because the Germans can see it out at sea." And she said, "Well they know where I am! Let them open fire! I don't care!" And she never changed it.'[3]

Despite her ostentatious patriotism and personality, Conti was actually the daughter of an impoverished Italian actor and had established the Academy in 1911 after 20 years of trying, unsuccessfully, to forge an acting career for herself. Together with her younger sister Bianca, she rapidly made the Conti's academy synonymous with theatrical training for children by hitting upon a success with *Where The Rainbow Ends*, an annual Christmas play that ran for decades and which was hailed as "the best of all the children's plays."[4] She owed this lucky break to a West End producer who had hesitantly agreed to back the venture, so long as the children "were off [his] hands!"[5] The producer's name was Sir Charles Hawtrey.

Cynthia Hayes: 'She was *the* teacher. It was a downgrade to go to anybody else. She always wanted to give you a stage name when you joined. I refused because I was happy with mine and didn't want to change it.'[6]

Needless to say, this is how Hartree became Hawtrey. The timing of Alice and George Hartree's visit to Conti was perfect. Sir Hawtrey had been dead for five years so wouldn't object to a young hopeful with a similar surname 'borrowing' his more august one, and rehearsals were well underway for the following month's production of *Where The Rainbow Ends*.

Charles Hawtrey: 'It was Miss Italia Conti's idea that my Christian name of Charles should come first, 'cause I've got several Christian names.'[7]

It's little wonder then why there isn't a single mention of his "son" in Sir Hawtrey's 1924 autobiography, *The Truth At Last* (an apt title). But even Hawtrey himself perpetuated this myth, long after Conti had encouraged him to do so.

Miss Italia Conti, c.1932.

"Charles Hawtrey –
The Angel Voiced Choirboy.
Emotional parts a speciality."

Bernard Walsh: 'Charles and I went into a chocolate shop and the lady behind the counter said, "Mr. Hawtrey, I am a great fan of yours but I loved your father, Sir Charles Hawtrey." When we left the shop I asked Charles why he let her believe he was his father and he said, "Well, I don't want to disappoint them."'[8]

The authors of the 1988 *What a Carry On, The Official Story of the Carry Ons* were duped, too: "Well into middle age he was still billed as Charles Hawtrey Junior, in deference to his father's memory. Charles Hawtrey is immensely proud of his father and when he is in the mood delights in telling anecdotes about him."[9] (Which anecdotes? The one about "papa's" barefaced homophobia? On the night Oscar Wilde was sentenced to two years hard labour for his dalliances with rent boys, Sir Hawtrey, together with Lord Queensbury and Charles Brookfield, threw a party at the Café Royal in London to celebrate. Like father, *unlike* son, for "Hawtrey Junior", in later years, would have his own adventures with hired young men and was one of the first openly gay celebrities.)

But his cover up was not limited to writers and the enquiring public. BBC Radio 4 Producer Martin Jenkins clearly recalls Hawtrey captivating the production team whilst making what would be his final radio shows in the early to mid-1980s. Over lunch, voluntarily, Hawtrey waxed lyrical about his family history, his links with the theatre and his famous father. He even gave the impression that he was taken round the theatres as a small boy by him.

It was obvious why. Bar Alice, he found his own family and social class deeply embarrassing. There was already a question mark over the identity of his father, so he latched onto the prestigious Hawtrey family tree. His blood lineage provided no relations remotely connected to the theatre or entertainment in general, only working-class labourers and workhouses. He desired a respectability that the Hartrees simply could not produce.

Charles Hawtrey: 'My dear mother could not afford [Conti's] fees, which were *enormous*! When she reduced it by half we still hadn't got the money so I passed out! And I wasn't acting. When I woke up my head was in her arms on the floor and she said, "You're devoted to the profession dear, I shall take you and don't worry, I can tell you how you're going to pay your fees." I said, "How Miss Conti?" She said, "I shall put you to work and deduct from the money what you earn!" Which she did.'[10]

Peter Byrne: 'She was terribly generous to poor children, kids who couldn't afford it, those that were dancing in the street or whatever. I got a free contract, by mistake, and we had a terrible row when she tried to charge me fees so she said, "Very well dear, I've got to get some money out of you somehow" so that's why she sent me out for every audition God created.'[11]

That Christmas, Hawtrey played one of the countless "Fairies, Dragon Flies, Bats, Elves, Hyenas, Frogs, Waterlilies, Moths, Mice and Rainbow Children"[12] in *Where The Rainbow Ends* at the Holborn Empire, London.

Charles Hawtrey: '[Conti] said at the time, "You shall play Noël Coward's[13] part, his suit will fit you," 'cause he was a very thin boy … and it did.'[14]

Peter Byrne: 'I was in *Where The Rainbow Ends* during the war and if you want to know what it was like, read Coward's *Present Indicative*. There's a sequence in there about him being in it and nothing had changed by 1944! The clothes, the props, everything was the same!'[15]

Cynthia Hayes: 'It was a very patriotic play with Saint George coming to defeat the Dragon King. It was a very moral story, but children loved it. I first saw it when I was five and the awful thing was that we had to fit into the same costumes years later! They hardly ever had new ones. These costumes were so disgusting! My mother got into trouble because she washed my fairy dress and of course it was a different colour from all the others!'[16]

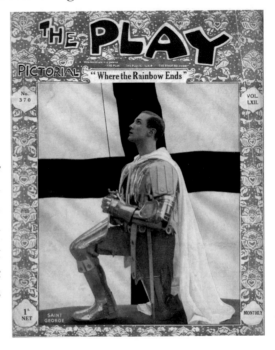

Preceding each performance of *Where The Rainbow Ends* was a short play by Bianca Conti called *A Child's Harlequinade*. This gave Hawtrey another more prominent part, that of "Pantaloon", a "silly old man, the butt of the clown's jokes, and his abettor in all his mischief".[17]

Cynthia Hayes: 'Pantaloon suited Charles because he was *always* old. He always looked like a little old man. It's so funny that out of all those I was with at Conti's, he's the only one I can remember anything about. He was thin and wiry and looked just the same as he did when he grew up. To me he never seemed to change, he seemed to be a little old man as a boy. There was something about him that made you feel he was years older somehow. He was a very strange character; he was just a character to me, more than just an ordinary boy.'[18]

Cynthia Hayes joined Conti's in the same year as Hawtrey and left two years later. From her own memory the students never earned more than thirty-shillings a week, which was paid directly into the child's Post Office account. She also remembers the incredible arguments the two Conti sisters would regularly have together.

Cynthia Hayes: 'They had a little office in the middle of the group of studios where we were and when the walls were shaking, when they were having one of their rows, we all knew we had to keep quiet!'[19]

Peter Byrne: 'Bianca, who was my teacher, she was the ugliest woman I ever met in my life. And yet they both had tremendous charisma and were wonderful teachers. Coward described Bianca as a "dragon in astrakhan" and that just about summed her up. But the two of them were so *unalike*; Conti had a small oval face with glittering eyes and a "crocodile smile". She was terribly mean but a great hard-nosed businesswoman.'[20]

Cynthia Hayes: 'Conti was quite a forbidding character but she was wonderful at getting things from children. She always tried to play down the fact that you might have any talent because *she* was going to bring you up. My mother went and said I was really a comedienne — I could always make people laugh — and she said, "Ah yes, but now she must try to be versatile and act in every way!"'[21]

Conti was a great believer in natural acting, *feeling* the words rather than *reading* them. It was method acting before the term had been coined. In fact it was Sir Hawtrey who pioneered this new approach, precisely the reason why he was Conti's idol, and even the boy Coward's: "[Coward] adored the acting which didn't look like acting; the naturalism. He was learning how to use his arms and hands; how to laugh on stage; how to produce actions and come out with lines that were so practised as to appear spontaneous."[22] (Though, probably, Sir Hawtrey was emulating Constantin Stanislavski, his Russian contemporary, renowned worldwide for "living the part". The actors Anthony Hopkins and Dustin Hoffman have both acknowledged adopting Stanislavski's technique.)

But Conti's own matriarchal, hands-on approach did not appreciate, nor tolerate, the restless minds of her young actors, of which Hawtrey possessed the worst.

Cynthia Hayes: 'One night, at the end of the show, where we all had to be "children of Where The Rainbow Ends", it was very subdued, peaceful and quiet … Charles danced onto the stage wearing a fairy queen's crown and a fairy wand in his hand! He was just dancing about, tapping us with the wand and we were all horrified, saying "Charles! Don't be silly!" and trying to stand in front of him, telling him to "Get off!" He was dancing up to the wings and the matrons were there, trying to grab him off, so he danced back again onto the stage! Someone *must* have grabbed him because it had to be the happy ending of the children meeting their parents in this land, so he couldn't have ruined the ending!'[23]

Perhaps it was karma when, in *Carry On Teacher*, Hawtrey himself suffered a similar act of sabotage as his character Michael Bean tries in vain to conduct the school's orchestra during the musical production of *Romeo and Juliet*, while the students pelt him with white paint and scenery.

Inevitably, Hawtrey was suspended from *Where The Rainbow Ends* for a week, yet clearly the punishment had very little impact on his rebellious streak, since there was more that followed.

Cynthia Hayes: 'I was also in *Quality Street* with him at the Haymarket Theatre in 1930. It was set in 1815 and there were two sisters who placed their money in the hands of someone who then lost it. The younger one, who was played by Angela Baddeley, falls in love with a doctor who went off to the war and comes back having lost an arm. The story is about their love affair. These two sisters have to start a school and we were the school children in it. One day, in the actual performance, the older sister, played by Jean Cadell, had to shoo us off the stage. She'd say, "Now children, time to go!" and we'd say, "Oh, please Miss Susan, we don't want to go! Must we?" — anything like that, we were allowed to adlib. But Charles just said, one night, "OK Suzie!" with a mock salute. Of course, howls from the audience and he was suspended again!'[24]

On the face of it this bravado could be interpreted as showing-off, but his classmates feel differently. They hold a shared belief that these outbursts were not designed to endear him amongst the cast. Merely, he behaved this way because of sheer boredom, desperate to make it funny, to shake things up and get the audience on his side.

Off stage, as with his friends in Hounslow, Cynthia Hayes and Peter Cotes remember him as a loner whose complexity and talent distinctly outshone the rest.

Cynthia Hayes: 'He obviously had no conscience about being naughty. My conscience would have troubled me if I was going to ruin a show by coming completely out of character. He didn't worry about it. In between the matinee and the evening show, Charles would make us draw the curtains in the dressing rooms and sit in the dark and he'd tell us ghost stories. Well, of course, the Haymarket is supposed to be haunted anyway, so he'd terrify us! When it came to the evening show we wouldn't go down. The matrons would say, "Come along, it's time to go down" and we'd say, "No, we're frightened, you take us down!" "Charles! What have you been doing? What have you been telling them?" To hold several children of his own age quiet enough to listen,and want more. I think that's pretty amazing, really. It shows the strength of his personality. He was alive to the reactions he would get; he would do things that he knew would have an effect. He would like to watch our reactions as he told us these terrifying stories. He had a marvellous gift for telling them.'[25]

Peter Cotes: 'It was never encouraged, but I recall those days at Conti's when Charlie would accompany himself at the piano, entertaining such fellow students as Jack Hawkins, Billy Speechley and myself, amongst others. We were all acting boy parts at night in West End productions and gratefully crowded round an old upright for a singsong in one of the studios after our dance lesson sessions had ended.'[26]

Sir Ralph Richardson: 'Hawtrey was such a strange little man; there really was nothing to him; you could hardly believe how he fascinated you, riveted you, and charmed you and held you; my goodness me, he was a magnet if ever there was one.'[27]

Left: Hawtrey (right) in *Babes in the Wood* at the Theatre Royal Exeter, December 1929. Right: "Master Charles Hawtrey" with American actors Mary Servoss and David Landau in *Street Scene*, September 1930.

Sir John Gielgud: '[His] infinite charm and regretful pathos. Everything [he] did on the stage was perfect, particularly his airy effect of enjoyment and leisure when he acted, passing off an embarrassing situation, eating a stage meal, or galvanizing undistinguishable dialogue.'[28]

The latter two, Gielgud and Richardson, are of course referring to Sir Hawtrey. But their descriptions (biographer Roger Lewis astutely noted Gielgud's) lend themselves brilliantly to our pre-pubescent starlet, especially in captivating those children with his horror stories and his uninhibited and unadulterated frivolity on the stage.

Within two years Hawtrey appeared in no fewer than six plays under Italia Conti's supervision. After touring with *The House That Jack Built*, he played the "Boy Babe" in *Babes in the Wood* at the Theatre Royal Exeter in 1929, picking up more notices as he went. "The clever youngster Charles Hawtrey [is] dainty and charming,"[29] said *The Stage* newspaper which also ran the first illusory link to Hawtrey's forebear:

"Master Hawtrey called on Miss Italia Conti, 'I would like to go on the stage, please,' said the youngster. Miss Conti must have heard this remark many times before but she appeared interested. 'What can you do?' she inquired.
'Do? It would be easier for me to tell you what I can't do,' responded the applicant modestly. Miss Conti became quite interested.
'What is your name?' she queried, unprepared for the answer which came along with unqualified assurance, 'Charles Hawtrey'. 'I can't turn anyone with that name away,' said Miss Conti, and that is how Exeter finds itself in temporary possession of a Hawtrey."[30]

Returning to the Haymarket, he then played in *Loves Labour Lost* ("… a clever lad bearing the familiar name of Charles Hawtrey as the shrewd and intelligent page Moth. This bright boy also rendered pleasingly at the end. We should hear again of Charles Hawtrey"[31]) and *Street Scene* at the Globe Theatre in 1930.

In March of that year his ability as a boy soprano landed him a record deal. He was paired with his Welsh counterpart, Evelyn Griffiths, and together they recorded six songs for the Regal label (Columbia Graphophone Co. Ltd.) at a studio on London's Shaftsbury Avenue: 'Hush Here Comes the Dream Man' and 'I Don't Want To Play In Your Yard' (15 March 1930), 'Home Sweet Home' and 'Sweet and Low' (24 May 1930), and 'While Shepherds Watched' and 'Hark the Herald Angels Sing' (13 September 1930).[32]

Regal's 1933 catalogue advertised them as "The Sweet-Voiced Children", while *The Gramophone* and *The Sound Wave* magazines used "Child Wonder Voices" and "Angel Voiced Children".

Evelyn Griffiths: 'I was only ten when I met Charles Hawtrey, after winning a competition in Cardiff to go to London and make a record with him. Charles was in the Westminster Boys Choir and was the official voice of England and I was the voice for Wales. We both stood facing the microphones, not each other, with the Stanford Robinson Orchestra playing along in real time. I remember it was so exciting to be singing with Charles Hawtrey and, when I saw him in the *Carry On* films, years later, he hadn't altered a bit. He was still the same as I remembered him when we made the records.'[33]

Listening to those 78 rpm gramophone recordings now, it is quite breathtaking to hear him as he was 80 years ago. Challenging, too, because

this is a side of Hawtrey the majority of us haven't known before. In their day they were extremely popular and much requested on the radio, especially on Children's Hour. "They say I sounded the cat's whiskers on your crystal sets," Hawtrey quipped in 1972. "But quite seriously, some of my records are still on *Open House*. The most popular is 'I Don't Want To Play In Your Yard'."[34]

Accustomed as we are to the *Carry Ons*, the brain can't help but want to try to connect "Dan Dann the Lavatory Man" or "Private Widdle" with the angelic tones that float from the speakers. Certainly the thought process isn't helped by memories of his merry rendition of 'There's No Place Like Rome' whilst sipping wine in the bathtub in *Carry On Cleo*; a sure-fire mental image when one listens to his original version of 'Home Sweet Home'.

Furthermore, although he sounds about eight, it's just as tricky to appreciate that he was actually 15 years old.

Years later, when Hawtrey's singing voice had finally left the soprano range, the producers brought in Denis Wright, another acclaimed and well-used 15-year-old boy soprano, as a voice stand-in. To explain away his character's sudden vocal change, in *Behind the Laughter*, broadcast in December 1941, Wright was required to improvise.

Denis Wright: 'During my weeks in London, I had requests from several producers of half hour BBC Radio programmes asking for me to take part. During this half hour programme, I had to "stand-in" for Charles Hawtrey and, during my singing, I had to pretend to make my voice break. This was very upsetting for my Mother when she heard the broadcast, as she thought it really had broken, and I had to reassure her it was just part of the play.'[35]

Conti insisted his page in the actor's directory *Spotlight* pictured him with the caption "Charles Hawtrey – The Angel Voiced Choirboy, Emotional parts a speciality."[36] Aside from his mischievous antics on stage, she recognised his unique gift as a boy soprano as well as one of her best child actors.

What nobody predicted was that he'd stay one for the rest of his career.

Charles Hawtrey: 'When I was a boy soprano my records were played by the first disc-jockey on radio ever, Christopher Stone. No offence, but I know you know nothing about me. Just the *Carry Ons*, that's all. Same as everybody else.'[37]

Errol Flynn and Hawtrey share the screen in *Murder At Monte Carlo* (1934). BFI.

CHAPTER FOUR
HERO WORSHIP

*That's the worst part of being a child
actor. It makes you sound so experienced.*[1]

Charles Hawtrey

Richard O'Callaghan: 'There was a young chap who got permission to come down to the set of one of the *Carry Ons* I did. He was doing a thesis on the *Carry On* films and Gerald Thomas, who was a very nice man, said, "Yes, as long as you don't annoy the actors. Don't bother them and don't get in the way of the technicians." Charles and I used to often go to the canteen, rather than the restaurant at Pinewood Studios because we were trying to save a few bob — they weren't terribly well paid. I think I got £500 for my first *Carry On* film! This boy found out we were going there one lunch time and asked if he could tag along, then he said to Charles Hawtrey, "Would you mind answering a few questions about your career?" Charles was really quite flattered and said, "I don't mind at all." They went into this rather long discussion and the boy asked, "Mr. Hawtrey, do you mind telling me, when did you make your first film?" And he got very coy and said, "I'm not going to tell you when I made my *first* movie, but I made my first *talkie* in 1932!" I'd never heard anyone talk in terms like that before — 'talkies' and 'silents' — I almost went under the table, I couldn't believe he'd said that! And the boy was completely stumped as well!'[2]

It had been nearly a decade since Charles Hawtrey last appeared in a film and a revolution had taken place in that time. When, in 1927's *The Jazz Singer*, Al Jolson opened his mouth and called out to the orchestra, "Wait a minute, wait a minute I tell yer, you ain't heard nothin' yet" he not only marked the arrival of "talkies", he instantly killed off the silent cinema. Actors, once swashbuckling heroes, now possessed squeaky voices. Actresses, previously debonair and enchanting, it sometimes turned out were, in fact, foreign and unable to speak English. And comedians, visually hilarious, had no choice but to try and tell a few jokes.

Hawtrey needed no re-invention. The two silent films he made as a boy were distant memories and not in the least bit relevant to his fledgling career now. He was 18 years old and before the decade was out would appear in a further 29 movies, beginning with his "first talkie" entitled *Marry Me*. Once again, as with the vast majority of those early 35mm nitrate films, it is highly unlikely that a viewable copy could still exist today. Fortunately, however, there does remain a handful of reviews within popular magazines of the period. The most insightful is an on-the-set article by *Film Weekly*, that pictures "a happy meal with Ian Hunter, Renate Muller, Maurice Evans and Charles Hawtrey Junior (son of the late stage actor)" and reveals that it was none other than Italia Conti who had supplied the "quite young boys" for the final scenes set in a German café (to look at him, even at 18, Hawtrey fitted that criteria).[3]

In a typed résumé he sent to the BBC in December 1954, Hawtrey claimed to have then featured in films such as *The Melody Maker*, *High Finance*, *Mayfair Girl*, *Trouble in Store* and *Kiddies On Parade* (which gave Conti another chance to show off her adolescent protégés). He even listed an Errol Flynn film from 1934 called *Murder at Monte Carlo*. While this could have been regarded as another of Hawtrey's delusions, thanks to an eagle-eyed archivist at the British Film Institute we have irrefutable proof:

a single photograph, immortalising the unlikeliest of pairings. Flynn is minus his bandana and rope from which to swing, Hawtrey is minus his glasses and looking as fresh-faced as ever.

Yet Errol Flynn wasn't the only cinematic legend Hawtrey was rubbing shoulders with. In 1935, the Italian film director Monty Banks used him in the Douglas Fairbanks Junior screwball comedy *Man of the Moment*, where he gaily sings 'Tiptoe Through the Tulips' in an office scene with Laura La Plante, herself a popular Hollywood actress whose most notable role was in the original silent version of *The Cat and the Canary*.

Hawtrey's CV also included the now lost *The Brown Wallet*, an early film by Michael Powell for whom he

Most probably from one of Hawtrey's many films for Warner Brothers and First National in the 1930s.

would later appear in *A Canterbury Tale*, and *Get Off My Foot* starring the music hall comedian Max Miller. At the same time, Alfred Hitchcock, the title designer from his first silent film, now one of Britain's leading film directors, offered him a short cameo in his espionage thriller *Sabotage*. Hitch and Hawtrey, the unlikeliest of pairings, part two. Thankfully, this particular film has survived and due to the proliferation of cheap DVDs has made its way into collections the world over.

Made in 1936, *Sabotage* gave Hawtrey an appearance lasting a mere thirteen seconds. Ostensibly, he's there to insert a bit of humour into an otherwise tense scene: in London Zoo's aquarium the terrorist has met his organisation's mastermind to obtain instructions for his next strike (eerily, a bomb on a London bus). Then, from out of nowhere, and without warning, Hawtrey glides past, incongruously linking his girlfriend, instructing her, and us, "… this rate of fertility is extremely high. After laying a million eggs, the female oyster changes sex!"

Hawtrey was working with the cream of the industry and mixing in the right circles. These glimpses into another world will have made him smile, riding back on the night bus to Hounslow and his doting mother once filming had wrapped for the day. But in the long term the benchmark that they set would cause irreparable damage. Sharing the screen with Hollywood actresses and Oscar-winning actors, in films by world famous directors, convinced elder Hawtrey to look back and regard these moments as his apex, all through a frustrated belief that try as he might he could never better them.

For now, the meantime continued to toy with his dreams.

Middlesex Chronicle, 14 November 1937

CHARLES HAWTREY IN FILM WITH WILL FYFFE

Charles Hawtrey, a Hounslow boy, is now playing the important role of Rupert MacNab in "Well Done, Henry" a Butcher's-Neville Clarke film starring Will Fyffe now in production at the Cricklewood Film Studios. Hawtrey started with a dramatic society in Hounslow at the age of eight. He then became a pupil of Italia Conti, with whom he played in "Where The Rainbow Ends" in the part of William (created by Noel Coward). Having completed his training, he went on the stage, giving a notable performance in "Street Scene". He was noticed by John Watt, of the B.B.C., who wrote a sketch specially for him. Since then Hawtrey has made over

With respected actresses Cathleen Nesbitt and Iris March in *Well Done Henry* (1937).

100 broadcasts in drama and musical comedy. He is a composer of popular musical numbers and recorded for Regal and Zonophone when he was 12. A month ago he broadcast with Cathleen Nesbitt, the distinguished stage actress, in "The Calendar." Incidentally in "Well, Done Henry" Cathleen Nesbitt plays his mother. Hawtrey has appeared in over 30 films, and usually has the same type of part, which he plays extremely well, that of a "nasty piece of work". He learnt the saxophone specially for the film. At Christmas he is playing the part of Slightly in "Peter Pan" with Charles Laughton.

"This has the making of a good film, but the character and dialogue are sketchy," reported *Monthly Film Bulletin*, without commenting on Hawtrey's "important role" but adding: "Will Fyffe has to take all the opportunities which the situations give, without much help from the rest of the cast, some of whom are exceedingly weak."[4]

Months later Hawtrey moved from Will Fyffe to Will Hay, the most famous and highest paid British film star of the 1930s. Nowadays, Hay's films, though considered classics, rarely show up on our TV screens. He was praised by one critic as "the best straight man there ever was" in homage to his beloved role as a bumbling schoolmaster who sniffs and rubs his face and double-takes at being upstaged by his students.

Will Hay pictured in his most memorable film *Oh, Mr. Porter!* (1937).

Patrick Newley: 'Most people came up to Hawtrey and wanted to talk about the *Carry Ons*. I was more interested in talking about the Will Hay films. His eyes lit up at this and he said, "Why would you be interested in Will Hay?" so I told him that I'd seen his films at the National Film Theatre and on late-night TV. He gave me the entire history of Will Hay and said, "I learnt everything working with Will Hay; the timing, the gestures. He taught me the business completely." He really did think Will Hay was God.'[5]

The strength of this idolisation was probably down to Hawtrey's paternal yearnings. Here was a man of a similar age to his absent car-mechanic father, yet hugely successful and intellectually brilliant. William Hartree, with his comparatively simple work on the Austin 7, had no chance against Hay's aviation credentials, expert knowledge on atomic fusion, amongst other complexities, and even an uncanny ability to write in reverse. Fluent in seven languages, he was also a published author (*Through My Telescope*, detailing his astronomical findings, including a significant discovery about Saturn) and was said to be an authority on comets.

But, above all, Hay was a kind and generous man who treated Hawtrey with respect and was appreciative of his experience.

Charles Hawtrey: 'It was the same every morning. He would say to me, "Have you had breakfast, Charlie?" and I'd have to pretend I hadn't because I knew he had already ordered breakfast for two. Over the meal he would say, "Have you learned your lines?" and I would say, "Of course I have."

Then he would ask me what I thought of the script. I knew what he was getting at. He was leading up to script changes. Between sips of tea he would read to me what he had written. If I didn't laugh, out went the line. If I laughed, in it went. On the set Basil Dearden would point out that we were in the wrong position for a particular shot and Will would tell him, "Oh, no, we've changed it." As for the dialogue changes, the scriptwriters were not usually around the set and by the time they found out, it was too late for them to complain.'[6]

Peter Byrne: 'Hay was two people. Off stage, like most comedians, he was a very serious man. He even had an observatory in his garden! He was a mathematician and had been a boxer in his time. He was a very, very serious, rather short man, squat, upright, with square shoulders and a large head with eyes, which were very, very shrewd. But he used to attract the women like flies around flypaper! He had this tremendous sex appeal, extraordinary because he always played this buffoon, a little man bluffing his way through life, and yet in real life he was the complete antithesis.'[7]

In total, Hawtrey made four films with Will Hay: *Good Morning, Boys!* (1937), *Where's That Fire?* (1939), *The Ghost of St. Michael's* (1941) and *The Goose Steps Out* (1942). He also appeared in Hay's BBC radio series *Diary of a Schoolmaster* for a number of months in late 1944 and early 1945.

Hawtrey's role throughout is that of a precocious know-it-all, the class softy, a teacher's pet, wide-eyed, prim and proper. He is Hay's nemesis, given that Hay is "an insecure, semi-educated drifter who finds himself propelled by chance into a position of authority for which he is intellectually ill-equipped."[8]

"You know, a critic described me as an actor who specialises in ageing schoolboys to Hay's headmaster," a touchy Hawtrey recalled, unimpressed by the label. "As a matter of fact I was in movies before Will. A silent [sic] film called *Marry Me*. Before *that* I was a real child. A boy soprano, would you believe it?"[9]

Hawtrey's debut for Hay was in *Good Morning, Boys!* His character Septimus is first seen during the school's French exam. Hay, in his recurring guise of Dr. Benjamin Twist, is desperate for his boys to pass so that he doesn't have to go "back on the dole". As a result he allows them all to cheat and turns a blind eye to their efforts in making Septimus, star of the opposing house, fail. Hawtrey's opening line comes after another

Opposite and Above Left: *The Ghost of St. Michael's* (1941).
Above Right: *Where's That Fire?* (1939).
Below: *The Goose Steps Out* (1942). All photos courtesy of Graham Rinaldi.

boy, Albert, played by one of Hay's other stalwarts, Graham Moffatt, stamps on his trademark spectacles.

SEPTIMUS: Oh dear, you've broken one of the lenses. What a calamity!

ALBERT: Sorry chum!

SEPTIMUS: I believe you did it on purpose!

ALBERT: What?

TWIST: What's all the trouble?

SEPTIMUS: He smashed my glasses.

THE DEAN: Clumsy young oaf!

SEPTIMUS: I shan't be able to see out of one eye.

TWIST: Well … Nil desperandum, dear boy. Remember what Nelson did with one eye … Ahem!

There is an element of Stan Laurel in Hawtrey's performance. Not only is his face as washed out and as pale as Laurel's, but he also uses the same blank expression given whenever an exasperated Oliver Hardy would try and explain things. There's also a glimmer of the future *Carry On* Hawtrey, too. Watch any of his scenes, especially with Kenneth Williams, and observe where his eyes are looking. When Will Hay is speaking to him, it's exactly the same: he doesn't make eye contact.

Peter Byrne: 'Poor old Will, he was a hypochondriac. In *The Ghost of St Michael's* there were stacks of these kids on the set and they used to run a sweepstake. They'd all put sixpence in and then you'd draw out, "I've got the flu" or "I've got a headache", but if you drew "I'm very well, thank you", you immediately tore it up. A different boy each day, when he came onto the set, would say, "Good morning Mr. Hay, how are you?" "Oh, I've got earache …" and they'd pay out!'[10]

Hay's biographers, Ray Seaton and Roy Martin, managed to persuade Hawtrey to contribute to their 1978 book *Good Morning Boys*. He regaled the authors with tales about the making of his final film with Hay, the 1942 Nazi comedy *The Goose Steps Out*. He bragged to them about their friendship and how, despite his youth, he wisely knew best. The scene in question sees Hay and Co. posing as German officers in order to sabotage an attack on Blighty, with Hawtrey, dressed in swastikas and the finest Third Reich uniform, looking every bit Goebbels's *doppelgänger*.

Filmmaking in the studio has its hazards. One scene in The Goose Steps Out required Charles Hawtrey to be involved in an escapade in an aeroplane, with Will and another actor playing a German navigator.[11] Charles was astonished when he arrived on the set to find there was no safety net below the suspended aircraft. "Where's the net?" he asked. "I'm not going to do it without one." Director Basil Dearden, who could be short tempered, exclaimed, "Stuff and nonsense. You don't need a net." Will, who was co-directing, didn't intervene so Charles insisted on being shown an insurance policy which covered him in the event of an accident. Dearden told him it was in the office. "Then I'll wait until someone gets it," said Charles. "I'm not going to do this scene without a safety net unless I'm properly covered by insurance." While the scene was being set up, the other actor fell from the aircraft, injured his spine and had a fit. A doctor and an ambulance were called and the actor was taken to hospital. Will went to Charles and said, "You were right. We should have listened to you. I've ordered tea for two." When anyone who had been in a dispute with Will was invited to have tea with him, he knew that all had been forgiven. Ordering tea, at any time of the day, was his was of saying, "Let's forget it."[12]

The next time Hawtrey laid down the law, however, the china did not make an appearance.

Peter Byrne: 'He played a character called "Smart" in the stage version of the Will Hay routine, *The Last Day of the Term*. There were three boys in the act: "Smart", who was the cheeky boy, played by Charlie; "D'Arcy" who was the younger boy with a giant brain and terribly polite to the old man, played by John Clark; and "Beckett", the fat boy, who was a complete idiot, played by Billy Nicholls. They did this act and, so the story goes, Charlie said to Will, "I want bigger billing." Well, Will told him to get lost and fired him. So when Will was going to appear in a revue, he held mass auditions at his Majesty's Theatre and I eventually got Charlie's part.'[13]

Hawtrey may have confronted Hay over billing after the success of *The Last Day of Term*, which was performed live from the Victoria Palace in March 1945, but his final radio programme was two months later, on 11 May, in a special VE Day episode of *The Will Hay Programme*.

Bryne concludes: "But Will Hay is the only person I ever heard Charlie say something nice about." Indeed, years later, in the early 1980s, Hawtrey repaid his gratitude to Hay by making regular visits to his dying widow in a nursing home outside Deal. And, whenever the opportunity arose, would always fervently eulogise "one of the loveliest people I ever knew who, indirectly, taught me a great deal. The great one and only, Will Hay."[14]

CHAPTER FIVE

THE MAKEUP BEHIND THE MASK

Camp isn't the word for him, I don't know what it is. He just has a strange, etiolated, epicene quality that is remarkable. And very funny.[1]

Stephen Fry

D ecades before the *Carry Ons'* McGill-styled opening credits started to feature alternatives such as *"Carry On Henry or Mind My Chopper"*, the Palladium's full title for its 1936 Christmas play was incredibly apt for regular cast member Hawtrey. He revealed in his radio interview with Brian Matthew that this was his fifth time in *"Peter Pan or The Boy Who Wouldn't Grow Up"*. He had started out in 1931 as the "First Twin" and gradually worked his way up through the roles in annual touring versions.

Dinah Sheridan, star of the 1948 film *The Story of Shirley Yorke* that gave Hawtrey an un-credited role, was another Conti student in awe of the young man's flair for entertaining his fellow child actors.

Dinah Sheridan: 'In 1935 we found ourselves on tour in *Peter Pan*, travelling to open in Dublin on Christmas Eve. We were all about 15 years old and a little home-sick over the holiday period. Charles, however, being a little older, kept us all amused by playing the piano to us and organising singsongs. The memory of him sitting at the piano in Dublin is very strong in my mind.'[2]

The following year, after turning 22, he was back in the West End playing "Slightly", yet another of Coward's old roles, with Charles Laughton and his wife Elsa Lanchester taking on "Hook" and "Pan" respectively.

Charles Hawtrey: That was the last one I did, because the only people who get a near living wage, are "Peter" and the "Hook". So I thought, no I'll do it this once with Charles. And a rather horrifying accident took place. I was sitting in the stalls, in front of Charles, because we were not in that scene, he referred to me as "Hawtrey". "Hawtrey!"
So I turned round and I said, "Were you talking to me?"
"Yes, Charles, I want to ask you a question."

With Dinah Sheridan, Derek Farr and Eleanor Summerfield in the crime drama *The Story of Shirley Yorke*, **1948.**

I said, "Yes, please do."

"What do you think of me as Hook?"

I said, "Oh, do you really want to know?" and he said yes. I said, "Well, forget your fan mail." Now, I was not being rude, 'cause you see parents had seen him in *Mutiny on the Bounty* and they were terrified that he'd frighten their children. And they said, "Please don't alarm our children." Well, unfortunately, he took that advice — 'cause children *love* villains — and he played Hook as a fool, got a very bad press report from all the papers, was so annoyed that he didn't turn up for the second performance or any other. The understudy had to play ... for the whole run.

Brian Matthew: How did he react to your comments though?

Charles Hawtrey: Oh, he took it quite nicely.

Brian Matthew: He did?

Charles Hawtrey: Because he knew very well what I was talking about.[3]

Maybe he did. "Charles Hawtrey," observed W.A. Darlington in his newspaper review, "shows a comedy sense not unworthy of his famous name",[4] whilst others had already started to call him a veteran actor.

But it's hard to believe that Charles Hawtrey, twelfth billed, gave such frank career advice to the star of the show, the winner of the Best Actor Academy Award three years previous. Based on other examples, it's just as easy to assume that this was another improvised moment of refining and exciting his anecdotes, something his *Carry On* co-star, Kenneth Williams, also felt compelled to do whenever there was an audience hanging on his every word. ('To the studio for *Wogan*. I did the Orson on vowels, Guinness on flies and Siobhan and the bishop and Edith Evans. The fact is on these chat shows I've been eating at myself for years ... just living off body fat ... and people say, "All he does now is go on and tell those *old* stories we've all heard before." Pathetic.'[5])

Three months later, in March 1937, Hawtrey performed alongside another soon to be Oscar winner, Vivien Leigh,[6] playing her brother in the comedy *Bats in the Belfry*. A flurry of eminent names followed with a stint compèring *Members Only* with Hermione Gingold in December 1937 ("Many of the comments by the gnomish compère are neat and aptly spiced"[7]), supporting Flanagan and Allen in *Happy Returns* in May 1938,

Marcus Barron, Lesley Wareing, Vivien Leigh and Hawtrey in *Bats in the Belfry*, March 1937.

and understudying Robert Helpmann's Gremio in *The Taming of the Shrew* at the Old Vic in March 1939.

That July, at the Duke of York's Theatre, Hawtrey embarked on his most successful play to date. *Counterfeit*[8] told the story of a Lancashire family whose rich cousin is murdered for his money, hidden somewhere within his palatial house in St. John's Wood, London. As his benefactors, "Joss" and his family travel down to the capital and, once there, are duly met by "the glamorous Countess of Ellerdale", their new housekeeper, who promises the northern dullards that they "shall see London with the lid off!" Gradually, Joss finds clues to the mysterious death of his cousin and, just before he is murdered himself, the police arrive and arrest the killer ("The Shadow").

But that wasn't the climactic twist.

"There is in this play one of the most successful jokes I have ever seen brought off at the expense of the audience," W.A. Darlington once again wrote in the *Daily Telegraph*. "I cannot tell you what it is for fear of spoiling it for you.

You must find out for yourselves. All I can say is that I was taken in completely and hereby hand the biscuit to the person or persons concerned."[9]

After three acts, comprising 20 scenes, Hawtrey, who had inconspicuously played "James Brixton" throughout the entire thriller, was spectacularly unmasked as the Countess, whom the programme and advertisements had fibbed was a young actress named "Charlotte Tree".

The critics loved it, with the *Daily Express* declaring Hawtrey "the hit of the show" for his female impersonation: "A genuine hit is made by Charles Hawtrey, who masquerades most persuasively and comically throughout the evening as a society woman."[10]

The Stage, like others, couldn't help but give the game away: "Charlotte Trees's portrayal of the bogus Countess is as absurd as it is improbable, and her telephone conversation to Covent Garden is as funny as a turn in a variety entertainment. At the conclusion it appears that the Countess is in reality a boy played by Charles Hawtrey, but one is under the impression that the person is Charlotte Tree."[11]

The Times wrote, "Mr. Charles Hawtrey, if indeed it is he who flaunts his tiara at the opera, amusingly deceives most of us."[12] And there were countless other reviews, praising Hawtrey, the new darling of the West End.

"Special praise is due to Charles Hawtrey's almost too convincing female impersonation" (*Brixton Free Press*)[13]

"Charles Hawtrey plays a bogus countess amazingly well, so well that the shade of his illustrious predecessor of the same name may not have been offended by the impersonation" (*Sporting Life*)[14]

"Let us congratulate Mr. Charles Hawtrey on his peerless peeress!" (*The Observer*)[15]

"Quite brilliant" (*The Star*)[16]

The **Daily Sketch's** picture sequence of the play *Counterfeit*, in which Hawtrey discreetly played the "glamorous Countess of Ellerdale" until the moment called for him to be unmasked.

With a mountain of glowing press tributes and a hit show, of which he was the indisputable star, Hawtrey's wish for stardom was coming true. Years later, when that brief taste of meteoric success was just a distant memory, Hawtrey proudly recalled *Counterfeit* to Kenneth Williams and Joan Sims on the set of *Carry On Teacher*.

Kenneth Williams: 'Mrs Hawtrey used to come with him sometimes and have a cup of tea. They were sitting there on the set and he was chatting away about this play he'd done, about playing two roles and that he'd gone on as a lady and come out as a bloke and so nobody knew who'd done the murder; a whodunit where he played both roles. He was in the middle of this long dissertation, when Joanie Sims said, "Charlie! Your mother's handbag!" 'cause she'd had a fag and it'd dropped into the open handbag and the whole of the reticule was ablaze. Joanie said, "Charlie! Your mother's bag, Charlie!" And Charlie had this cup of tea and he said, "Oh, yes," and he flung the tea into it and she snapped it shut and the whole sodden-mess was confined. And he continued with, "Eric Portman said to me after that show, 'Well, I'd like to meet that girl!' — 'cause he'd only seen me come on as a bloke — and I said, 'Darling, you've met her!'" So he was totally unconcerned with the fire in the bag!'[17]

Imagining Hawtrey as a woman isn't particularly hard; he committed a few female appearances to film, such as Lady Puddleton in *Carry On Again Doctor* and, unforgettably, his "Agatha" opposite Kenneth Williams's "Ethel" in *Carry On Constable* (wherein the two newly-recruited policemen think it a wise idea to go undercover as ladies in order to catch department store shoplifters).

But glancing over the surviving photographs of Hawtrey posing as the Countess, wearing pearl earrings, black arm gloves, a long black dress and blonde curly hair, it is no surprise the audience were fooled. The outfit gives him a natural feminine look, rather than that of a bloke in a dress.

"I was most amused by the performance of Charles Hawtrey," said the *Daily Sketch*. "His portrayal of the Countess of Ellerdale would have been a neat bit of comic characterisation had it not been female impersonation."[18]

Of course, it was the *realism* that was essential in deflecting any suspicion the audience may have had; anything less than a genuine woman and they would have smelt a rat. His next film, however, a 1940 comedy entitled *Jailbirds*,[19] gave him a chance to don his blonde wig and long black dress in a couple of scenes purely for laughs. It can't be

"Do you know, I haven't done this since I was in the army — at a camp concert!" Hawtrey in drag years later, as "Agatha" for undercover work in *Carry On Constable* (1960) and "Lady Puddleton" in *Carry On Again Doctor* (1969).

happenstance why the script has to explain early on the reason Hawtrey's character "Nick" ends up behind bars in the first place.

NELSON: What are you here for?

NICK: Nothing.

NELSON: Nothing! What, you don't know what you're here for?

NICK: I haven't the slightest idea.

NELSON: Well, what were you before you came here?

NICK: I was a female impersonator. You see I was performing and some detectives came out and took me away. I think they must have made a mistake.

NELSON: Why didn't you tell that to the beak in court?

NICK: Well, I told him I was not guilty. He didn't believe me either.

With Albert Burdon in *Jailbirds* (1940), the film that gave Hawtrey his first real shot at a starring role. Butcher's/Cinema Museum.

To attempt a break out, he and his fellow inmate (played by Albert Burdon) disguise themselves in ladies' attire. Occasionally it raises a smile, but the same visible aspect as the *Counterfeit* Countess remains: Hawtrey hardly resembles a music hall grotesque-dame, but a young lady, blonde and slim, wearing lipstick and batting his eyelashes. (Even the bass in his voice has disappeared, leaving an utterly bona fide vocal imitation to match.) There is no hint of awkwardness or self-consciousness to help generate maximum comedy effect. No signal to the audience that he, in reality, is actually a 26-year-old bloke in a dress. He's incredibly *femme*, unlike "Agatha" or "Lady Puddleton", when his female impersonations had finally developed into full-blown caricatures. He clearly relishes the sex-change.

And it didn't stop there. While other men, including his brother Jack, went to fight in the Second World War, Hawtrey was a conscientious objector, choosing instead to stay at home and entertain the troops. So, for the next three years, in as many revue shows, he carried on, delightfully playing perfectly believable women.

His chief contribution to *New Faces* in 1940 *should* be remembered as his piano playing for Judy Campbell's debut of the now classic song 'A Nightingale Sang in Berkeley Square'. Instead the reviews concentrate on his roles of "Natasha" and a "Vivandière", chirping away to camp ditties such as 'Under Which Flag' ("Charles Hawtrey makes a palpable hit in his female impersonations"[20]). *The New Ambassador's Revue*, the following year, at least had Hawtrey attempting a send-up. But in 1942's *Scoop* he's back — or, rather, *she's* back — in two roles, one sporting wild hair and huge hooped earrings, and another captioned in the programme: '"Oh, Madame Rene, you're as good as Toscanini." Charles Hawtrey as leader of a ladies' café orchestra.'

"Charles has returned to the stage to give us some of his deliciously absurd female impersonations," cooed the *Dancing Times*, "which are so completely convincing that, until he removes his wig at the end of the sketch, you wonder who the tall, elegant young woman in slinky green satin can be!"[21]

For a man who weighed 8st. 8lb. Hawtrey's shameless effeminacy was unbelievably daring and exceedingly courageous in an era when homosexuality was illegal and punishable by jail.

Judy Campbell: 'If I came back early, or looked in on rehearsals, there'd be Charlie entertaining everybody, doing my numbers, in full drag. I was so

Left: "'Oh, Madame Rene, you're as good as Toscanini.' Charles Hawtrey as the leader of a ladies café orchestra in 'Listen to the Band.' Charles Hawtrey was in *New Faces*. He is another old member of the Gate [Theatre], and, incidentally, the only boy to play Peter Pan (on the radio)." (Caption within a review for *Scoop!* in April 1942.)

Above: "Your tiny hand is frozen." Hawtrey and Madge Elliot in the sketch 'Violetta' in *The New Ambassadors Revue*, July 1941.

"Give them my buns with strychnine in them …" Ernest Thesiger and Hawtrey are 'The Amazons'.

Hawtrey (far right) pictured in a scene from *Claudius the Bee*, December 1943, with Nigel Clarke, Derek Lansiaux and Bruce Winston.

fond of him — we were so young; it was such a beautiful beginning — which makes it all the more tragic; the dreariness later, in Deal. Charlie was so good at doing my numbers, I said, "Have them." He was much funnier than I'd have been, and he grabbed them. So he did the Vivandière's song ["Women and War"] which was meant to be mine and that's how they got to give me "Nightingale" instead, which stopped the show in the most extraordinary way. You see, it was the early years of the war, when we thought we were losing. There was this incredible atmosphere of danger and uncertainty, and of excitement. The air raids were on. The show was constantly interrupted by bombs falling. The cast and the audience would sometimes be marooned in the theatre until two in the morning. It's funny — up in the night sky, Hitler's bombs; down below, Charlie Hawtrey, with that beady face and huge specs, in a dress.'[22]

Richard O'Callaghan: 'I think he was the first gay man that I ever met — the first man I was told, "He's queer", as they said in those days. As a boy I just thought there was something pretty eccentric about him.'[23]

Richard Dyer: 'I have always loved him, yet he does embody one of the things that the Gay Liberation movement tended to disapprove of — the stereotype of the effeminate gay man. And no doubt much of the straight laughter at him is oppressive laughter. He confirms that gay men are ineffectual, trivial and, worst of all, like women. Yet for all the hatred that this expressed through the stereotype, it is also the case that Hawtrey was much loved — and anyway, I'll take the comparison with women as a compliment, thank you. Besides, who cares what people think? The most attractive thing about the turn to "queer" in recent years is that it implies a rejection of worrying about what people will think. In his way, Charlie was like that too. What I relish most about him is his utter disregard for what anyone else may think. He just gets on with being himself.'[24]

In his lecture 'Carry On Regardless: The Genius of Charles Hawtrey' at the National Film Theatre in October 1989, Dyer, Professor of Film Studies at London's King's College, poses an interesting question: did Hawtrey play gay characters? Sure, he plays a gay stereotype, yet conversely there is something about him which is not typically gay. Compare Hawtrey's characters to John Inman's Mr. Humphries in the BBC's sitcom *Are You Being Served?* for instance. Both are perennial bachelor boys, but while Humphries minces about and practically *sings* his catchphrase ("I'm free!"), Hawtrey is indistinct. He is never suggestive.

While this ambiguity may be true of later roles, what these drag performances in *Counterfeit*, *Jailbirds* and the revue shows presented, in effect, was a chance for Hawtrey to 'come out' without having to say it. He was gay; there were never any personal uncertainties about that.[25] But until his mother died and the Wolfenden Report recommendations eventually decriminalised homosexuality in 1967, Hawtrey would choose to channel all his energy into his promising career. He had every faith that the forties would be a very busy and very successful decade.

Script meeting with Ted Ray and his gang for the radio hit _Ray's A Laugh_.

CHAPTER SIX
DESPERATE TIMES

April 7th 1956

Dear Sir,

I have just been listening to one of the "Norman and Henry Bones" adventures and enjoying your voice again.

Will you allow me to say I hope more occasions will be found for you to use the Norman Bones voice, whose quality is much admired and gives much pleasure.

Yours faithfully,

(Miss) M. Roomes.

Fan mail to Charles Hawtrey,
BBC Written Archive

A mongst the thousands of files, scripts and working papers, dating back to its formation in 1922, the BBC's Written Archive in Caversham, near Reading, holds nine files on Charles Hawtrey. They contain contracts for his radio and television broadcasts, correspondence between the corporation and his agents, and the occasional personal letter to a BBC acquaintance (written in Hawtrey's own hand). Not to mention *hundreds* of his begging letters, imploring, what must have been, nearly *every* BBC producer to "Remember how anxious I am to broadcast more frequently in the future"[1] and "If there is anything remotely for me, please keep me in mind".[2]

These letters are undeniably desperate, often hysterical in their regularity, since, according to the pile of surviving contracts, Hawtrey was appearing pretty much weekly on their radio network. He played the lead in *Norman and Henry Bones, The Boy Detectives* from 1943, Hubert Lane in *Just William*[3] from 1945 (complete with his first catchphrase: "How's yer mother off for drippin'?") and, like Ted Ray, Peter Sellers and Kenneth Connor, featured in the hit *Ray's A Laugh* from 1952.

Hawtrey, one must conclude, had finally realised his inevitable destiny. Each of these roles was adolescent, none more so than the character Norman Bones who was an adventurous 14-year-old boy and who Hawtrey would play for the next *seventeen* years, alongside Patricia Hayes.

Richard O'Callaghan: 'One of my mother's specialities was playing boys on the radio. We used to live in Brighton, originally, and she would catch the train up to London to record them. *Norman and Henry Bones* was written during the war by a vicar called Anthony C. Wilson, who lived somewhere like Norfolk, and he used to send these scripts in at irregular intervals. Hawtrey's voice really did sound as though it'd only just broken. As you can tell if you watch a *Carry On*, it's just on the edge of being broken almost, isn't it? So it sounded like a boy's voice — but what a strange pair, Hawtrey and my mother, to be playing *boy* detectives.'[4]

The series included episodes such as *The Curse of the Camdens* and *The Mysterious Lodger* and was produced by Josephine Plummer, another woman, like his mother and Italia Conti, whom Hawtrey highly respected.

Richard O'Callaghan: 'Josephine Plummer was a tall woman, good fun, quite strict — she wouldn't stand for a lot of nonsense — but generally warm. I think in those days you weren't allowed to broadcast until you were twelve years old, so on or about my twelfth birthday I found out her number and rang her up and said, "Josephine, this is Richard here and I'm twelve now so can you give me a job?" I think she put me in one of the *Norman and Henry Bones*.'[5]

At almost 30 years old, Hawtrey had gone from playing the over-grown school boy in the Will Hay films to a teenager in a radio series listened to by the entire child population. Equally pigeonholed were his cameo appearances in films around this time; he shows up as an art student in George Formby's *Much Too Shy* and in Alastair Sim's *Let the People Sing* he plays "young Orton". Even his role of Thomas Duckett, in Michael Powell and Emeric Pressburger's *A Canterbury Tale*, is quirkily childlike in so far as his station-master character is precociously superior and bossy. (Note that aside from the narrator, not only does Hawtrey have the opening line in this masterpiece, but in the black-out at Chillingbourne Station, his is the only face to be lit, while the rest of the actors remain in the shadows.)

To see the predicament of casting-directors, seek out his 1945 short film, *The Ten Year Plan*, directed by Lewis Gilbert (eventually a James Bond director). Hawtrey's first major role since 1940's *Jailbirds* is disappointingly poor, mainly the fault of an unsuited casting. Unless you count his telephone call to his "girlfriend", there isn't a single moment of comedy, just a dire plot and dire acting. It is a propaganda film in which Hawtrey, as a cocky reporter, is sent out to see for himself if pre-fabricated homes are the future. The answer is a resounding yes, since the government, who were keen to build thousands of these things, funded the film. For want of a better phrase, Hawtrey just couldn't do straight. What should have came across as a self-assured and sceptical newspaper correspondent instead looked self-satisfied, forced and uncomfortable.[6]

In the theatre, too, the typecasting continued to persist. Hawtrey played "Walter Wilkins" in *Merry England* ("a witty and elegant performance, though on a rather miniature scale"[7]) and "Peter Crawley" in Richard

Tauber's *Old Chelsea* ("There is no comedian's part in the strict sense of the word, but Charles Hawtrey gives a lively performance as a kind of eighteenth century English Puck"[8]).

Charles Hawtrey: '[Tauber] called me "Baby Schnappler" and he called my mother "Mamma Schnappler". Incidentally, in his apartment at Grosvenor House, I used to be invited for tea, etc. We'd sit side by side at his grand piano and he'd play one end and I'd play the other — 'cause one of his hands was paralysed. You remember how he always used to sing with a clenched fist in front of him? Well that was the reason. It wasn't a gesture at all, the hand was paralysed.'[9]

To combat the juvenile typecasting, and steer clear of roles that were clearly out of his depth, Hawtrey worked on a shift in career to behind the scenes, not just in cinema but also the theatre. Throughout the second half of the 1940s and early 1950s, Hawtrey produced and directed over 20 stage shows around London, beginning at the Q Theatre with the comedy *Temporary Ladies*.

Peggy Cummins: 'It was a tremendous theatre outside of London, at Kew Bridge. Everybody used to go to it. All the agents went to it because so many actors worked there. I do remember we got *nothing* for the work — very little. It was in May, just before I went to America in September 1945. It was a very amusing and very funny play. I liked Charlie very much. He was a very good, clever director. He had a great sense of comedy. He left us alone to get on with it and built us up. People knew he was a good director and so he always got big names. I was very fond of him indeed. And, at times, when I came back to England to make the film with Rex Harrison [*Escape*, 1948], I saw him several times because we kept in touch. But somehow it disintegrated. I don't know what happened.'[10]

"There are plenty of laughs and realism provides an antidote for a skilful plot," reviewed *The Stage*. "The dialogue is lively throughout. Peggy Cummins is outstanding. She is full of personality and has a delightfully skittish manner which renders her actions all the more funny. Charles Hawtrey's production succeeds in bringing out the finer touches of the comedy."[11]

Cummins was right about his reputation as a good director since there were more favourable notices toward his skill. On *Oflag 3*, *The Stage* again wrote, "Charles Hawtrey, who produces the play, makes a good impression by his clever handling of the large company"[12] and later, for *The Blue Lamp*, "Charles Hawtrey's production never flags for a moment."[13]

It is worth noting the number of people Hawtrey cast who, like him, had appeared in an Alfred Hitchcock film or two: Desmond Tester, in Hawtrey's production of *Mother of Men*, was the small boy who unknowingly carries the bomb onto the London bus in *Sabotage*; Mary Clare, star of *Happy Birthday*, was in *The Lady Vanishes* and *Young and Innocent*; and Gus McNaughton, the lead actor in *Trouble in the House*, played in *The Thirty-Nine Steps*.

His other stars had their claims to fame, too: Bessie Love, in Hawtrey's adaptation of *You Can't Take It With You*, started out with legendary Hollywood director D.W. Griffith; Joan Greenwood, in *Chinese Bungalow* and *Czechmate*, was one of this country's finest actresses; and Wally Patch, star of *Uncle Harry*, had appeared in a whopping 214 films, many of which had crossed-over with Hawtrey.

Charles Hawtrey: 'By a fluke, I did direct two films. One was called *Dumb Dora* [*Discovers Tobacco*], which was the history of tobacco treated comically, starring Henry Kendall, Claud Allister — do you know Claud Allister, the man with the monocle? He played algy [Algernon] parts, that sort of thing? The other one was called *What Do We Do Now?* which was a musical. I had three bands, no less, and a group of real old timers.'[14]

What Do We Do Now? was the first to be made. In 1945, Hawtrey, with well over 30 films under his belt and a burgeoning career as a theatrical producer, now had enough experience to convince Grand National Films that he was ready for his directorial debut. Though, whether it really was "a fluke" or dogged schmoozing of the company is anyone's guess.

Monthly Film Bulletin describes the plot: "Lesley and Wesley, comedians awaiting their turn at the Skewball Hippodrome, appoint themselves amateur detectives in order to find a diamond brooch which is supposed to have been stolen from Biddy, a music-hall artist. Eventually Biddy's hen-pecked husband admits that he pawned the brooch, and though the two comedians find that their detective work was a failure, their success as comedians secures them a London contract."[15]

It doesn't sound too dissimilar from other screwball comedies being churned out at the time, indeed another reviewer from *Kinematograph Weekly* labelled it as a "pathetic attempt at a British *Hellzapoppin*."[16] It may

Page 108–111: This set of lobby cards is the only surviving insight into Hawtrey's first film as a director, *What Do We Do Now?* Cinema Museum.

be coincidental, but the comparisons are strong: it had two main comedy characters, George Moon and Burton Brown (the equivalent to Americans Ole Olsen and Chic Johnson) and it centred around British music-hall, whereas *Hellzapoppin* based itself on burlesque revue.

Quite unlike its American predecessor, *What Do We Do Now?* was criticised for its poor humour, romance and musical numbers. "Comedy material, especially dialogue, is artless and unoriginal in extreme, while farcical situations take second place to musical treatment as regards entertainment value," said *Today's Cinema*. "Typical music-hall variety turns include a characteristic act of two comedians, one or two songs from a girl crooner, operatic parody and modern orchestrations from rumba and swing bands. The footage, which is excessive considering the lack of acceptable material, could have been sensibly reduced by the omission of an extraneous streak of romance and various comedy sidelines of a rather well-worn character."[17]

Other reviewers were beyond scathing: "Crude and witless British musical extravaganza, with a provincial music-hall setting. It traces the chequered fortune of a top-line comedy team, but neither George Moon, Harry Parry, Jill Summers,[18] Ronald Frankau and other well-known members of the profession loosely embraced by its feeble story shine individually or as a team. Its intentions are honourable but wit and showmanship are lacking. Its laughs can be counted on a mittened-hand. We'll say no more," *Kinematograph Weekly* scoffed, before assuring Abbott and Costello that their position in the double act hierarchy was far from threatened by Moon and Brown.[19]

Hawtrey's direction received only a single mention ("unpretentious"[20]) yet, despite the failure, Grand National had already agreed to finance another film, *Dumb Dora Discovers Tobacco*.

"The 'Dumb Dora' in the title of this frivolous little offering is a nit-witted girl reporter whose editor assigns her the task of chasing up a story on the history of tobacco," described *Today's Cinema*. "Her ludicrous exploits, though intended to amuse, are so ponderously handled that the onlooker is inclined to experience the same exasperation as her unfortunate editor. Adequate direction, modest portrayal, weak comedy script. Fair lightweight offering."[21]

Last seen on American television on 24 August 1953, *What Do We Do Now?* is now believed missing and, until recently, *Dumb Dora Discovers Tobacco* was considered to have suffered the same fate. Mercifully, when the British Film Institute sent Ronald Grant of the Cinema Museum, London, a list of titles they were looking for, he vaguely remembered his archive holding some reels of its negative.

While the BFI's Conservation Centre painstakingly transfers those nitrate rolls to safety film, restoring and preserving *Dumb Dora* for future audiences, we're unable to see how "adequate" his second attempt at film-making was — although the trade press at the time was collective in its decision that it was another turkey. Other industry reviews sent out to cinema bookers included: "Very third rate quota fill-up"[22] and "This film is ruined by its light-hearted vein and the ridiculous behaviour of the childish journalist."[23]

"The film has a good basic idea but it is indifferently carried out," sighed *Kinematograph Weekly*. "There are flashbacks of Flora Robson as Queen Elizabeth, Charles Laughton as Rembrandt and Barry K. Barnes as the Scarlet Pimpernel, but the spectacle, borrowed from 'old masters' and the re-enacted period scenes do not blend smoothly into the biography. The trouble with the film is that it tries to be too funny and ends up by being a pathetic bore."[24]

Even the impressive star line-up couldn't sway the film critics into better reviews: "Pamela Stirling grossly overacts as Dora, and Henry Kendall fails to make the best of a bad job. Claud Allister and Gene Gerrard are also off the beam in their costume character roles."[25]

Hawtrey re-cut and re-released the film in 1947 as *Fag End*, which marginally helped, but not where it mattered. *Kinematograph Weekly*'s original mention of its "Indifferent editing" was upgraded to "Exceedingly well edited", and "Unfunny commentary" became "Easy commentary helps considerably." [26]

Throughout Hawtrey's valiant attempt at an alternative career behind the camera and behind the curtain, he didn't let up on his letter-writing campaign to badger BBC producers into taking him seriously. He was appreciative of his work on Children's Hour; it always guaranteed a regular income, but he knew it was pigeonholing him and besides, television was clearly the future.

In his BBC files Hawtrey's personal correspondence stands out, either typed on his rickety old typewriter or written in his skeletal scrawl, often on hotel notepaper.

Aubrey Phillips: 'He would never buy an envelope and he would never buy paper. So if you got a letter from Charles, from home, it would be nothing to see the "Grand Hotel Scarborough" stamped on it. He'd gather the paper everywhere he went, like when you stopped on a motorway with him, on a journey, you'd get the tea and the coffee, Charles would get *handfuls* of these little sachets of sugar! Twenty, thirty of them on the tray just for his cup of tea! Once a girl looked and said, "Do you really need all that sugar, sir?" And he said, "Yes, I'm making jam when I go home."'[27]

Variants of the word anxiety make an appearance in nearly every letter he ever sent to the BBC's producers, but Hawtrey, in true comedic style, made light of his deep-rooted despair.

30 September 1946

My dear Charles,

Further to our delightful conversation at B[roadcasting] H[ouse] the other day, you devil you.

May I remind you of my anxiety to broadcast? As you know my make-up is unbelievable, and my wardrobe very smart, so what more do you want?

Bless you,
Yours very sincerely,

Charles Hawtrey

In the summer of 1947, his persistence paid off and he finally got his first taste of television. Hawtrey appeared in two episodes of *New Faces* for fifty-two guineas, broadcast live from Alexandra Palace.
Then, irritatingly, it all went quiet again.

15 January 1948

My dear Henry [Caldwell],

I trust this finds you well.

My present engagement [playing Dick Bultitude in Vice Versa at the Q Theatre] terminates on January 31st, that is in less than three weeks time, after which I am free. If you could suggest anything for me, I would be very grateful. I think I am unknown to most Television Producers, if you could help me in this respect I would again, be very very grateful.

Looking forward to seeing you again,
With kindest regards,
Yours sincerely,

Charles Hawtrey

Caldwell wrote back, thanking Hawtrey for his letter and assuring him that although he had "nothing quite in your line at the moment", he would pass his letter around the drama and variety producers. Hawtrey, meanwhile, had heard about plans to begin televising children's programmes and, as one of their biggest stars on Children's Hour, felt they should be considering him.

11 February 1948

Dear Miss Adams,

CHARLES HAWTREY

This artist has now finished his theatre engagement and is most anxious to work for you in the new Children's series [For the Children] which I understand you will be producing shortly.

I am sure you know his work, particularly in the "Norman Bones" series, and I do hope you will be able to find a spot for him in your productions.

Yours sincerely,

Josephine Burton
Al Parker LTD. (Representation in New York and Hollywood)

Getting his agent involved seemed to have done the trick. The BBC offered to see Hawtrey on 8 March but ended up cancelling the meeting that very day (a handwritten note reads, "Phoned Miss Burton putting him off"), for which no reason was given. A fortnight later, to appease her client, Josephine Burton tried a different tack, with a different executive.

23 March 1948

Dear Bill Ward,

CHARLES HAWTREY

Although this artist is well known for his work in straight plays and musical productions, he has a "Songs at the Piano" act, which he is very keen to televise. May I make an appointment for him to come and run through it for you?

Yours sincerely,

Josephine Burton
Al Parker LTD. (Representation in New York and Hollywood)

Again, the agent's intervention paid off and another contract followed; another fifty-two guineas to appear in two episodes of *Tell Her the Truth*, which generated much backslapping between Hawtrey and its producer, Michael Willis.

19 June 1948

Dear Michael,

May I take this opportunity of thanking you for my very enjoyable engagement in Tell Her The Truth and for your patience and help in production.

Although I have filmed a great deal, I am not yet familiar with the technique of television, but I trust that you were satisfied with my performance.

I look forward to renewing our acquaintance and the pleasure of working for you again.

With grateful thanks and best wishes,
Yours very sincerely,

Charles Hawtrey

25 June 1948

Dear Charles,

Thank you very much for your letter.

In replying to it I would like to say that I thought your performance in 'Tell Her the Truth' was excellent and that is the opinion of all those viewers with whom I have been in contact. The show itself seems to have been most popular. I feel that it is a reflection on the mentality of our viewers that they would prefer such 'escapist' material like this to all other things, but, who are we to sit in judgement to the public who have to be given what they want.

I have not received details of what is being put on my plate in the way of productions in the Autumn but you can be assured that should there be any part that seems to me to respond to your particular gifts, I shall not forget you.

Thank you again for writing.

Yours sincerely,

Michael Willis

Aside from these sporadic appearances on television, Hawtrey continued to turn up in films such as *Meet Me At Dawn*, as a reporter at a fairground, and another for Powell and Pressburger entitled *The End of the River*, this time unshaven, sweaty and *sans lunettes* in the role of "Raphael Morralis", a bar tender, opposite Sabu.

A similar appearance was called for in *Passport To Pimlico*. Again, minus the aid of his trusty specs, Hawtrey played shaggy-haired glass collector and pub pianist "Bert Fitch" in what is widely regarded as one of the greatest Ealing comedies.

Patrick Newley: 'When we once met in London we talked about *Passport To Pimlico*. I brought it up because in the late seventies I handled the press for Hermione Baddeley who starred in that. Charlie said how much he had liked her and would I pass on his regards to her, as she was living in

Hollywood then and only visited here occasionally. I think Charlie was probably in admiration of her, far above the cast of the *Carry On* films — that sort of thing would have been 'beneath' Baddeley — and he probably envied her lifestyle. After all she was a British comedy actress who had made the big time in Hollywood and was immensely wealthy. She made pictures for Disney and the like, and Charlie that night said of her, "She did well for herself didn't she?" So you can see that line as perhaps being a bit wistful, i.e. "I'd like to have done that."[28]

24 July 1948

Dear Michael,

I am at the moment filming in Passport To Pimlico, at the Ealing Studios and a bombed site at Lambeth. A little hut is built for us at Lambeth, which we refer to as the Prefab. and there between scenes we have a merry poker session, that is Hermione Baddeley, Stanley Holloway, Betty Warren and myself.

I trust this finds you well, I look forward to working for you soon.

With kindest regards,

Charles Hawtrey

In January 1955, when writing to one of the BBC's musical producers touting for work in their department, Hawtrey made the audacious boasts that "I was leading man in the Richard Tauber operette [sic] *Old Chelsea* at the Princes Theatre [and] in the film *Passport To Pimlico* I composed the music and played it in the picture. So if anything turns up in your musical productions, please don't forget me."[29]

Nowadays it's not unheard of for people to embellish previous employment on their CVs, usually with topics that are hard to question. Hawtrey, on the other hand, chose to elaborate the big ones. Firstly, Richard Tauber was himself the leading man in his own opera, while Hawtrey (as "Peter Crawley") appeared in just three out of the show's 18 scenes. Secondly, in so far as his piano-playing character tinkled cheerily on the keys in a pub scene in *Passport To Pimlico*, perhaps he did compose a ditty or two. But Hawtrey did not, as he'd have us believe, compose the

Bert Fitch, *Passport To Pimlico* **(1949).**

film's entire score, which was written by the prolific movie composer Georges Auric and brought to life by the Philharmonia Orchestra.

This helpless need to exaggerate, to prove his versatility and self-worth, wasn't the only insecurity that was beginning to consume Hawtrey. More than any other was a growing obsession with star billing. Exactly ten years after he played Mr. Wellington in the 1938 production of *Chain Male* at the Richmond Theatre, he was offered the same role for its television adaptation. His initial reservations over the reduced fee quickly moved onto his position in the programme's credits.

What had first presented itself with Will Hay would continue to be a sore point of Hawtrey's in the years to come with *Norman and Henry Bones*, *The Army Game* and, ultimately, the *Carry Ons*. Billing was fast becoming his Achilles' heel.

28 October 1948

Dear Charles Hawtrey

I quite see how disappointing to you the fee offered for Wellington was, but I don't honestly see what I can do about it. I am allotted an overall figure for the whole cast and I just have to ration the money out in a very matter-

of-fact way in proportion to the length of the part. As you know, Wellington, although an excellent part, is a short one and that is how the Bookings Department arrived at the fee they offered. Naturally, I would be very glad to get such a performance as you would give in the part and heartily agree with [the writers] [A.R.] Rawlinson and [Michael] Pertwee that you are the best man in the part. I should not, of course, be asking you to attend all rehearsals and I am sure we could come to some amicable agreement which would leave you free for odd days' filming, which would mean the whole of rehearsal time was not a dead loss to you.

I would be most grateful if you would think the offer over and let Mrs. Birch know.

Yours sincerely,

John Glyn-Jones

Hawtrey was playing with fire. He had worked hard to win over the BBC's television producers, of which Glyn-Jones was one of the most respected, and now he was haggling over deal-breaking conditions. But he had good reason. Some months previous his agent had, at Hawtrey's behest, negotiated a half-baked plan to reduce his radio fee in an effort to generate more work. ("It is, of course, to be clearly understood that our client's agreement to meet you regarding terms will in no way prejudice his professional status as a radio actor: after all, he had been broadcasting steadily since 1929, and has always been happy to co-operate in any way."[30]) When Hawtrey thought it had backfired, he had fired his agent, Al Parker, and began to represent himself. Now it looked as though he would have to take a similar pay cut with his more lucrative television work. His only consolation would be for Glyn-Jones to give him top billing.

29 October 1948

Dear Charles Hawtrey,

I have been into the question of possible star billing for "Chain Male" and am very sorry to say that I don't see how it can be managed. I don't want to give any star billings for this show and if I had to do so it would obviously be very invidious to single out your part from others of equal size on the grounds that it is being played by an artist of your experience. I am sure this will not comfort you much, but I hope that on reflection you will see that were we to do as you ask it would involve us in a never-ending series of requests from artists in a similar position to yourself.

I still hope that you will find it possible to play the part for me, but if you do feel it would not be worth your while, perhaps you would let Mrs. Birch know.

Yours sincerely,

John Glyn-Jones

30 October 1948

Dear John Glyn-Jones,

Thank you very much for your letter, and for your efforts to secure for me comparable billing with my former Television engagements,[31] in this case desirable since my fee has been cut by fifteen guineas on the grounds that I shall not be required to attend many rehearsals.

I note that no artist will receive star billing for the production of Chain Male. I shall be happy to accept this engagement, provided the Television Booking Department do not base future fees for future engagements on my acceptance of a cut fee for Chain Male.

Looking forward to working for you,
Kind regards,

Charles Hawtrey

Over a year later, a haughty Hawtrey confronted his former agent over their deal with the BBC's Drama Booking Manager. "Regarding my Broadcasting activities," he wrote to Josephine Burton. "The last thing you did on my behalf, prior to cancelling our agreement covering Broadcasting & Television, was to accept a 25 per cent cut for a trial period of six months, with an assurance from David Manderson, that a greater number of Broadcast engagements would follow this acceptance. During those six months I have, in point of fact, Broadcast less than at any other time, notwithstanding the Booking Department's knowledge of my availability. I would appreciate your observations."[32]

Our observations would include the reverence with which he treated broadcasting (he continually capitalises the word), his misconception over an "assurance" and "six months trial period" that had never been discussed, and his false assertion that he had broadcast less in this time (see Appendix).

Hawtrey's desperation was lost in translation. His hauteur was, in fact, another manifestation of his anxiety, his nervousness and the result of watching all his peers moving onto bigger and better things, whilst he languished on Children's Hour.

Manderson didn't hold back in shattering Hawtrey's delusions.

25 July 1949

Dear Miss Burton,

I must confess to a little surprise at the contents of your letter, as I hardly think I should be foolish enough to have given any artist an assurance that, on the reduction of their fee by 25%, a greater number of engagements would necessarily follow than had been the case over a specified period in the past.

In Hawtrey's case, it was simply a matter of the Head of Children's Hour agreeing with me that 15 guineas was quite adequate for the type of engagement he did for them. In fact, with the reduction of his fee it was very probable that the rate of his future engagement with them would be greater than if he insisted in remaining at the higher fee. This is an entirely different matter as I think you will agree.

In any event, it seems most unlikely that you would have been a party to creating such an impression as Hawtrey now expounds. Your letter to me of the 15th June, 1948, certainly gives no such indication.

Anyhow, I fail to see why Hawtrey is grumbling, because, without going very closely into the actual figures, it appears from his file that he has done more work for us during the past 12 months than he did over a similar period prior to the new arrangement, which, may I remind you, first became effective with a programme on 26 June last year. If we take Children's Hour engagements alone, there were 10 before and 16 following the new rate over the two-year period I have reviewed.

It is true that he has been asked for only very rarely at the 20 guinea rate which, as you know, applies to engagements involving 2 to 3 days rehearsal, and on this score I can only assume that in such productions the type of parts for which he is generally cast have either not cropped up, or that the 20 guinea fee involved put off a number of producers who might have used him if it had been more reasonable.

Yours sincerely,

David Manderson
Drama Booking Manager

Or could it be word was getting round the BBC that Hawtrey was difficult and above his station?

The advent of the 1950s did not bring new challenges. *Norman and Henry Bones* continued, as it would do for another ten years, supplemented by a sprinkling of offers to appear on other Children's Hour programmes and radio plays on the Light Programme.

In May, Hawtrey wrote another of his letters, expressing his surprise that "in all my years of Broadcasting, I have never attempted an audition for the [BBC] Variety Department … I have had much experience in Cabaret in which I sing amusing and popular songs at a piano, and I propose doing this for you, that is, if you will kindly grant me an audition."[33]

A date was eventually set in September, but as the judges' notes clearly suggest, it wasn't worth the wait:

'Sang a song he called "The Passing Twenties" but he should have burlesqued the period and not sung the song straight. His "straight" song was sung in the same vein.'

'Does not make the grade as a songs–at–the–piano merchant. Old fashioned material sung straight but no good nowadays.'

'He should stick to his acting. No use to us.'

WINTER GARDEN THEATRE

DRURY LANE, W.C.2   Tele.: HOLborn. 8881 & 9020

Licensed by Lord Chamberlain to RICHARD HERBERT DEWES
Proprietors : WINTER GARDEN (LONDON) LTD.

HUSBANDS DON'T COUNT—(?)

ADAPTED FROM THE FRENCH OF ROGER FERDINAND
BY PATRICIA HOLLENDER

A FARCICAL COMEDY

NIGHTLY at 7.45

SATURDAY at 5 o'clock and 8

At the Winter Garden Theatre, 1st October, 1952

'Oh, Charles, no. Let us draw a decent veil across this. Stick to acting.'[34]

"Many moons ago," Hawtrey wrote four years later in December 1954, still waiting for his calling, "I was given an audition by the Variety Department and judging by the letter following, passed it but nothing has happened yet."[35]

Within Hawtrey's BBC files lives a carbon copy of that letter, alas no mention of his passing the test.

29 September 1950

Dear Mr. Hawtrey,

Thank you for attending the audition of Monday 25th September 1950, as the result of which we now have full details of the nature and standard of your performance.

You will, no doubt, appreciate that the selection of artists from the large number suitable for broadcasting is governed by our programme requirements. If, however, an opportunity should occur to offer you an engagement in Variety programmes broadcast from our London studios, we will, of course, communicate with you again.

Yours faithfully,

Geoffrey E. O. Riggs.

Whilst holding out for Mr. Riggs and the Variety Department to "communicate with [him] again" he appeared as the judge's head clerk in a provincial tour of the play *Husbands Don't Count*, describing it as "weak but very, very funny, helped I think by the recent films".[36]

Amongst those films, *Brandy for the Parson* and *You're Only Young Twice*, both made in 1952 for Group 3, stand out as the most significant.[37] He features heavily in the second half of *Brandy for the Parson*, playing the comedy element, George Crumb, who takes a liking to a carafe of pear sherry. In *You're Only Young Twice* he is billed third (much lower is a certain Ronald Corbett) and keeps the tedious 81 minute film afloat. This time, in a characterisation worthy of his elderly self in Deal, Hawtrey, as the goody-two-shoes son of the hated Professor Hayman, is forcibly inducted into the world of alcohol by the other university students. But after a night trashing a café and falling off chairs and getting into brawls, he discovers he has a taste for it and spends much of the time happily inebriated. It's a fine bit of comedy acting and a clear sign of things to come, both professionally and personally.

HAWTREY: (slurring) Officer, I have a "friend" sitting on a bench in McCleven Park. He's drunk!

POLICEMAN: Do you tell me that now?

HAWTREY: I am but a *child* in these matters …

POLICEMAN: Yes, yes.

HAWTREY: Will you *kindly* tell me … what I can do … to restore my "friend" to sobriety?

Sloshed on screen in *You're Only Young Twice* (1952). Group 3/Cinema Museum.

POLICEMAN: Tell your "friend" to go home and lie down like a good boy and he'll be fine. Does your "friend" know the way?

HAWTREY: Perfectly ... He's not going home, you know? He's going to see Nelly!

Throughout all of this cinematic success, Hawtrey's stream of begging letters to the BBC remained unbroken, telling each recipient that he was finding his "Televising, long overdue". It certainly was. Between 1948 and 1953 his written output had been in vain, failing as it did to generate a single casting. Finally, the role of "Arty" in *All On A Summer's Day*[38] came along, which by his own account — as well as a variety of random people he had met — was a great triumph.

25 June 1953

Dear Campbell,

I trust this finds you well. I have received a multitude of glowing comments regarding "Summers Day" [sic] — those of which I must quote.

"Yorkshire Man" — "Ee that was a damn good story, best we've ever seen. Nearly laffed me bloody 'ead off."

"Two Australians" — "The most typically English play we could ever see — we saw the repeat also."

"Metropolitan Gas Board Fitter" — "Better than anything we've seen, because it was about real people, played realistically too."

Kindest regards to you,

Charles Hawtrey

It could have been the turning point, but it wasn't. No matter how many letters he wrote or names he dropped ("Dear Mr. Norman Rutherford, I was talking to a mutual friend today, — Lady Ulick Browne — Elma, and she was horrifed to learn that I didn't televise more frequently"[39]), the few television roles that he secured were minuscule.

They included an office boy in the *Fred Emney Show*, the "Caterpillar" in *Alice in Wonderland* and a couple of appearances in the sitcom *Life With the Lyons*. Career progression it was not.

His turning point would come two years later, in 1957, when Hawtrey would finally get his chance to become a household name. For now, he'd just have to carry on.

CHAPTER SEVEN

ON THE UP

> *A half hour domestic comedy series about life at the Army Camp at Nether Hopping, Staffs, a forgotten Transit and Surplus Ordnance Depot where Major Chessington, an incompetent C.O. who keeps pigs on the side, drags out an unruffled existence, disturbed only by the arrival of a new draft in Hut 29. Hut 29 contains as motley a draft of scrimshankers, scroungers, dodgers, binders and lead swingers, as ever got scooped up by the National Service Act, and it is the never ending war between Sergeant Bullimore and the C.O. on the one side, and that "unspeakable shower in Hut 29" on the other, that forms the basis of the series.*[1]

The Army Game, original pitch,
9 May 1957

As far as Charles Hawtrey was concerned, the formation of Independent Television in 1956 meant he, and others like him, were no longer at the mercy of the BBC, until that point, Britain's sole broadcaster. He was still representing himself and still sending letters, only now it was to two companies.

This increase on postage stamps quickly paid off when he secured his first offer from ITV, an appearance on the Saturday night prime-time *Dickie Henderson Show* on 6 April 1957. However, Hawtrey's debut was curtailed by his collapse thirty seconds after the programme went live, leaving the producers to scramble a replacement.

'TV actor taken ill in sketch,' screamed Monday morning's *Daily Telegraph*. 'After welcoming Dickie Henderson to the barber's shop Charles Hawtrey was not seen again. Without notice or rehearsal the leader of a vocal group, Barney Gilbraith, who was about to go home, was requested to go on in his place to save the show. The producer and director, Brian Tesler, said to me yesterday: "Barney had never rehearsed in the sketch and knew none of the many lines during the six minutes it lasted. He was given his first line, then 'fed' the others one by one." At his home in Hounslow Charles Hawtrey told me yesterday that he was still feeling "a bit shaky." He is 42 and has appeared in many plays and films since 1930."'[2]

Whether it was genuine illness or alcohol-induced, it was a disappointing start to his relationship with the network. He had been given the lead role in the barber's sketch and the exposure would have done him good. Luckily for Hawtrey there was no further speculation and soon after he was delivered a second offer to co-star in Granada Television's *The Army Game*. It would become ITV's first popular comedy sitcom. Says *Carry On* historian Robert Ross: "It tapped into the public's consciousness and delivered a regular feast of cheap, low-brow laughs and likeable, accessible characters."[3] Written by Sid Colin, who with Talbot Rothwell had been writing *Ray's A Laugh* (the radio series Hawtrey had appeared in from 1952 to 1953), it was this phenomenal success that would eventually lead

William Hartnell, Norman Rossington and Hawtrey, to be offered roles in the 1958 film *Carry On Sergeant*, joined later by Bernard Bresslaw.

Frank Williams: 'Clearly, Charles's character, "the Professor" — the rather fussy, prissy man who did knitting and so on — there was a lot of Charles in that. His campness was of the *prissy* kind, I think. He wasn't a person who impinged on one. He wasn't a big personality so it's possibly why my memories of him are rather hazy. It's rather curious.'[4]

Williams, best remembered as Reverend Timothy Farthing in *Dad's Army*, became a regular member of *The Army Game*'s cast in 1959, but he had played various parts in the series beforehand. Although he considers his recollections of Hawtrey as poor, it is consistent with what Ernest Maxin felt when he later produced Hawtrey in two other television series in the early 1960s.

Ernest Maxin: 'You never saw him go or arrive! It was amazing. You'd get in for early morning rehearsals, chatting to people like Hattie Jacques and Norman Rossington, greeting people as they arrived and he'd just appear like a ghost! Same too when he left, he never said goodbye. After we did *Best of Friends*, I never saw him again … he just disappeared! I often used to ask people if they'd seen Charles but no, and the strange thing is nobody ever spoke about him. It was almost as though he wasn't a real person.'[5]

Hawtrey's elusiveness is also recalled by Francis Matthews, who appeared with him in the *The Army Game*'s movie spin-off, *I Only Arsked!* in 1958:

Francis Matthews: 'I don't think I ever spoke to him, I don't think he ever spoke to me. I don't think he spoke to anybody. I can't remember him being in it, that's how nebulous he was. I'm not being rude about him, but it's simply true and I think many people will tell you that. He wasn't one of the lads. Normally, when you're on the set you have giggles and fun and go eat together in the canteen, I never saw him. It's like he wasn't there.'[6]

Frank Williams: 'I seem to remember there was quite a to-do during a photo-call because he had it in his contract that he wouldn't be filmed without his hairpiece and, therefore, he wanted to be filmed either with his

Norman Rossington, Bernard Bresslaw, Hawtrey, Alfie Bass, Michael Medwin and William Hartnell in the ITV sitcom *The Army Game*.

army cap on, or somebody had to go and get the hairpiece and stick that on him.'[7]

Hawtrey was back to being anxious, fiercely ensuring that his public image mustn't be imperfect, and that his colleagues should always be acutely aware that they were in the presence of an experienced star.

Frank Williams: 'He was always quite amusing in not using ordinary language that the rest of us used. He would always elaborate it. He would always call a taxi, a "taxi-metered cabriolet" or he would always refer to it as "Boots Cash Chemists". It was quite deliberately to make an effect.'[8]

Francis Matthews: 'He was a bit strange, quite frankly. I found him rather weird. He was a fish out of water, he wasn't one of us, you know? I think he must have had psychological problems because he wasn't an ordinary human being. I don't know what his life was. I don't know what his relationships were. I never found anything about him. I don't know what made him tick.'⁹

The Professor.

Granada's DVD sleeve for *The Army Game Collection*, released in 2008, implies that of the 31 episodes Hawtrey appeared in, only three have survived, those entitled *The Mad Bull*, *The New Officer* and *W.R.A.A.C.S*. However, the author has unearthed another. By chance, the newfound programme revolves around Hawtrey, with a letter sent from his mother to the Commanding Officer pleading for her son to be made a success in the army. Consequently, having his rank upgraded to Corporal compels Hawtrey to become a credit to her, resulting in him throwing his new power around and putting on airs and graces, much to the chagrin of his comrades; an obvious echo of the sitcom's set.

On the whole, like the *Carry Ons*, in these four remaining *Army Game* examples, Hawtrey doesn't actually say very much. Unlike the *Carry Ons*, due to the dated script, what he does say is not particularly funny. But what he brings to the small screen is that unique comedic charisma, the *look* we now regard as classic Charles Hawtrey. To that end, *The Army Game* was the bridge for his rising level of absurdity, from the idiosyncratic yet priggish bit parts of previous films to the cheery eager-beaver characters of the future *Carry Ons*.

Surrounded by a plethora of bad acting, over-acting and unrefined comedy, he easily outshines them all in *The Army Game* (bar perhaps Bernard Bresslaw), in a literal sense as well as in his performance; it may well be the lighting but while the other cast members look grey in the face, Hawtrey is glowing white. At times it makes him look superimposed, like an actor inserted into a reworked scene for a biopic of his life.

I Only Arsked! The Army Game **feature film, made in 1958, that starred the original team.**

His entrances aren't built up in the way they were in the *Carry Ons*, but he still manages to get whoops of laughter from the studio audience with his dainty steps, coy grins and exaggerated eye movements. Likewise his character's knitting which, like him, is intricate and delicate, not fast and frenzied as one would expect of a proficient knitter. It is precise and methodical. This could be because Hawtrey hadn't the faintest idea how to knit, but it works with the Professor's character and whenever the scene opens on him knitting the audience gives a roar, quite the opposite of Bresslaw's catchphrase "I only arsked!" which just about generates a muffled titter.

Frank Williams: 'After they'd all moved on from *The Army Game* to the *Carry Ons*, I once wrote to Peter Rogers saying, "I must be the only comedy actor in Britain that's never been in a *Carry On* film." He said he'd do something about that, but he never did.'10

Peter Rogers: 'Was Hawtrey in *The Army Game*? What was he doing in *The Army Game*? Charlie Hawtrey was in *The Army Game*? Oh, maybe he was in *The Army Game*. I don't know, I didn't see it.'[11]

It was hard to work Rogers out sometimes. As producer of the entire *Carry On* series, he always maintained that he suggested: "to keep down budget levels it would be an idea if the artists form a kind of repertory and take percentages of the films' profits" (the cast and their agents have denied this) [12]; that the *true* stars of films were the two words "Carry" and "On" ("I told you, nobody knew who was in them! As long as they were called *Carry On* nobody cared!"[13]); and, finally, he was seriously suggesting he had no idea Hawtrey was in *The Army Game* — which formed the very basis for his first *Carry On* film. (Hawtrey himself casts doubt on his feigned ignorance: "I was seen in a television series playing an army man. That gave him the idea that I'd be right for this part."[14])

Peter Rogers: 'I used to think of a title in the bath, in the morning. Then, I'd ring up Norman Hudis and tell him the title and how I think it should go. He'd do a draft and we'd have a meeting about it, and he always, quite rightly, boasted that script conferences on a *Carry On* were the shortest he'd ever known. They only lasted ten minutes because I knew I was always going to work on it myself. And the script was the blueprint; once that was on the floor nobody changed a thing. Not a word. Nobody was allowed to invent a line, or adlib. Quite impossible.'[15]

Norman Hudis: 'Hawtrey gave the impression, to me at any rate, on and off the screen, of being two feet off the ground, someone who floated through life rather than paced or plodded. I must have been aware of this when I named him "Golightly" in *Carry On Sergeant*.'[16]

SERGEANT: Now, you lads are in uniform for the first time and I think you'd all agree with me you don't look like soldiers. It would be stupid of me to expect that …

GOLIGHTLY: It would that. (To the others) He's very fair.

SERGEANT: That man there! Private Golightly, someone should have told you, you're not to talk when you're on parade. It's not the custom, so don't do it! Understand?

Golightly being pulled out of the mud by Galloway (Gerald Campion), *Carry On*
Sergeant **(1958). Canal+/Cinema Museum.**

GOLIGHTLY: Oh yes, I understand.

SERGEANT: Now, where was I? What was I saying?

GOLIGHTLY: How stupid you are …

SERGEANT: Stop talking on parade will you!

Gerald Thomas, the *Carry Ons* director, shouted "Action" for the first
time on 24 March 1958. The total budget for *Sergeant* was £73,000.

Charles Hawtrey: 'Well, it was made for about thruppence, and we were
paid about a ha'penny, and then Peter hawked the film around and nobody

**Future Dr Who, William Hartnell, observes Hawtrey on the set of *Carry On Sergeant*.
The curious look makes one wonder what is going through his mind: is it admiration
or, in the words of Kenneth Williams, the "irritating desire to be intriguing"?
(KW Diary, p.569)**

would take it. Finally, one company did take it and it made a fortune, hence
the series.'17

Peter Rogers: 'How he ever managed to do the drill in *Carry On
Sergeant*, I don't know to this day! We went to Guilford Barracks,
where the Queen's Regiment were going to do their passing out
parade. It was a very hot, sunny day. There was a regimental sergeant
major there, a very short chap who, I think, was no bigger than four-
feet high. He drilled our artists for two hours, when we were shooting
something else, so that they could take part in *their* parade — and they
did. But if you'd watched Charles Hawtrey, sloping arms, and
presenting arms ... you don't know how he did it, but he did it. He
didn't do it properly, but he got there. And no one would notice it. If

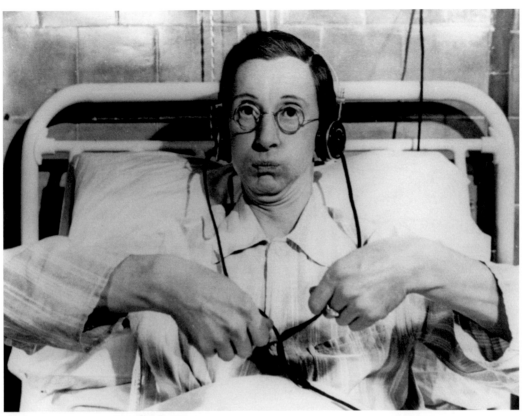

Mr. Hinton, *Carry On Nurse* (1959).

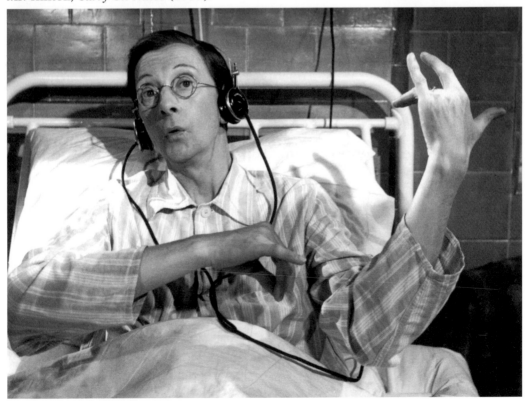

you run the film a hundred times, you wouldn't notice any difference. And, incidentally, on that parade, it was only the regular officers who fell out and fainted!'[18]

The film eventually grossed £500,000. The actors who stayed on for the sequel, *Carry On Nurse*, continued to play the same type of roles: Kenneth Williams remained the intellectual snob; Kenneth Connor, the hypochondriac; Shirley Eaton, the eye candy; Hattie Jacques, the matronly figure; and Hawtrey, the skinny ninny who "skips happily through life with a child–like unawareness of the dotty impression he is creating on others."[19]

The foundations of typecasting, the curse of the *Carry Ons*, were being laid.

It's a beautiful role he plays in *Carry On Nurse*. Confined to his hospital bed and lost in his world of hospital radio, Hawtrey, as "Mr. Hinton", steals the show with his snappy appearances. He vigorously conducts the orchestra[20] and mimes the pianist he's listening to, he cries like a big girl at the latest instalment of *Mrs Dale's Diary*, and shares with the man in the next bed "*the* most marvellous recipe" he's just heard for "Campus Jamboree Folly" ("You take a couple of red raisins, two whites of eggs, one grated earphones … earphones? Oh, you wicked, bad girl! I shall miss the next programme!").

These films may have been in black and white, but Hawtrey stands out like a rainbow.

Aubrey Phillips: 'If you examine them, you know, Charles never had huge parts in them. They were always cameo roles. A lot of it was his facial reactions, probably deliberate.'[21]

Richard Dyer: 'He's always on. Quite often he isn't given much to do but stand around, but nonetheless he is perpetually animated. His eyes dart bird–like behind his wire rimmed glasses, he nods at everything people say, looks delighted or crestfallen. No actor ever gave better value on the reaction front.'[22]

When the second series of *The Army Game* came to an end in June 1958 so did Hawtrey's involvement. At the time, he publicly claimed it was his decision to leave because he "was disenchanted with the script quality of the show and [was] reluctant to be swallowed up by his

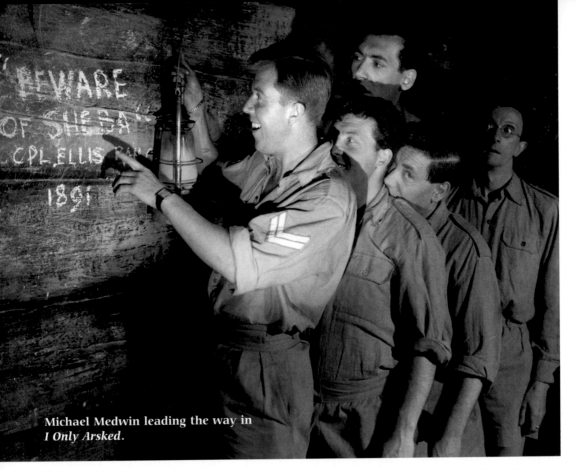

Michael Medwin leading the way in
I Only Arsked.

characterisation as the Professor."23 But, not surprisingly, it was another one of his yarns. When he gave his final interview to *The Sun* in 1988, he admitted he was actually dropped at the end of the first series and suggested his co-stars Michael Medwin, Bernard Bresslaw and Alfie Bass "whispered [him] out." 24 He makes no mention of the fact that it was actually thanks to Medwin that he had been given a second chance.

Michael Medwin: 'He was popular in the first series and when [the producer] fired him, I insisted he be re-instated because of his popularity.'25

Norman Rossington: 'It is true that Michael Medwin had him re-instated for, although he actively disliked him, he was also aware that Charlie was of paramount importance to the series.'26

Given the problems between Hawtrey and his fellow cast members, when, to the disbelief of the producer, he brought up a request for star billing and increased wages, there was no offer of another bailout at the end of the second series.

Norman Rossington: 'He was one of the most professional actors I have ever met; he could do a retake that was exactly the same as the scene he just played to the letter, with every detail, no matter how small, logged in his memory. But for all his professionalism I found him very difficult to work with, as *The Army Game* team were a sociable bunch and had a lot of fun together. However, Charlie was never part of this, preferring to stay apart from the others and was a painfully private person. I can remember how surprised I was to find that he was an alcoholic, because he never drank a drop on set but made endless pots of tea. With regard to his dismissal, as far as I was aware, Charlie was sacked for unreasonable demands for more money and not because of his addiction to the bottle. What I remember so clearly about him, aside from his tea making, was his knitting on set; the Professor knitted, so he took to knitting too. He was one of the most strange people I have ever met, in dress, speech, stature and personality. Utterly bizarre in everyway.'[27]

Michael Medwin: 'I am afraid I do not have any affection for him whatsoever. He was never a team man in *The Army Game*. One acted with him, devoid of contact, and he was a sad pain in the arse.'[28]

With Hawtrey now off the small screen, his new agent since May 1958, Eric L'Epine Smith, wrote to the BBC to try and kick–start a new television series.

10 June 1959

Dear Eric [Maschwitz],

I wonder whether you think it would be a good idea to feature CHARLES HAWTREY in a series? [The word "NO" is written in pencil beside this question.]

As perhaps you know he has had a tremendous success in Carry On Sergeant and Carry On Nurse and is in Carry On Teacher, which has yet to be shown, and he is doing another Carry On later in the year.

He is enormously popular and his fan public is amazing, which started chiefly when he was the Professor in The Army Game, which, according to many people, has not been quite the same since he left the programme.

I have a feeling that teamed with the right woman, either comedienne or straight, he could be a great success in television.

If the idea appeals to you I would like to discuss it with you and get down to something more concrete. It is only an idea at the moment.

Kind regards,
Yours sincerely,

Eric L'Epine Smith. Ltd
Governing Director

Despite the negative comment scribbled on the letter, Maschwitz, the Head of Light Entertainment on BBC Television, replied saying it would be dependent entirely on the script and if L'Epine Smith could find a "first–class idea and the writer to carry it out", he would be interested.

11 January 1960

Dear Eric,

You may remember sometime ago I wrote to you regarding the possibility of Charles Hawtrey appearing in a television series for you and you showed interest.

I am enclosing a brief format entitled "Ask Aunt Harriett" or alternatively "Send For Harriett". This is by Brock Williams, who incidentally sends his regards to you. I think it has the makings of a good idea and would like to get your reaction. I have not approached Hattie Jacques as she is not under management to this office but Hartnell and Hawtrey are and they would be very keen to embark on such a series.

Kind regards,
Yours sincerely,

Eric L'Epine Smith

Sadly, the synopsis is missing from the BBC's files.
Maschwitz sat on the proposal for a couple of weeks and eventually

"Charlie, essentially, always played fey, no matter what the role. The public loved it so why would he monkey with the persona? Speaking for myself, I was pleased to write for him in this vein." Norman Hudis offers a new reflection on the man who played his characters in, amongst others, *Carry On Teacher* (1959).

wrote back saying, "I regret that this would not fit in with our plans for the coming year."29

Evidently, Hawtrey's reputation at the BBC was terrible, and he wasn't about to help matters that September when his latest dispute brought an end to his 17-year run playing Norman Bones on Children's Hour. This time, his quest for star billing meant he was heading for an acrimonious split with the very department that had kept him in regular work since 1943.

6 September 1960

Dear Mr. Gould,

I wish to confirm our agreement on Charles's billing as follows:

Charles Hawtrey
and with Patricia Hayes

Perhaps you could be good enough to confirm this. ["No! We should not agree to this" is written in pencil beside this question.]

Yours sincerely,

Eric L'Epine Smith

8 September 1960

Dear Mr. L'Epine Smith,

Thank you for your letter. Since speaking to you, the arrangements for the new lay-out of Radio Times have been announced and so our proposed billing for Norman and Henry Bones would be, e.g.

The Pink Pearls
Starring
Charles Hawtrey
and
Patricia Hayes

Another adventure of
Norman and Henry Bones, the boy detectives

I think this is probably an improvement on our original idea.

Yours sincerely,

Graham Gauld
Children's Hour Department

12 September 1960

Dear Mr. Gauld,

Thank you very much for your letter of the 8th September with regard to the proposed lay-out for the billing of the "Pink Pearls" in the "Norman and Henry Bones" series. Unfortunately Mr. Smith is away on holiday at the moment and I am not fully aware of what has passed between Mr. Smith and yourself, but I have had a long talk today with Mr. Hawtrey and he still disagrees with the billing of "and Patricia Hayes". Although Charles fully appreciates your position in this matter he feels that at this stage of his career he could not agree to this and would wish the billing to be:

Charles Hawtrey
with
Patricia Hayes

He, therefore, feels that if this could not be agreed to then you would possibly be able to re-cast the part with perhaps a younger artist.

I do hope this has not caused you too much inconvenience but I can assure you that Mr. Hawtrey is adamant on this point.

Yours sincerely,

Terry Carney

Hawtrey was demanding and anxious to prove who's the star, bluffing the BBC with a reminder of his lengthy career and a cocky suggestion that they re-cast the part he'd made his own over the last 17 years. Hawtrey was crying out, "Go on, I dare you" and, to his shock, the BBC did.

"We regret that we are unable to accept Charles Hawtrey's proposed billing," concluded Graham Gauld, "so we shall be very sorry to lose his services."[30]

It's just as well he had the *Carry Ons* to fall back on; they were going from strength to strength, so who needed the BBC anyway? Plus, ITV were in talks to give Hawtrey not only another chance, but his *own* television series. And this time he'd get it.

CHAPTER EIGHT
CARRY ON CHARLIE

I may be gay and play camp characters but I think that I am a professional. My work has always come first. My private life is my own and I simply wish to be left alone.[1]

Charles Hawtrey

E rnest Maxin: 'I produced two series with him, one called *Our House* and the other *Best of Friends. Our House* was the *Carry On* team — you know, Joan Sims, Charles Hawtrey, Hattie Jacques. *Best of Friends* was Charles Hawtrey and Hylda Baker, they were the stars. For *Our House* we did thirty-nine, live, one-hour shows.'[2]

Trying to capitalise on the success of the *Carry Ons*, by then up to its fourth instalment with *Carry On Constable*, ABC Television hurriedly put together a new sitcom for ITV which used the same people, both in front of the camera and behind.

Ernest Maxin: 'Norman Hudis wrote *Our House*, because he'd written the *Carry On* films and [ABC] had already booked the artists, but didn't have a story! So we got together and we worked out the story of all these people who meet in an estate agent's office and, finding the properties to be too expensive for each of them, decide to club together and buy a house between them. They all had their own duties in the house, rotated of course, and the stories each week were built around each individual.'[3]

Joan Sims: 'Hattie played Georgina Ruddy, a librarian who needed to make a great deal of noise at home to compensate for having to be quiet at work, Charlie Hawtrey, again the eccentric loner, worked in the council offices, and I was Daisy Burke, who moved from job to job on a regular basis.'[4]

Ernest Maxin: 'When I say live, we shot them *as live* because there were so many people in the cast. We didn't edit them and they went out about a month later. There were three commercial breaks in it so we'd film right up to the first one and then change a set or two, do the middle twenty minutes, another quick break, then the final twenty. We'd rehearse all week in the rehearsal room and go into the studio on a Saturday and rehearse with the cameras and lighting. On the Sunday, we'd come in and have a rehearsal from 9.30 in the morning until 6pm. The audience would arrive between 7 and 8pm — about 300 people; they were at one end of the studio and we'd go straight through to get their laughter. We never used canned laughter in those days. You couldn't make a mistake because having got the laugh, you'd never get the same response if they'd seen it before. It became a very big success.'[5]

In "Simon Willow", Hawtrey had clinched another co-starring role in a hit television series. He could take comfort in achieving second billing beneath Hattie Jacques, whose broad style posed no threat to him. Now and again, when the plot revolved around his character, he even got top billing. Coupled with his increasing fame in the *Carry Ons*, it made the 1960s look the most promising of decades so far. He knew he was playing

"Charles Hawtrey makes his big decision and joins the rest of the new tenants in ABC Television's new comedy series, *Our House*, which starts on the ITV network on Sunday, September 11th [1960] at 3.25pm." (Publicity picture and accompanying caption.)

up to the stereotype of the weedy incompetent, but the allure of fame and making his mother proud was too great to curb his inner conflict. Alice was a potent force to succeed.

Ernest Maxin: 'As far as I could tell, his mother had a great influence on him and he felt that he had to please her all the time, as well as do well for himself. He showed me a photograph of him with her in the garden of their house, probably taken about twenty years before, and she looked exactly like him! I remember Norman Hudis saying to me, "She's like Charles Hawtrey in drag!" He felt responsible for her and loved her, but didn't want to show anyone that he was a loving son. He wanted to appear more independent and stronger. He was an emotional person who was frightened to show emotion in case people thought he was weak. So he always sat in a corner and wouldn't enter into conversation with anybody. I think he was so dominated by his mother that he was still a little boy. I think he drank a lot too.'[6]

They both had begun to drink a lot; Alice to ease her senile dementia, and Hawtrey to quell the pain of seeing his beloved mother gradually slipping away — in addition to the physical strain she was placing on him as her fulltime carer. But, before her death, Hawtrey's drinking was confined to the privacy of their family home in Hounslow, as those who were around him at the time will verify.

Ernest Maxin: 'Charles was wonderful to work with. He took direction extremely well. His delivery of lines was excellent. He never forgot a line, he was always word perfect. We'd give him all the visual things because he was funny; you'd only have to show him once and he'd do it. I never saw him under the influence of drink; he was always the perfect professional. And, as I talk about him now, I still have that liking for the man himself.'[7]

Peter Rogers: 'He was a professional. He was a gentleman. He was always a gentleman, whatever happened; a carefully spoken, well mannered gent.'[8]

Norman Hudis: 'Hattie Jacques held the opinion that Charlie was eccentric because what else could you expect from someone who lived with a forgetful mother and an alcoholic cat? I confess I have no direct knowledge in this area and if I have wronged either Mum or the puss, I unreservedly apologise in advance. But Hattie was a shrewd one and merits quotation.

Playing his own Aunt Wilhelmina in the *Simply Simon* episode of *Our House*. ABC/Cinema Museum.

Did his eccentricity, on and off screen, arise from or depend on alcohol? I doubt it. He was self-admittedly vulnerable, but I never saw him take a drink. In fact when he did a personal appearance for me at our local Red Cross at Rickmansworth, when we still lived in England, he wouldn't even sip a sherry with me at lunch beforehand. And when he'd successfully and sincerely declared the fête open and they gave him a book by way of modest thanks, this deceptively skilful actor had to turn away to hide tears — brought on by strangers thinking of him to this extent, routine and formal though anyone else might have considered the gesture. To him, it was love, for which, I feel, he forever sought.'[9]

By the end of the decade, when Hawtrey's drinking had fully penetrated his work, these tributary comments would make way for derisive and pathetic descriptions. Yet for the time being he was a valued performer, always unfaultable and dependably creative on screen.

Norman Hudis: 'In one episode of *Our House*, I'd written in a huge wall-safe behind Charlie's desk (he was playing a Civil Servant). The set safe was already built when we changed the story and the safe was no longer needed. Nothing for it but to leave it there, unexplained and unused. "Pity," said Charlie, "it's a lovely prop." Just before we recorded, live, with audience, he asked director Ernest Maxin to keep the camera on him for a moment at the end of a certain scene. Maxin did so and, unrehearsed, Charlie opened the safe and took out his sandwiches. Perfect for the character, and a huge laugh.'[10]

Judging by the three of the 39 episodes that evaded ITV's cull of its archive and are now circulating amongst collectors, Hawtrey was getting many huge laughs. He is perfect in providing the main source of laughter for Hudis's trademark blend of comedy and pathos, playing up to the studio audience with deliberate smirks and glances and playing up to the camera by looking directly at the viewer, just as he would in the *Carry Ons* — the only member of the team to get away with it.

The Stage, 15 January 1960

This is an original teleplay by Norman Hudis. To me, it looked as if somebody were trying to write a book about how-to-write television comedy. "First, remember it's a visual medium," then follows a list of visual gags;

throw a shoe at a chamber-pot, which pings; have someone sneeze so that a character's headpiece falls off; spill ink on a chair and have somebody sit on it; have a foot stuck in a wastepaper basket; cover a character with plaster. They're all in Our House. We were introduced to a number of old gags and a number of people. There were: the newly-weds who won't live with in-laws. A librarian and a bank clerk who are thrown out of their digs by the landlady for playing the wireless too loud. An elderly husband and wife. A young man studying law, and an odd-job girl. They have something in common – nowhere to stay. Inevitably they buy a broken-down house. The episode closes with the difficult local government man wanting to take a room. This part is played beautifully by Charles Hawtrey.

In the 13 half-hour episodes of the follow-up series, *Best of Friends*, which began broadcasting in January 1963, Hawtrey played Charles, an insurance salesman who works next door to a café run by his housemate Hylda Baker.

Producer Ernest Maxin, wanting to make sure it was different in style from the previous sitcom, used his brother Gerry, Bob Block and Brad Ashton to write the scripts, instead of Norman Hudis. "We feel that in *Best of Friends* we have the very best parts of *Our House* comedy and in the shorter half-hour format, the humour runs swiftly and with greater accent," Maxin told the press. "Charles and Hylda really play their parts to the hilt."[11] None of these programmes is available.

With his name at the top of the pile in the show's credits, Hawtrey had finally conquered star billing. Baker, however, being equally as strong-willed, didn't see it that way and the growing friction led to hostility on both sides.

Brad Ashton: 'Originally the series was to be called Charles and Hylda but Hawtrey and Baker disliked each other so much that we decided to change it to Best of Friends, and had Kenneth Connor and Patricia Hayes under a stand-by contract to take over the lead roles at a moment's notice. It was a particularly difficult series to write because though they were supposed to be such great friends, they refused to actually appear together in any scene. On screen they only actually spoke to each other on the telephone or on the other side of a door so we could record them separately and cleverly edit it afterwards. They both frequently demanded unnecessary script re-writes just to exert their clout as stars.   During heated arguments I threatened to resign several times, but Ernest Maxin was a fantastic diplomat and managed to get us to cool down and return to an even keel.'[12]

Ernest Maxin: 'If I gave Hylda something funny to do, Charles would say, "Hmm, I think her bit's funnier than mine." I'd have to think very quickly and say, "No, I've got something else, *as well*, for you to do." And I'd give him something — just on the spur of the moment, think of something — or if I couldn't think of something, I'd say wait until the tea break. Although they worked very well together, and they bounced off each other extremely well when performing, they never spoke to each other. As soon as they finished their scene they never spoke to each other! There was that "I don't want you to get more laughs than me" so I was always the one they came to.'[13]

Hawtrey's attitude was not misogynistic, despite his earlier quarrel over sharing the bill with Patricia Hayes in *Norman and Henry Bones*, but another outbreak of fretfulness at not being acknowledged as the show's outright star, particularly since Baker's comedy was in danger of taking over his own. Like a small child, scared and afraid, he didn't have the nerve to confront Hayes personally, nor in this case Baker with whom he had gladly partied in his house in Hounslow. ("Cars were up the road, there was lots of noise and dancing, and then they came out doing the conga!"[14])

In later years, Joy Leonard revealed, Hawtrey was keen to give her a crank phone call, his favourite way to channel his bitterness with past acquaintances.

Joy Leonard: 'There were a lot of artists that he used to slate like mad in the end. I went round there once and we were sitting on his settee, and he said, "Who don't you like?" So I said, "Hylda Baker." "Why don't you like her?" he asked me. "Because she's a nasty old woman," I said, and I told him that we'd been in this variety show and she'd thrown her weight around. So he said, "Let's go through the names of those we don't like and then we'll phone them up and be rude to them! I'll phone Hylda Baker first …" Well, thank God she wasn't in!'[15]

Brad Ashton: 'To be fair, his performances in *Best of Friends* were faultless. He played his part very well. I'm sure we would have been booked for a second series had the first not been so fraught with backstage problems.'[16]

Ernest Maxin: 'You had to treat him very delicately. He was physically not a strong man. You would sometimes feel, when you directed him, that you had to be very careful to make him feel that it was all his own and that he wasn't being told what to do. Charles was a little bit touchy about these things. I always felt very sorry for him, he was a very lonely man and odd in type. He was rather like a character that you read in a comic, a drawing rather than a real life person. I always felt that when I was speaking with him, with Hattie and Bernard I was speaking to real people, but with Charles it was more like a Disney character. I couldn't imagine him existing at home, doing normal day-to-day things like going to the toilet! The only times I saw him walking was on the set! It was spooky in a way. I honestly don't think there was a real Charles Hawtrey. I think when Charles went home he took the character with him, and slept on him.'[17]

Maxin makes a shrewd observation, especially about the Hawtrey we see on the screen in the *Carry On* films; he and his fellow 'Carry Onners' are like a zoo of extremes and over-the-top caricatures, each looking and even *sounding* like cartoon characters, with their elongated vowels and yelps and comedy giggles.

Off the screen, in a complete reversal, as Maxin and others have also pointed out, Hawtrey was aloof and insular.

Barbara Windsor: 'You'd get Hattie doing the *Times* crossword, Bernie Bresslaw doing the *Telegraph* crossword, Joanie Sims would be standing there talking about the price of meat in Tesco's. You would have Kenny holding court where I would be — 'cause you know he'd be telling you these jokes, making everybody laugh. There'd be Sid who would start a poker school. And there would be Charlie, miles away, sitting in his chair, in the back, drinking sherry ('cause he did like a tipple) and like kind of saying, "What am I doing in these dreadful films?"'[18]

Aubrey Phillips: 'He never drank sherry. He drank Sandeman's port. It had to be Sandeman's. Same as with lemonade, it had to be R. White's. And when it came to champagne, it had to be Moët et Chandon, preferably pink.'[19]

Peter Rogers: 'In the canteen at Pinewood, they used to say, "Oh, there's another *Carry On* coming in, so we'll have a happy time in the restaurant." And they did. They used to sit together and laugh and scream and tell each other stories, but Charles didn't take part in that. He wasn't a team man at all. He always stayed on his own. He was an old man. He'd been in films long before they'd been born.'[20]

In his late forties, Hawtrey was hardly an old man. But what Rogers is undoubtedly describing is the same superiority Hawtrey had brazenly projected toward his colleagues on the set of *The Army Game* and *I Only Arsked!*

Barbara Windsor also comments: "I think Charlie looked down his nose at the *Carry Ons*."[21] And she was exactly right. Unlike others on the set, Hawtrey never approached his work half-heartedly or with indifference.

"His interest was entirely of coming into work, getting the job done, going home, making sure his lines were right for the next day. He lived purely for the profession," adds Ernest Maxin.[22] In that respect, he was the antithesis of every *Carry On* role he played; while his characters floated along, full of fun, carefree and naïve, in real-life he was tense, anxious and in no mood for levity. It was a trait inherited from the masters he had encountered over the years. "[Richard Tauber] was a disciplinarian. I approve of *that*," Hawtrey later stressed when talking about the Austrian tenor and his approach to work.[23]

If there was one person who would not kow-tow to his self-imposed detachment, it was Kenneth Williams.

Jon Pertwee: 'There'd always be rows going on between Kenny and Charlie, because Charlie used to come onto the set with his plastic bag, with his newspaper in it, his packet of Woodbines[24], his sandwich and bottle of lemonade. Every single day, Kenny Williams would hide it and when he wanted to sit in a corner and do his *Times* crossword, or whatever it was that he had his pencil for, and eat his sarnie, it was gone. And there'd be this terrible ruckus that went on, all the time. It was so tedious — the same joke.'[25]

Jack Douglas: 'He kept away from the general enjoyment of the team and appeared to prefer to sit alone and had a bit of a "them and us" attitude towards actors and was rather a snob. The general feeling was that he wasn't a member of the inner circle, so to speak, through no fault of theirs, but self-inflicted.'[26]

Aubrey Phillips: 'He got on with Williams all right. I know that to be true because I have been in their company at the same time. He got on with Joan Sims, very well indeed, and Hattie. He absolutely hated Kenneth Connor. I went to see [*Stop It Nurse!*] that Charles was doing at a theatre in Torquay, with Bernard Bresslaw and Kenneth Connor.[27] When I went backstage to see Charles he was tucked away in a small dressing room, in the side. I said, "What the fucking hell are you doing down here?" — Because it was number five or six, this dressing room. He said, "At least it keeps me away from bloody Connor, otherwise I'll be passing him all the time, so I only see him when I'm on the stage!"'[28]

Joy Leonard: 'No, he didn't like him. "He was a snake, an all round snake!" I think one of his favourites was Joan Sims, because they used to sit drinking together and they'd chat over old times.'[29]

Kenneth Williams: 'He talked with a sort of *Telegraphese*[30], which Joanie understood perfectly. She'd always interpret everything that Charlie was saying, I certainly couldn't — some of this was absolutely beyond me. It was so code-ish.'[31]

It was only a matter of time before Hawtrey's exasperation with the team's merry camaraderie would lead to his first outburst with Peter Rogers. This occurred, according to *The Carry On Companion*, during the making of *Carry On Regardless*, in late 1960. He argued vehemently for a rise from third to first billing, and was displeased with the "lack of funny lines" Norman Hudis had written for him. "I am a comedian!" Hawtrey shouted at Rogers — who probably shot back that the only thing ever to be billed first were the words "Carry On".[32]

Norman Hudis: 'This is the first I have heard of Hawtrey complaining about material I wrote for him. I think Peter Rogers would have told me of any such unhappiness on Charlie's part. I don't recall any such report. Also if Hawtrey ever read the original script he would have seen an entire sequence devoted to him — one in which he has to hide in a wardrobe and report on a woman's night-time dreams, etc.

The censor killed it so perhaps it wasn't ever filmed. I simply don't know. Paranoia? Maybe. If so, very sad. If not, rather inexplicable.'[33]

CARRY ON REGARDLESS (extract from cut scene)

GABRIEL DIMPLE (Hawtrey) stands in for DELIA KING (Liz Frazer) when she fails to turn up for an assignment from Helping Hands, an agency run by BERT HANDY (Sid James) designed to help people in any way they wish. The assignment is to sit in the bedroom of MRS RILEY (Eleanor Summerfield) while her husband is away, and write down everything she says in her sleep. But GABRIEL does not know this when he arrives at the door of her flat:

GABRIEL: Madam – what possible good can I be to you in the wardrobe?!

MRS RILEY: Plenty – with a notebook.

GABRIEL: A notebook?!

MRS RILEY: Do you have one?

GABRIEL: No madam, I do not! One way and another, I seem to be singularly ill-equipped for this job. I really think I'd better go … WHOOP! (he's grabbed)

MRS RILEY: Don't! I'm desperate!

GABRIEL: I'm sorry, madam, but there's clearly been the most awful mistake.

MRS RILEY: Oh, not too awful really – though I *did* ask for a *woman*.

GABRIEL: A *woman*?!

MRS RILEY: Well – if you were in my shoes, wouldn't you?

GABRIEL yammers.

MRS RILEY: Oh *really!* Man, woman – what difference does it make, so
             long as you use your ears?

GABRIEL: (wriggling a finger in each) I can't be hearing right!

MRS RILEY: Oh *do* help me! I do it every single night. And the awful thing
             is – I don't *know* what comes out. That's why I need a
             Helping Hand.

GABRIEL: And an 'elpful ear?[34]

Any hint that Hawtrey was aggrieved with this part doesn't come
across in an interview he undertook whilst making the film, though this
almost certainly was before he knew that one of his scenes would end up
on the floor. On paper, at least, he had the opportunities to sparkle on his
own. In his scenes in *Carry On Regardless* he was the star and not a
supporting cast member. There was no Kenneth Williams or Kenneth
Connor to share the screen and the laughs with.

Charles Hawtrey: 'You can quote me as saying that this is, in my honest
estimation, the funniest *Carry On* so far. It is a little different from the
previous four in so far as there are fewer group scenes and therefore more
individual performances. Nevertheless, the humour is more mature, more
sustained and plentiful than ever. I am very glad to be back and if possible
I would like to work exclusively in films. It is true that many actors move
easily from one medium to another without apprehension, but speaking
for myself, I think that anyone seeking a career in films can suffer from
the overexposure of television. If people see too much of an artiste in their
own homes they are less likely to put themselves out to see him in a
cinema or theatre. My point is that artistes with film aspirations are wise
if their television appearances are not over-frequent.'[35]

But it wasn't Hawtrey's wisdom that brought about the scarcity of
his own television and theatrical engagements. Moreover, his claim to
want to work solely in film contradicted what he continually told
producer Ernest Maxin.

Ernest Maxin: 'It was the theatre more than the film industry that he
talked about and loved. I remember him saying to me, "People should

always be in the theatre before they enter films. Because you're out there on the stage in front of all those people and you mustn't make a mistake. When you're filming you can make mistakes and shoot it again." He felt that the theatre was far more professional than the "movies", as he called them.'[36]

His previous demands for top billing in television (*Chain Male* and *The Army Game*) and radio (*Norman and Henry Bones*) had failed, but Hawtrey had proved it possible in film where his small roles in *Please Turn Over* (1959) and *Inn For Trouble* (1960) were credited as "Guest Star" (a condition specified in his contracts). Now, as an indisputable mainstay of the *Carry On* team, Hawtrey refused to back down and when Peter Rogers offered him the role of "Wilfred Haines" in the next *Carry On* film, his terms and conditions went even further. It was a daring risk, considering Rogers was his sole employer.

Peter Rogers: 'He priced himself out of *Carry On Cruising*! There was a film publication called *The Cinema* and there was a man called Williamson, "Willie" we called him; and he said something about, "There's a new *Carry On* film being made and if doesn't include Charlie Hawtrey, it's can't be worth seeing" or words to that effect. Of course, next thing we know his agent, Eric L'Epine Smith, wants ten times the money he had before, a star on his dressing room door, and one thing or another. Eric wouldn't have thought of such a thing; he did what his artist asked him to do. That's what an agent's for, to save you doing it yourself. Either you're too morally cowardly or you haven't got time. So I told him to "Piss off!" and we used Lance Percival instead.'[37]

Brad Ashton: 'I'm sure Charles never realised how difficult he was to work with and was exceptionally upset and complained to me bitterly when he was dropped and his role given to Lance. He couldn't understand why, because he thought Lance was "this useless guy" who killed the part he could have done better.'[38]

Gerald Thomas: 'It was a difficult situation. But with the best will in the world we just could not bill him above Sid James, for example.'[39]

Peter Rogers: 'He reached a point where he did not fit into the team, and team work is vital if these films are to be made in the allotted time. He

Being that close to Kenneth Connor in 1963's *Carry On Cabby* would not have pleased Hawtrey. For reasons known only to himself, he considered Connor "a snake – a viper!"

was not pulling with us, but standing alone. He used to say I was drunk with power, but power is something I have very little use for. But on the next *Carry On* he came back in normal circumstances, as though nothing had happened.'[40]

With an important proviso: that he would never be billed anything less than third place. Hawtrey returned to 1963's *Carry On Cabby*, the first to be written by Talbot Rothwell. The role of "Pint-Pot Tankard" was the perfect embodiment of his now established on-screen character: delicate, adorably happy and busting a gut to please, innocently carrying on regardless no matter what.

Other books on the series have claimed that Hawtrey couldn't drive before the filming of *Carry On Cabby* and was given a crash course by Pinewood staff. This, it now transpires, is incorrect.

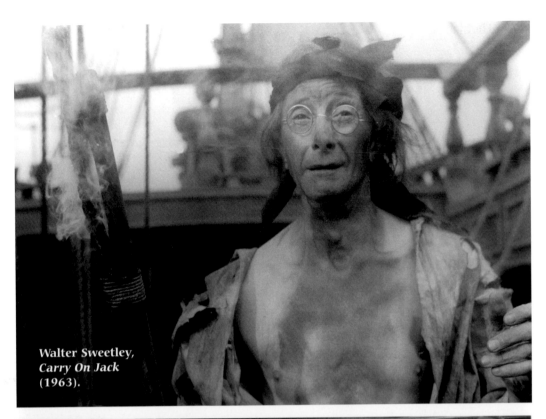

Walter Sweetley,
Carry On Jack
(1963).

A PETERS ROGERS PRODUCTION
"CARRY ON JACK" (A)
starring
KENNETH WILLIAMS · BERNARD CRIBBINS
JULIET MILLS · CHARLES HAWTREY
DONALD HOUSTON
and GUEST STAR—CECIL PARKER
EASTMAN COLOUR
FROM ANGLO-AMALGAMATED FOR WARNER PATHE RELEASE

Peter Rogers: 'Rubbish. Rumours and rumours, really! What nonsense! In the same way that if someone can't ride a horse, you get someone else to do it!'[41]

John Hartree: 'Uncle Charles loved fast cars, but had a bad accident in his early years and never drove after.'[42]

Richard O'Callaghan: 'Kenneth Williams told me some extraordinary story about how, in some town like Staines or Reading, a motorcycle policeman came along this huge queue of traffic and got right down to the front, and there, at the set of traffic lights, which were green at the time, was an abandoned car and a man, who'd climbed up the traffic lights and was peering into them. It was Charles Hawtrey, very drunk, with a very drunk mother in the back, singing rude songs. The policeman got him down and said, "What on Earth do you think you're doing?" and he replied, "I was trying to see the pretty colours!"'[43]

Incredibly, there is a certain amount of truth to what sounds like another Kenneth Williams' fable. In June 1963 Hawtrey was indeed caught drink driving, twice in fact, and addressed the authorities just as comically as Williams's tagline.

The Daily Telegraph, 13 September, 1963

2 DRINK CASES IN 8 DAYS — ACTOR FINED AND BANNED

Charles Hawtrey, the actor, was fined £25, with 10gns costs, and disqualified from driving for four years at Middlesex Sessions yesterday. He was said to have committed two offences of driving while under the influence of drink in eight days. Hawtrey, 38,[44] of Cromwell Road, Hounslow, appeared under his real name of George Hartree. He pleaded guilty to driving in Kingston Road, Staines, on June 5 while unfit through drink. Mr. John Blofield, prosecuting, said that a policeman saw Mr. Hawtrey driving erratically in Kingston Road. He stopped him near Staines police station and he was unsteady when he got out of his car.

Age question

Hawtrey, who was with his mother, was found to have consumed the equivalent of 6 ? pints of beer. When asked his age he said: "I never tell anybody that. Say I am 35." He said he had had three whiskies with water. When told by the doctor that he was unfit to drive Hawtrey said: "Doctor, you have a terribly boring time." Inspector Walter Meech said Hawtrey was summonsed for driving while under the influence of drink on June 13. On July 9, at South-Western Magistrates' Court he was fined £25 with 15gns costs, and disqualified for 12 months for this offence.

"Not unusual amount"

Mr. Ivor Stanbrook, defending, said that Hawtrey had what was for him a not unusual amount to drink. He considered himself quite capable. He did not accept that he was driving fast. His manner of driving might have been accounted for by the fact that he had lost his way. The Hon. Ewan Montagu, Q.C., chairman, said that the court would deal with the penalty side of this as a first offence. He had regard to the fact that Hawtrey had the courage to admit to his offence. "When we come to the disqualification, one cannot disregard the fact that it has been proved that you have been under the influence of drink on two occasions." Hawtrey was allowed seven days to pay, with an alternative of three months.

John Hartree: 'Sometimes Uncle Charles would get himself in trouble and my father would go down there and get him out of trouble! He would go to the races, drink too much, drive the cars and dad would have to go round and make sure he was pulled out OK and that he got home. That's the way it was.'[45]

Although Hawtrey's increasing alcoholism had been kept away from his working environment, 1963 was certainly the year in which the two worlds collided. The man whom the interviewer described as a "conscientious worker" on the set of *Carry On Regardless*, had started to fill up his R. Whites' Lemonade bottle with booze soon after.

Nearing his 50th year, Charles Hawtrey, the determined professional who persevered and fought hard for respect and appreciation, was giving up the battle.

Jack Douglas: 'As a young man he never touched it. His alcohol dependency wasn't particularly intrusive to begin with, but as the years rolled by, and the work became easier, he relied on it more and more, putting strain on others if he behaved badly on set.'[46]

Kenneth Williams: [diary, 10/9/63] 'Pinewood [for *Carry On Jack*], arrive at 7.45. Tank sequence. All day in the bloody rowing boat. Charles Hawtrey was pissed. Breath smelled appalling. It's a disgrace. Still, one must be charitable.'

Barbara Windsor: 'I met Charles for the first time on *Carry On Spying*. As spies, we were captured and held over a vat of boiling oil to make us divulge our identities. There were doubles and stand-ins on call, but Gerald preferred us to do our own stunts. It was a tricky scene to do, and when I'd unstrapped myself, I looked behind me to say something to Charlie. "Gawd, he's fainted!" I yelled. We got him down and saw that his eyes were glazed and he was white as a sheet. "Brandy, get him some brandy!" "You're joking," exclaimed Gerald. "That's what's done it … the bleedin' brandy!" I didn't know Charlie had a drink problem, did I? I soon learned though. There were always one or two occasions on every film when he got really pie-eyed and would pass out. When that happened they would shoot round him. An hour or so later Charlie would come round and throw up. Once, I took over a bucket when he was throwing up in a corner — everyone else was ignoring it. But Charlie seemed to resent it. "Oh, why

Above: Secret agent Charlie Bind (Double-O ... Ooooh!) with Barbara Windsor's Daphne Honeybutt, Bernard Cribbins' Harold Crump and Kenneth Williams' Desmond Simkins in *Carry On Spying* (1964).

Below: The cast and crew of *Carry On Spying*.

don't you piss off?" he said. "You're always trying to be so kind and good to everyone." It was so sad to see this wonderful comic actor, who I admired so much, ruining his life with booze.'[47]

Kenneth Eastaugh in his 1978 *The Carry-On Book*, which dubiously paid thanks to Hawtrey for co-operating, was extremely frank about his condition. "Hawtrey is basically a loner," wrote Eastaugh. "Though outwardly he can appear defenceless and vague, he is inwardly tough. However, he brings out the mothering instinct in women, and Joan Sims and Hattie Jacques keep a caring eye on him, maintaining contact even when no *Carry On* is in production. Barbara Windsor has cleaned up for him when he has been ill during afternoon filming."[48]

Elsewhere, Hawtrey was routinely painted as an idiosyncratic character, "wander[ing] through Pinewood stages, muttering lines and studying race form."[49]

Peter Rogers: 'Well, his love of drink was his love of drink. Just like anybody. If you like it, you like it. And if you like it too much, you don't know when to stop. And sometimes, he didn't know when to stop. I mean he would turn up and do his best. Sometimes when he couldn't stand up, he couldn't stand up. You know how it's done? Like with Ralph Richardson on the stage sometimes, you gather people around so you know he's not going to fall over. You don't make it obvious. But he knew his lines and, oddly enough, at the end–of–picture parties he would have a pot of tea. And, if he had a boyfriend come down, he was beautifully behaved all through the film.'[50]

More often than not, it was his mother who would accompany him to the studio. With Alice Hartree's mental health waning fast, leaving her home alone with their cats was no longer an option. Marlene Hargrave, a bus conductor on routes around Hounslow, remembers that Hawtrey would sit three rows from the front leaving Alice to climb up and sit alone on the top deck, her favourite place. ("A friend of mine used to be quite friendly with Charles and she did invite me to go along for a drink one morning. We didn't get offered a coffee or a tea. We got offered a gin and tonic!")[51]

Peter Rogers: 'The whole of the corridor, in front of the stage, was covered in toilet paper that she'd thrown around, so he had to keep her shut in his dressing room. She was a dear old soul but a bit doo-lally. So, what with his mother and his bottle, he had quite a busy time.'[52]

Barbara Windsor: 'One day he forgot to turn the key and she got out. We were coming back from a take and we heard this rasping voice, echoing through the corridors. "Have you seen my Charlie? I've got his tea ready and he hasn't come home from school yet!" We turned a corner and there was Charlie's old mum quizzing Sir John Gielgud.'[53]

Aubrey Phillips: 'I never met the mother so I don't know what the situation was. But other people told me she was just as bad with the drink. That would be Charles's generosity I suppose; "Mother, have one of these!" I don't think film-land helps because I visited Pinewood Studios once, and all they had to do was pick a phone up, even at ten in the morning, and they could have what they wanted; alcohol was delivered! And there was a bar, just off the set, which was open for alcohol at anytime! Doesn't really help, does it?'[54]

Jack Douglas: 'Charles had a tendency to be false, for want of a better word. He created a big public persona that he was unhappy with himself, as a way of an escape. His care of her needn't have been quite so public and he was just attention seeking.'[55]

It is a view shared by Hawtrey's nephew, John Hartree, who maintains his parents were there to assist in her care, but found it difficult because "they were poles apart in personality".[56]

Whoever is right, one thing can be certain: nobody was there in March 1965 when the paralytic pair stumbled home for the final time.

CHAPTER NINE

DEATH IN HOUNSLOW

'A problem for Rogers and director Gerald
Thomas, from time to time, has been
Charles Hawtrey. Though one of the
longest-serving members of the Carry On
team, Hawtrey has always been
something of a loner and is extremely
wary of strangers. 'There is so much
cardboard in show business that one must
take a long time before accepting people,'
he says. It is a statement he bases on
forty-two years as a performer, making
his first appearance on stage in 1925 and
in films in 1930. When he knows you and
trusts you he is full of funny stories about
the people he has met and worked with —
people like Groucho Marx and Will Hay.
A dedicated actor, he has also directed,
produced and scripted plays. Though he
has had no music lessons, he has an acute
ear. Whistle a tune and he will play it on
the piano. He also plays the horses.
Like Kenneth Williams, though more
privately, he rates professionalism among
the front-ranking qualities that he looks
for in others. His own supreme
professionalism is one of the facets which
has kept him a member of the Carry On
team for so long.[1]

Kenneth Eastaugh, *The Carry-On Book*

Recognising that the cheap and cheerful *Carry On* films had become the pinnacle of his career, Charles Hawtrey, for the first time in his life, was allowing his professionalism to erode. He hadn't worked for BBC Television in eight years, BBC Radio in five, and ITV in three. Apart from a one-off sketch with Peggy Mount at the Palladium in 1959 and another with Anna Neagle in 1964,[2] his last theatrical engagement was in the early 1950s and the regular offers to play bit parts in other films had also dried up. The annual *Carry On* films, bringing six weeks of filming and an overall fee of £2000, were now his only reliable work. Some years were fortunate and brought two, but each appearance augmented his typecasting all the more and led him into further despondency and alcoholism.

It wasn't without its rewards, however. Audiences loved Hawtrey's "Oh, hello!" entrance which he purred grinningly, clearly savouring the only catchphrase in the series, fully aware that these two simple words would guarantee him one of the biggest laughs of the film. It also confirmed, in his own mind, his senior status within the cast. But this belief was not shared by others on the *Carry On* sets at Pinewood Studios where the team and its producers were growing tired of Hawtrey's behaviour and attitude.

1965 began auspiciously with promising offers for a couple of television roles secured by his new agent Michael Sullivan at the Bernard Delfont Agency. In February he played a pilot in a David Croft series called *Hugh and I*, shooting his scenes on location at Gatwick Airport, and was due to play the "Voice of the Chaise Longue" in the *Comedy Playhouse's Memoirs of a Chaise Longue* when an unexpected tragedy struck.

Middlesex Chronicle, 19 March 1965

FAMOUS ACTOR IS BEREAVED — Fall in lounge led to mother's death

Famous comedy actor, Mr. Charles Hawtrey of 217 Cromwell Road, Hounslow, told a Coroner's Court in Twickenham on Monday, that when he took his 84-year-old mother out on March 1st she was wearing stiletto heels and shortly after midnight, when they returned, she had a fall. He said that his mother, who was getting rather unsteady on her feet, tripped in the lounge of his home while he was speaking on the telephone. Mr. B. Wynn Davies of West Middlesex Hospital said that Mrs Hawtrey was admitted, unconscious, at 1.40am. He said that, although she was X-rayed and no fractures could be diagnosed, Mrs Hawtrey died on March 10th. Mr. P. Bowen, pathologist, said that a blood clot had formed in her skull after the fall and bronchial pneumonia had developed and was the cause of death. The Coroner, Mr. H. G. Broadbridge, said that the clot had been formed as a result of the blow on the head when she fell. He recorded a verdict of accidental death.

Neighbour Violet Humphries not only recalls how Alice Hartree's senile dementia had been an increasing source of pressure and embarrassment for Hawtrey ('He used to yell at her "Come out of that garden, now, 'ere have your dinner, and shurrup!"') but quite innocently pokes fun at the octogenarian's unconventional footwear, not realising that they were what had probably led to her fall ('His mother used to wear very high heels and she used to totter along').[3] Along with other neighbours, Humphries also remembers seeing Hawtrey and his mother regularly staggering back from the local pub, Henekey's, late at night after their extended "liquid lunches".

Because of such benders and because it was he who had left her unattended to make a late night telephone call, it is quite clear why Hawtrey never stopped grieving after his mother's death. He was racked with guilt and that made her demise doubly hard to bear. "Most of all I miss Alice," he wrote to a friend in Hounslow some 21 years later. "I am comforted knowing that she is in that better place."[4]

The six or so people at Alice's funeral saw for themselves the depths of his bereavement. "He was heartbroken. I've never seen somebody so upset," remembers Maureen Hartree. "It was even more than a mother dying to him."[5]

As a consequence he withdrew from *Memoirs of a Chaise Longue* in May ("Charles Hawtrey does not now wish to take part, although, of course, he has signed his contract. We are releasing him from this engagement"[6]), but managed to return to Pinewood in July for the role of "Big Heap", the Indian chief, in *Carry On Cowboy*.

Re-watching him now, one could never spot the pain Hawtrey was suffering inside. He lights up the screen, darts about like a meerkat and,

On the set of *Carry On Cleo* (1964) with Kenneth Williams, his mother Louie and aunt Edith (seated in front of Hawtrey).

adroitly as always, delivers his comedy lines with precision. He hides his grief so well, which is testament to the professionalism that all his colleagues describe — and all wish had remained. Big Heap's love of alcohol (in this case "firewater"), something Hawtrey's character had shown a taste for in the preceding film (*Carry On Cleo*), was an in-joke of how things had become when the cameras weren't rolling.

Another suggestive wink to the audience was Hawtrey's isolation from the cast and crew, with each script characterising him as a loner. Composer Eric Rogers even represents him in the musical score by a solitary flute. He almost seems like an afterthought, which "Dan Dann, the lavatory man", living out his lone existence in a gent's washroom in 1966's *Carry On Screaming*, is proof of.

Whilst Peter Rogers maintains that for the first time there wasn't a role for Hawtrey, *Carry On* author Robert Ross says the casting of Hawtrey was done at the eleventh hour: "C.H.B. Williamson wrote a piece in *Today's Cinema* noting that for the forthcoming entry in the *Carry On* series, much respected comic great Charles Hawtrey would be absent from the cast. He expressed his sadness at this and wondered whether the box office returns would be affected by the omission of this vital player. To publicly deny this as simply a rumour and to satisfy panicked distributors and backers, Rogers cast Charles in a minor supporting role."[7]

If true, this back-pedal by Rogers would have fuelled Hawtrey's belief that he *was* the star of the series and, as a consequence, quite indispensable. Jack Douglas, astutely, is the first to raise the subject of narcissism which Hawtrey, with his delusions of grandeur, surely indulged in.

Jack Douglas: 'His eccentricities were, to begin with, his own creation and over the years they'd become as much of a part of him as one of his limbs. Charles was unhappy with himself and the way that he looked. He was an amazingly tiny man, almost a bird–like appearance, which he did not enjoy and the result was vain to the point of obsession.'[8]

Charles Hawtrey: 'I wasn't included in [*Carry On Screaming*] until production was nearly over. When I did my first scene there were only a few days left and even then it was touch-and-go. In this one I'm Dan-Dann! I've just got to give you the name and you won't ask any questions — "Dan, Dann the lavatory man." Right? Disgusting. I demanded compensation for that. And I got it. At the end of filming, fifty pound notes in an envelope.'[9]

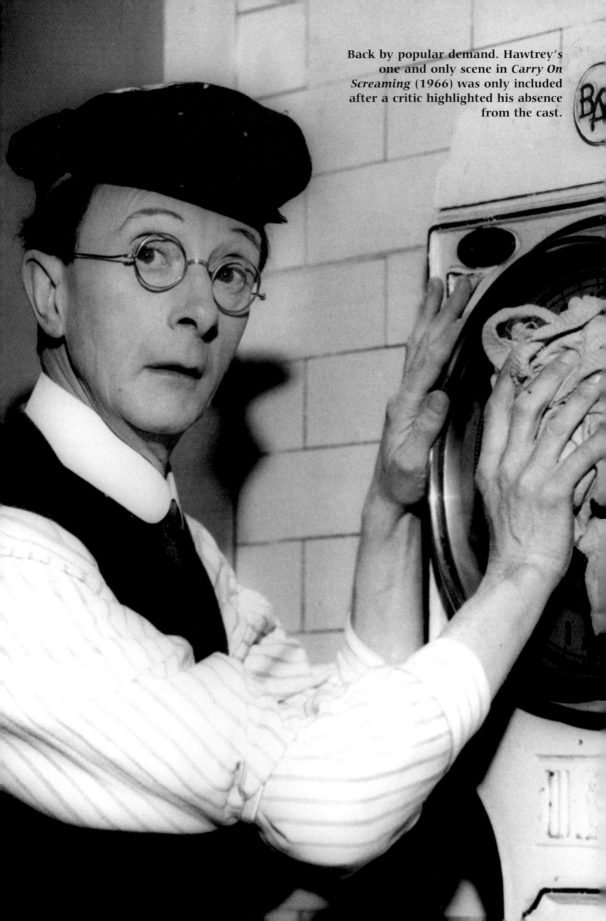

Back by popular demand. Hawtrey's one and only scene in *Carry On Screaming* (1966) was only included after a critic highlighted his absence from the cast.

Duke de Pomfrit, *Carry On Don't Lose Your Head* (1966).

As the *Radio Times* revealed to its readers in 1973, Hawtrey liked to profess distaste and had a typical stance when it came to anything like toilet humour. He consistently refused to blaspheme, which meant he would not say the word God in any context nor say a joke line that did not have a clean meaning to its *double entendre*. "It's not fair on the parents in the audience," he told the *Radio Times* reporter who went to visit him in Deal.[10]

In September 1966, a mere six months after the completion of *Carry On Screaming*, the cast were back before the cameras. Hawtrey played the "Duke de Pomfrit", an aristocrat rescued from the guillotine by the "Black Fingernail" in *Carry On Don't Lose Your Head* ("I have an urgent message for you my Lord." "Drop it in the basket. I'll read it later!"). He clearly enjoyed playing the regal type and, by all accounts, had fun whilst making it, even insisting on performing his own stunts.

Joan Sims: 'He was a wicked corpser, too, and in my scene with him in the arbour, [he] took great delight in looking mischievously at me as I delivered the line, "My brother — the Count — wishes to meet him," with the result that I could scarcely stop myself cracking up while still in shot.'[11]

Joy Leonard: 'He was courageous. He was swinging from chandelier to chandelier and they were terrified in case he broke his neck. "No, no," he said, "the public came to see me and I'm not going to let somebody else have the parts!" So he used to do it himself.'

Through this mix of self-importance and self-imposed need to safeguard his place in the *Carry Ons*, Hawtrey was giving it his all. But he was only getting through it by drinking which had sharply increased. Kenneth Williams continued to record in his diary a pathetic and forlorn Hawtrey in stark contrast to his delightfully happy Dann and Duke.

Top: On location at Camber Sands for *Carry On Follow That Camel* (1966).
Above: With Peter Butterworth, Jim Dale and Kenneth Williams.

Kenneth Williams: [diary, 21/10/66] 'Pinewood. They gave a party for the end of picture. One of the waitresses told me that Charles Hawtrey asked her for a carrier bag full of leftover snacks from the buffet, to take home with him. The sadness of it all.'

Joan Sims: 'Charlie's greatest love was his cat, and everyday at Pinewood he'd nip off to the canteen to scrounge food for it.'[12]

Peter Rogers and Gerald Thomas knew that giving Hawtrey a significant role would more than likely backfire and his erratic conduct could well jeopardise the tight filming schedule. After meeting with him to talk about the role of "Le Pice", Captain to Kenneth Williams' Commandant in *Carry On Follow That Camel*, they ignored his plea for a more substantial part.

"The part of Batman of Beau [Simpson] gives a real opportunity of being funny," he wrote in a letter to Thomas. "I can only hope that Peter can be persuaded to give this part to me — and am certain that both you and he would not regret doing so."[13]

Instead, "Simpson" went to Peter Butterworth and Hawtrey was stuck with their original offer, though it wasn't an entirely bad decision. Supporting Jim Dale as his loyal manservant would have stifled Hawtrey's chances to be as funny. There would be no quips at the raising of the "Spring bloomers" or getting the men of the French Foreign Legion to sing 'Oh, We Do Like To Be Beside the Seaside'. More to the point, he and Williams bounce off each other as only the two can. They're a terrific comedy duo whether Hawtrey liked it or not.

If Hawtrey thought Le Pice wasn't substantial enough, in *Carry On Doctor* his role was minor still. As Mr. Barron he spends the entire film in a hospital bed, going through his wife's labour pains, believing he's the one who's pregnant. There aren't many lines, just a few visual moments reminiscent of his Mr. Hinton role in *Carry On Nurse*. Again, Rogers and Thomas clearly felt a bed-ridden Hawtrey would ensure a smooth shoot, having the ability to film around him if he was drunken and passed out.

The film was also the first of two to feature Frankie Howerd whose role as "Francis Bigger" was offered to him after Kenneth Williams turned it down. According to Aubrey Phillips, Hawtrey declared himself personally responsible for Howerd joining the team at the last minute.

Aubrey Phillips: 'He'd met Frankie Howerd in some bar in London and Frankie said he was near destitute, he'd had no work in a long, long time,

To the residents of Deal this image is hard to believe: Hawtrey happily signing an autograph for a young fan, July 1967.

and could Charles recommend anything. Charles was just going to start *Carry On Doctor* the next week at Pinewood and said, "Come down to Pinewood, pretend you're visiting me and have a word with Peter and Gerald." Apparently he did exactly that and got the part.'[14]

Yet in no way is this confirmed in Howerd's autobiography *On the Way I Lost It* and, as previously exposed, Hawtrey's white lies were told to excite intrigue in his life and bolster his reputation with friends, colleagues and interviewers. (That isn't to say the pair didn't know one another. In the mid-50s, he had appeared briefly in Howerd's film *Jumping For Joy*.)

Despite his personal traumas, Hawtrey's run of iconic and memorable performances in the *Carry Ons* continued. In *Carry On ... Up the Khyber* he plays Private James Widdle, defending the Indian/Afghan pass single-handedly (well, Snowdonia) and in *Carry On Camping* he's Charlie Muggins, wandering hobo-like through the British countryside at the height of summer (well, October and November).

Since his mother's death he had purposefully stayed away from their Hounslow home, even agreeing to go on a nationwide tour of *A Funny Thing Happened On the Way To the Forum* once filming for *Carry On Cowboy* had come to an end in early September, 1965.

Unlike Widdle and Muggins, Hawtrey couldn't face being alone, especially in the house he and Alice Hartree had shared for half a century.

Aubrey Phillips: 'He was very upset when his mother died. He felt he had to get out of that house in Hounslow, so he bought this house very quickly in Mortlake — 66 Lower Mortlake Road, because he was upset about living in an empty house with his mother dead. But he was conned into buying it.'[15]

The Rank Organisation Presents
A PETER ROGERS PRODUCTION
SIDNEY JAMES · KENNETH WILLIAMS · CHARLES HAWTREY
ROY CASTLE · JOAN SIMS · ANGELA DOUGLAS
TERRY SCOTT · BERNARD BRESSLAW · PETER BUTTERWORTH
in
CARRY ON ... UP THE KHYBER IN COLOUR 'A'

"Who goes ... Oh! Now what was it now?" With Bernard Bresslaw's "Bungdit Din".

Roy Castle: 'Sometimes [on the set of Carry On … Up the Khyber] he used to stand in a corner talking to himself. He owned a block of flats when we were filming; he lived in one of them. He had a tenant who had to be evicted. It caused him a lot of trouble and preyed on his mind so much that he'd sit in a corner practising his conversations with the absent tenant.'[16]

Aubrey Phillips: 'This beautiful house, in its own grounds, obviously in need of a coat of paint, gardens hadn't seen a gardener for years, everything growing wild, lovely big staircase when he opened the front door. He said, "Come in this way, dear". He goes to the left, opens a door — and this is what would have been a lounge years ago — everything that Charles possessed was in this one room; bed, settees, table, kitchen. I said, "Charles, what on earth are you doing in this one bloody room when you've got this great big lovely house?" The house, apparently, was in four flats. Peter Butterworth was renting one of the flats, and the previous owner had said, "Oh, it's with vacant possession. All the other people will be gone by the time you take over." And that wasn't true at all; he couldn't get rid of anybody, so all he'd got was this one bloody room. He was very unhappy there. He said, "Shall we have some pink champagne?" The pink champagne was stored under the bed! I felt very, very sorry for him when I saw this room. I never ever went to that house again because it was a mess.'[17]

Kenneth Williams: [diary, 5/4/68] 'Peter Butterworth told me the saga of Hawtrey moving into the one room at his house. It was unbelievably sordid and terribly funny.'

    It was towards the end of 1967 when Phillips, a theatrical impresario staging his fourth season of Jack and the Beanstalk at the Victoria Theatre, Salford, telephoned Hawtrey's agent, Michael Sullivan.[18]

Aubrey Phillips: 'When I first booked him, I'd never seen a Carry On film. I'd heard of him but I wasn't a great cinemagoer. When I rang, I'd actually rang for an availability and price on Kenneth Williams who I did know and had seen many times in revues in the West End. He said, "Well, he's not very good in pantomime, he doesn't like it and he's a very difficult man to get on with. He's also a bit of a big head and I can't see him wanting to go and work in Salford. Can you really afford it? He'd want two thousand pounds a week." Well, admission prices in those days would be something like seven shillings and sixpence, so that obviously was out of the question. He offered me Charles and I said, "Now, which one is Charles Hawtrey?" He said, "The little fella with the glasses." I said I'd remembered him from the Will Hay films, and also *Passport To Pimlico*, but not the *Carry On* films 'cause I'd never seen one. I got him for £250 per week. On tour we'd always pay his travel expenses and accommodation, but it never went beyond £350.'[19]

In his last pantomime, over 40 years earlier, Hawtrey had trod the boards with Charles Laughton and Elsa Lanchester in *Peter Pan* at the London Palladium in the heart of London's glittering West End. Now, at 53 years old, he was playing "Simple Simon" opposite Ronnè Coyles in a rundown theatre outside Manchester.

Ronnè Coyles: 'I first met Charles on the first day of rehearsal. He looked exactly as he did in the films; you just couldn't fail to recognise him. We went down onto the stage to rehearse and, unknown to me, he'd put tapes all over the stage. Aubrey said, "Charles wants them down so he knows where to walk." So, we start rehearsals, you see, and we came to a scene where he's selling my belongings, because I'm going to be evicted from my home, and he's stood on a box in the middle of the stage. I come on and say, "Oh, Simon, what's going to happen?" Come the opening night, I went on stage for this particular scene and did my line: "Oh, Simon, what's going to happen?" and he just stopped and looked at me. There's a full house there and I looked and said, "Simon?" He just looked back at me and I thought, "Oh, he's going to do a *Carry On* funny or something."
He said, "Have you finished?" So I said, "What Simon?" He said, "Have you finished?" I thought, "What's going on here?" So I said, "Yes" and he said, "Good! Then I shall begin!" And then he delivered his lines and went through it fine. I came off to do a quick change and Aubrey dashed around from front of house. "What the hell's going on Ronnè?" he asked me. "Don't ask me! Ask him in Number One!" Well, after we'd finished the show Charles asked for me to go into his room, so I went in and asked him what it was all about. He said, "You know what you did, don't you?" I said, "No? What did I do?" He said, "All through rehearsals, when you walked away from me and turned to deliver the line, you counted five steps. Tonight you did about eight!" I said, "Charles, tomorrow I might do twelve!" He said, "Don't you dare!" It was very, very weird.'[20]

Unlike the strict well-known rule in filming the *Carry Ons*, the cast of *Jack and the Beanstalk* were encouraged to adlib and have fun with the script. Hawtrey wouldn't deviate. He offered no adlibs, just "funny walks and funny faces". Ernest Maxin, when producing *Our House* and *Best of Friends* earlier in the decade, had also witnessed his obsessive attention to detail: 'He never adlibbed, not a single word. He was a real professional.'

Ronnè Coyles: 'It was the same with one of his entrances. I was waiting in the wings with him, waiting to go on, and he said to me, "Don't talk to me please!" And he stood there waiting for his cue to go on and he's mumbling to himself, then his cue came: "Where's Simon?", and he starts counting, "One, two, three, four, five, six, seven, eight … Oh, hello!"[21]

Gossip quickly circulated around the cast that Hawtrey's peculiarity was due to alcoholism. They discovered a crate of booze behind a makeshift curtain in his dressing room, began to notice how often he sprayed his mouth with Listerine and, eventually, saw the gravity of the situation for themselves.

Ronnè Coyles: 'He invited me along to his hotel one night to have a drink with him. This lovely grand hotel, and there was some lounge music playing and a load of people having their drinks. We ordered our drinks and sat down. People recognised him and were coming over. He was loving it. The majority of these people worked at Manchester Airport, pilots staying there overnight. Things got pretty hectic after a while, the drinking went on and on and he became drunk, and the music was some blues tune and he just decided to strip and he took off everything. *Everything.*'[22]

Kenneth Williams: [diary, 22/5/68] 'The barman said Charles Hawtrey consumed two and a half bottles of port, a whiskey and a pot of tea last night! Last night I heard him shouting and bawling on the stairs. It's not the eccentricity, or the grotesquerie, or the homosexuality that puts one off Charles: it's the excruciating boredom.'

Jack Douglas: 'Although in the published diaries it appeared that Kenneth disliked him, this was not the case. But he did feel exasperated with him and Charlie seemed unable to cope with his faculties and appeared in later years to have lost his dignity which was something that Kenny could not abide.'[23]

Jack and the Beanstalk ran from 22 December 1967 and was extended until 3 February 1968 because of an excellent box office. A sold out tour immediately followed to towns such as Llandudno, Buxton and Leek. Hawtrey was praised as "an expert in creating this family party-type of atmosphere … wonderfully persuasive."[24] While another plaudit used more fitting words: "The veteran of many films came across with a warmth and sincerity that clearly demonstrated the amount of fun and *good spirits* he was putting into his performance."

In time, Aubrey Phillips would replace Peter Rogers as the only producer willing to employ Hawtrey, whose mental state was rapidly nose-diving.

Ronnè Coyles: 'I heard him talking to himself in his dressing room — who he was talking to I don't know because I tapped on the door and said, "Is someone in with you?" He said, "No, come in dear, I'm just here by myself." I went in, sat down and we chatted, then I got up and walked out

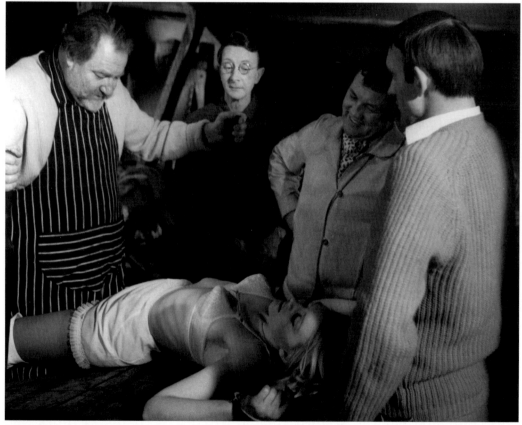

According to the Internet Movie Database, Hawtrey was the second choice to play "Swyne" in 1969's sexploitation movie *Zeta One*. The first choice, whoever he may have been, was not available.

again, went back into my room next door and he started talking again, as though someone was in the room with him.'[25]

Patrick Newley: 'The word everyone says is "paranoid". He was paranoid. Then there were great depths of despair and hatred and black moods. He just felt that nobody wanted him and that there were "enemies."'[26]

Hawtrey confided as much in a letter to Kenneth Williams in late 1969: "I am surrounded by enemies and traitors, but soon I will leave these evil shores FOREVER."[27]

Actress Peggy Mount had also noticed this when working with him on stage at the Palladium, and during the filming of *Inn for Trouble* in 1960.

Peggy Mount: 'Although I found him easy to get along with and a wonderfully professional actor, he was ridiculously camp and utterly bizarre. He had from time to time, in varying degrees, strong degrees of feelings of persecution and was convinced that people were out to get him, to the point where it affected life and movements completely. He always felt at ease with me because he felt none of the usual threats of having normal one to one relationships with fellow actors.'[28]

She was right about the effect this fantasy had on his life. Williams, in his autobiography, also writes that during the wrap party for *Carry On Again Doctor*, Hawtrey announced "he was going abroad. 'I'm taking a false beard and travelling under an assumed name, to allay suspicion. I'm meeting my companion at Smith's bookstall at the airport." It was all cloak-and-dagger.'[29]

In May 1969, while in Johannesburg to appear in South African TV series *Stop Exchange* with Sid James, Hawtrey confided to the press that, "I don't want to go back to England. I love the sunshine here. I think I'll find a wealthy widow with a gold mine and settle down."[30] Upon his return, he wound up in a low-budget science fiction film entitled *Zeta One* which is as far as is possible from *Carry On Camping* and *Carry On Again Doctor,* his other films in 1969. This soft-core pornographic tale about the "race of topless, large-breasted women from the planet Angvia"[31] sees Hawtrey, not to mention James Robertson-Justice, incongruously strapping a semi-naked girl to a rack, as well as other scenes of suggested bondage. Compare this to Charlie Muggins ("I knew I shouldn't have eaten those radishes!")

Private investigator James Bedsop,
Carry On Loving (1970).

or Dr Stoppidge ("Sir, I do not object to jiggery but I take exception to pokery!") and one realises that Hawtrey's bid for stardom was pretty much over.

Consciously or not, producer Peter Rogers, in the run up to what would be Hawtrey's final *Carry On*, was continuing to limit the amount of time he allowed him on screen. In *Carry On Up the Jungle*, released in 1970, Hawtrey's "Tonka the Great", a role originally written for, but declined by, Kenneth Williams, appears for the last twenty minutes, and "James Bedsop", the conspicuous private investigator in *Carry On Loving*, for just five. With roles this brief, Rogers brought up the sensitive issue of billing, but Hawtrey refused to be billed anything less than third and swiftly reminded him of their gentlemen's agreement back in 1963. Desperate to have him play Bedsop, Rogers uncharacteristically backed down and continued to accommodate Hawtrey's drinking on the sets of the remaining *Carry On* films and television specials in Christmases 1969 and 1970.

One would like to think that he temporarily curbed his alcoholism when playing in the children's TV series *Grasshopper Island*, made around this time. The modern fairytale tells of three orphaned boys who decide to run away and finish up by an old boat at the docks. "The owner wasn't like any sailor they had seen," says the nonchalant voiceover, "he wasn't exactly young. He wasn't exactly old. He was more a sort of elderly boy."

Naturally, it's Hawtrey. Complete with a bird in its cage, reminiscent of Bobby his budgie in *Carry On Constable*, and balls of wool and knitting needles from *The Army Game*. He agrees to sail the boys to "an uninhabited island" and they set off for twelve short episodes, though by the second, entitled *The Elderly Boy*, he's already passing round mugs of his rhubarb wine.

"The elderly boy explained that it was his favourite drink," says the voiceover, without any inflexion to suggest it might also be his favourite in real life.

After landing on the island, the boys have grown weary of Hawtrey and his black and white angora sweater, skin-tight jeans and bright yellow 'man bag'. He's cramping their style. So, after falling down a sand dune, he gives in trying to keep up and lets the youngsters explore by themselves. When they come back he's left them a goodbye note and isn't seen again for the rest of the series.

It's a quirky little role. And for Hawtrey it's the perfect epitome of his life and character: Charles Hawtrey was in his mid-fifties but wanted to be a ten-year old child again. He dressed in bizarre clothing and his mincing along the sand is probably how he'd have done it in Deal. Kenneth Williams would later recall how he'd shout out to the men painting their boats, insisting it brought some "glamour into their dull lives". One can see why. It's Quentin Crisp without the mascara and purple rinse. He's a lush but at this point it's amusing, not yet tragic.

Similar comparisons can be made with his next film, the last for the series that had kept him on the big screen for 14 years and 23 appearances. His swansong in *Carry On Abroad* gave another, more accurate, depiction of how Hawtrey, the man, existed in real life 1972. Writer Talbot Rothwell had made subtle references to Hawtrey's drinking before, going back to *Carry On Cleo*. But Eustace Tuttle, a camp, mother-dominated alcoholic, was a deliberate send-up. It was a severe and definite prod, not like *Grasshopper Island's* playful dig.

The press booklet even went as far as calling the character "schizophrenic".

Patrick Newley: 'The first time I met him was through Aubrey Phillips, when *Carry On Abroad* was playing in only one cinema in London. He came to visit him when Aubrey was playing the Wimbledon Theatre. He just turned up to say hello, and he was the little bit worse for wear. He looked dishevelled, he had his glasses on, he was always wearing a raincoat, and carrier bags. I don't know what was in them.'[32]

Aubrey Phillips: 'After we'd done *Jack and the Beanstalk* for the first time, we met up in London some weeks later and had one of Charlie's boozy nights. We ended up in Edmundo Ros's club. He was a member there and was welcomed at the door, showed to a table near the front and the cabaret was just going on, and in a loud voice he said, "Oh no, not another fucking magician!" But the magician was the top of the bill, a very famous man named David Nixon, who wasn't very happy about this comment. Charles ordered champagne, then after a little while the restaurant manager came over and asked if he could have a word with him, quietly. So Charles got up and left and was away for a good quarter of an hour to twenty minutes. I got a bit worried about it so I followed him, because he was quite well "oiled". I discovered that the last time he'd been in he'd walked out without paying the bill. He was in no state to bloody understand what they were talking about, so in the end I went back to his carrier bags at the table — can you think of anybody else walking into a nightclub with a

Sir Roger de Lodgerley,
Carry On Henry (1970).

On location in sunny Brighton for *Carry On At Your Convenience* (1971).

Above: Dr Goode carries on with Matron (1971). Right and below: Hawtrey's twenty-third and final character, Eustace Tuttle, in *Carry On Abroad* (1972).

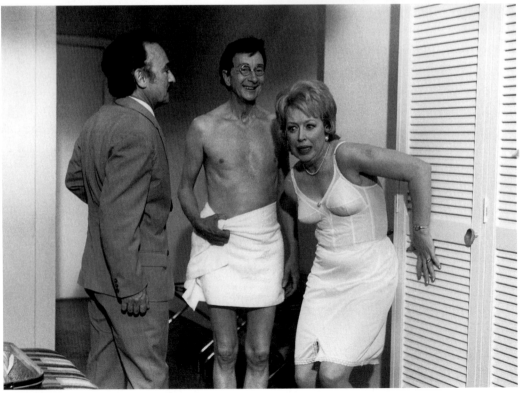

carrier bag? — found his chequebook, went back, filled it in for the amount of money that he owed and eventually got him to sign it so we could carry on with the evening. It was very embarrassing.'[33]

Sir Laurence Olivier: 'I was coming down the Pinewood road [and] I saw this pathetic figure in an old mac, with two brown carrier bags struggling along the road, and I was sure I knew him. So I lowered the window and called out, "Isn't it Charles Hawtrey?" and the figure looked up and said, "Oh, yes, Sir Laurence." So I said, "Come in and I'll give you a lift." He told me he struggles along that road every day, getting the tube from Uxbridge, to film the *Carry On* pictures which must make a lot of money. Surely they'd provide a motor-car for him?'[34]

The sight of Olivier and taking that drive to the studios in his chauffeur-driven Rolls Royce will have been a powerful reminder to Hawtrey of missed opportunities, of a lifetime's ambition that was never fulfilled. Years before, they had worked with the same people, performed in the same theatres, directed and produced their own productions but, ultimately, because of the latter's juvenile looks and perpetual typecasting, were always poles apart.

"Larry" became a Knight Bachelor, Life Peer and recipient of the Order of Merit. Hawtrey became "that funny fella with the glasses".

Patrick Newley: 'He was, in a sense, grateful that they gave him a living. But I'm not sure that he respected the performers that he worked with. If you look at the films that he'd done, prior to the *Carry Ons*, he'd worked with some wonderful actors and great directors. I think he felt that he was cheapening himself, as an actor. He always regarded himself as an actor, but in his depressions he thought they were beneath him and his talents. When you talked with him in-depth that's the way it came across.'[35]

During negotiations for Thames Television's 50-minute *Carry On Christmas* special in 1972, Hawtrey refused to accept second billing beneath Hattie Jacques, whom Peter Rogers and Gerald Thomas considered a greater pull for television audiences. On this occasion his argument was logical: Sid James and Kenneth Williams, who ordinarily would take first and second billings respectively, were not appearing and considering their agreement. Rogers and Thomas should duly promote Hawtrey from third to first place.

Both parties stood firm, playing a game of bluff. Eventually, the day before they were due to film, Thomas rang Hawtrey in one last attempt to entice him. But his call was in vain; Hawtrey, this time, in *Carry On* terms, "could not bear letting Jacques go on top."[36]

Gerald Thomas: 'I found him having lunch at Bourne and Hollingsworth and, again, over the telephone, tried to talk him into changing his mind. In the end, I said: "Well, this is it. You have to make up your mind finally right now, before you hang up. Will you accept second billing or won't you?" There was a pause at the other end of the line, then he said: "No," and hung up. I was very, very sad about it. Charles [was] a bit of a lonely man, I think, more so than any other member of the team. He used to volunteer to go to various cinemas all over the country to help promote one of the films. Of course he would be wined and dined and made a big fuss of and all I can think is that possibly this gave him a false sense of his own importance.'[37]

Charles Hawtrey: From that moment onwards I thought, "Charlie, this is where you make an exit." And I did, very politely.

Brian Matthew: 'Cause, successful as they were, you were required to do the same thing virtually every movie.

Charles Hawtrey: Oh, I didn't worry about that. But what did worry me was the dialogue, instead of being *double entendre*, with two meanings, became only one meaning, which was vulgar. And I thought, "You're going to lose a lot of people who are kind to you in the audience if you use language like that." So I thought that was the time to say "No".

Brian Matthew: Did it affect your career very badly when you made that decision?

Charles Hawtrey: Not at all — touch wood. Course, I was hated by lots of people![38]

More grandiose, paranoid fantasy; bar the second-rate stage work and handful of guest appearances on television and radio, turning his back on the *Carry Ons* killed his film career and being "hated" existed in his mind only.

Whatever spin Hawtrey wanted to put on his exit from the series, he would get another chance some years later when Peter Rogers, in *The Carry-On Book*, was quoted as saying, "Nobody is dropped for ever from the *Carry Ons*. They can all come back".[39] Indeed, Aubrey Phillips does recall efforts to coax Hawtrey to return, though by this point the quality of the films had slipped to a new low.

Aubrey Phillips: 'He refused the last two or three *Carry Ons* because they wouldn't put his money up and they had to be shot in six weeks and Charles hated the fact they wouldn't do retakes when he thought it was "bloody awful". For six weeks' work, getting up at half four in the morning, a seven day week, still at it 'til late in the evening, two grand wasn't a lot of money. The other thing that annoyed him, and I think this was the last reason they fell out; they were starting to put the old ones on the box and they were issuing contracts saying they were buy-outs so you could never earn any more money from them. You wouldn't get away with that today. Obviously that Peter Rogers is still making a lot of money out of it, they're forever turning up, aren't they? So they wouldn't put his money up or include the clause about television royalties and that annoyed him and he said no. I suppose they thought they'd enough bloody trouble keeping him sober, why should they pay him any more money? But the last few were a disgrace, weren't they?'[40]

Phillips was now Hawtrey's only trustworthy friend, and the only man willing to employ him. At first it seemed like a bargain: a *Carry On* star for £250 per week. But, eventually, he too would have trouble keeping him sober and realise it wasn't worth the effort.

Eamonn Andrews, presenting Patricia Hayes' *This is Your Life***, asks Hawtrey to recall their days on the radio playing Norman and Henry Bones, April 1972.**

CHAPTER TEN
DRINK! DRINK! DRINK!

He undoubtedly had a mental problem which, combined with drink, contributed to his downfall. There were many occasions when we would literally have to hold him up on stage because he'd had too many in the pub at lunchtime. It was very, very sad to see one of our comic greats reduced to this.[1]

Aubrey Phillips

The death of his mother in 1965 had left Charles Hawtrey like his famous typecast character: alone, vulnerable and lost. From the very beginning, Alice Hartree had nurtured his talent, ordering his older brother to convert their father's old pigeon coop into a mini theatre and serving homemade lemonade to the children who came to watch her youngest son perform. She had given him unconditional love and support so concentrated that it led to the separation with her husband William and alienated her other son, Jack.

John Hartree: 'My grandmother and grandfather split early in life but didn't divorce. I was told by my father [Jack Hartree] that his father stopped him from going to work overseas as he had to stay home and look after Grandma Alice and his brother Charles. My parents looked after Grandma and Charles as best they could although being miles apart in personality. But Uncle Charles made a scene of every situation he found himself in, and being a successful actor was his main concern.'[2]

Alice shared Hawtrey's enthusiasm and determination in becoming a revered entertainer. She had constantly showered him with praise; he was special, a star, the son of a millionaire car manufacturer, etc. Until he could reach the stardom they both believed was owed him since childhood, he could never appreciate life and could never grow old. That he spent five years playing in *Peter Pan* is an interesting and notable paradox. And, like a small boy who didn't get what he wanted, Hawtrey had spent his career routinely throwing tantrums and refusing to co–operate. Even at the age of 58, he'd demanded more money and star-billing from *Carry On* producer Peter Rogers, leaving the series because this was not met. He had pointed out to many different producers over the years that he was the only one with any talent in their series and if they wanted to keep him it'd mean more money and a star credit. Each of his ultimatums ended in tears.

His mother had been his motivator and best friend, inspiration and biggest fan, but her own high hopes and expectations were an added burden for Hawtrey to carry. Alcohol alleviated the pressure when those hopes were dashed and her mental condition deteriorated, reversing their roles so that he had become the adult and she the child.

Now she was gone, yet Hawtrey refused to believe it.

Aubrey Phillips: 'I often, when we were on tour, had a bedroom next to his and you'd hear him late at night, particularly when he'd had a drink, talking to his mother. Then having an argument with her, he'd do that as well! One of his favourite expressions to anybody, even when he was in a bar and wanted to stop someone from arguing, he'd say, "Oh, shurrup!" And that "Shurrup!" I could often hear through the wall. Bryan Johnson knew a lot more about those things, because he seemed to get the room next to Charles more than I did! He'd often come down to breakfast and say, "That bugger kept me awake again last night!"'[3]

Paul Denver: 'In 1970 he didn't have a drink problem on stage. As far as I can remember he waited until he got across the road afterwards. But once he got into that bar he certainly could knock it back. This bar had a very large Alsatian called Sheba and, about one o'clock in the morning, Charles would invariably start a conversation with the dog, telling her what had been happening, the way of the world and about the show. Often he would do this, and the dog would wander off and he wouldn't notice, he was so pissed. So he was talking to an invisible dog.'[4]

At work on the *Carry On* set Hawtrey knew his drinking had been tolerated, but for his new employer, Aubrey Phillips, he initially tried hard to keep the two separate. An admirer of Paul Denver's ability as a straight man, Phillips paired him with Hawtrey in *Carry On Holiday Startime* at the Gaiety Theatre, Rhyl, in the summer

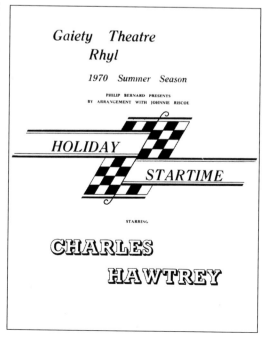

Gaiety Theatre
Rhyl

1970 Summer Season

PHILIP BERNARD PRESENTS
BY ARRANGEMENT WITH JOHNNIE RISCOE

HOLIDAY

STARTIME

STARRING

CHARLES

HAWTREY

of 1970. Before they met for rehearsals, Hawtrey insisted on doing as much preparation with Denver as possible.

Paul Denver: 'There were *long* telephone conversations, because he asked me to write the sketches out *word for word* and I would send him the script. Then he'd send it back having underlined things; I may have written things like, "Do you mind?" and he'd write back saying, "I can't say that because Kenneth Williams says that!" Lots of niggling things, but he wanted it right so I went along with it.'[5]

Aubrey Phillips: 'We took a lot of the old double–act sketches from a lot of the people who had died, people like Sid Field. There was a routine called "The Golf Sketch", which was a play on words: "Keep your eye on the ball" so Charles would get on his hands and knees and put his eyes next to the ball, you know? "Address the ball", meaning with your golf club. So he'd say, "Dear Ball ..." Absolutely stupid things.'[6]

Paul Denver: 'I'm the straight man, the expert golfer, and he's the one that gets everything wrong and misconstrues everything I say. The straight man gets frustrated, almost on the verge of losing his temper. I remember doing it on one particular night and he came off quite frightened because he really believed that I was shouting at *him*.'[7]

Aubrey Phillips: 'We had another sketch, which belonged to a couple of Scottish comedians. We called it "The Machete Routine"'[8]

Paul Denver: 'The idea is that I suggest to Charles that he'd make a very good bullfighter and he doesn't seem too keen. But then I mention the senoritas and the advantages of being a bullfighter; being like a pop star with the women chasing him. So he was playing the gay character,

CHARLES HAWTREY

Charley Hawtrey has spent a lifetime in entertainment. From the moment he first stepped on to the stage as a child actor in "The Windmill Man," he became enveloped in the ever-changing pattern of show business.

Opera, Shakespeare, Musical Comedy, Musical Play, Revue, Vaudeville, Drama, Farce, Cabaret, Records, Radio, Films, Television . . . you name it, Charles has embraced them all.

A true professional, which dates back to his early training days at the well-known Italia Conti School in London, Charles has appeared with the best-known and all-time "greats" in the business; with Will Hay in films and variety, with Scottish comedian Will Fyffe; with Richard Tauber in the record-breaking stage musical, "Old Chelsea."

Although Charles is an accomplished actor and also a pianist, it is his comedy talent that has endeared him to audiences of all ages. The proof of this is in his outstanding record of appearances in 24 "Carry On" Films.

Charles also enjoyed considerable personal success when he toured in the West End show, "A Funny Thing Happened on the Way to the Forum."

Highlights of his career? Undoubtedly his brilliance in a revue that packed the Comedy Theatre, London, entitled "New Faces," his appearances in "The Army Game," his production in the theatre, and his direction of various films, plus, of course, the "Carry On's."

but butch at the same time. It was full of *double entendres* so what you had to put in the audience's mind was that his *machete* was his *penis*. He'd get in the bullring and say, "What do I do?" and I'd say, "You whip out your machete!" and we'd wait for the laugh from his expression.'[9]

Aubrey Phillips: 'Charles was a master of double-take, the facial double-take. He really was very good at that.'[10]

Carry On Holiday Startime was well received. "Visitors need have no fear that [Hawtrey's] performances on stage do not reach the quality accepted within the film world," *The Stage* enthused to its readers. "His personality enlivens each passing scene — that personality which has so delighted and endeared itself to so many thousands."[11]

Denver's evaluation of that personality's sexuality, however, is a common misinterpretation. Hawtrey's characters were neither gay, nor butch. As Richard Dyer also pointed out in his 1989 lecture: "He plays men, but without butchness. He does it with campness."[12] And, as we should remember, effeminacy does not constitute being gay. Indeed, Hawtrey's sexual ambivalence ceases to exist when he gets Valerie Leon to help him "stick [his] pole up" in *Carry On Camping*, is thrown out of a

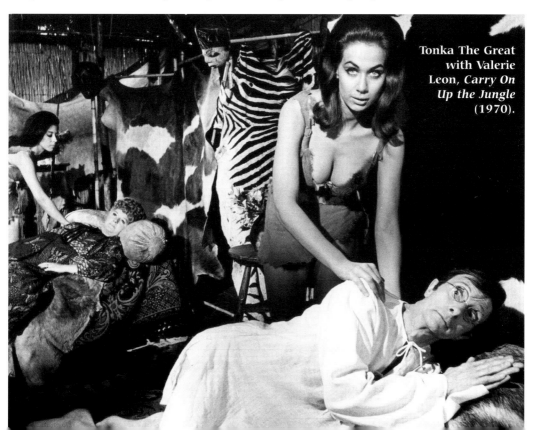

Tonka The Great with Valerie Leon, *Carry On Up the Jungle* (1970).

brothel in *Carry On Abroad* or, as was the case in Rhyl, lust over the senoritas Denver was describing to him.

No, Hawtrey's characters were in fact as straight, as blatant and as lecherous as Sid James's: in *Carry On Up the Jungle* he is the promiscuous ruler of his own harem ("King of lovers, master of women, father of countless"); in *Carry On at Your Convenience* he badgers his landlady (played by Renée Houston) for games of strip poker; and in *Carry On Cleo* he's practically a sex pest, coaxing maids to "play with his duck" and to "take it in [your] hand (it won't bite)" before ending up in Cleopatra's bed-chamber.

CARRY ON CLEO

SENECA   (Hawtrey), surrounded by CASEAR (Kenneth Williams), CALPURNIA (Joan Sims) and MARC ANTHONY (Sid James), reclining on a chaise longue, comes round after having "one of his visions".

SENECA: Oh, hello …

CAESAR: Well? Did you see anything?

SENECA: Oh yes, and it was lovely. There was this room, see? And it was filled with lovely girls, all lying about in things you could see right through

CALPURNIA: Daddy dear, you've been eating cheese again!

SENECA: Daughter darling, no I haven't … And then Caesar came in and there was a lot of soldiers.

CAESAR: Yes, well what happened to me?

SENECA: Oh, I don't remember that, I was busy looking at the girls!

CARRY ON AT YOUR CONVENIENCE

COOT: Has Victor gone?

THIS WAY TO
THE TOMB
OF
SANTA CECILIA

Chaos ensues when
Hawtrey is thrown
out of a brothel in
Carry On Abroad
(1972).

SPANNER:	Yes Charles. We're all alone.

COOT: Good. How about it then?

SPANNER: Oh I don't know. I really ought to do the dishes first.

COOT: Oh, they can wait! Just a quick one?

SPANNER: I do find it hard saying no to you.

COOT: You know how much I like it as much as you do.

SPANNER: Very well, I'll draw the curtains …

Heterosexual audiences, to add to Dyer's point, think of Hawtrey as the naughty schoolboy, rampantly chasing the girls but never catching them. (Apart from when his Sir Roger de Lodgerley impregnates Joan Sims's Queen Marie of Normandy in *Carry On Henry*.) To them he's the class clown, funny but un-cool. "In terms of being gay, Hawtrey both 'obviously' is and isn't," wrote Dyer in a chapter on Hawtrey for his subsequent book *The Culture of Queers*. "He just sails plain through the unremitting heterosexual sexism, making straight masculinity look absurd and so making it looking much more delightful to be a queen. Besides who cares what straights think? He is not defiantly queer; he just loves what he loves."[13]

Pay close attention to the *Carry On* films and you'll see the same applies to Kenneth Williams: he fends off Hattie Jacques not because he wants a man, but because she's the token McGill fat woman; his characters are often married, too, or desperate to become married; he'll leer over Barbara Windsor's bottom as she boards the coach in *Carry On Camping* or fall in love with a young impressionable girl, such as his assistant in *Carry On Abroad*.

The Jolly Roger, *Carry On Henry*'s unlikely lothario.

When the two do camp it up, there is always an ingenuous explanation. *Carry On Again Doctor* is a good example. Hawtrey's Dr Stoppidge takes exception to the "pokery" amongst the other doctors, is jealous of Jim Dale and agrees to dress up as a woman to get the secret diet serum, because he wants to be Williams's favourite "Senior House Surgeon" (the teacher's pet). You could, if you were so inclined, believe he loves Williams and wants him for his own. But looking at it from the perspective of an eight-year-old child, Hawtrey is jealous purely because he's losing his friend.

The characters played by Hawtrey and Williams were androgynous, maybe, but certainly not gay. This innocence is why they have great appeal and are adored by children; they're one of them, uninhibited and carefree, whilst feeling a latent sexual twinge. They're two funny men and that's that.

Though, in reality, it was a completely different story. Hawtrey did not enjoy life or find any part of it fun. He was now a lonely old man, broken-hearted and wholly dependent on alcohol to get through the day.

Paul Denver: 'We shared a hotel across the road from the theatre and it had an upstairs residents' bar. Charles was there every night, drinking champagne and smoking his Woodbine tips. I found him a very curious man because he'd spend a fortune on champagne but as little as possible on cigarettes. At the end of the season, so the story goes, the landlady re-carpeted the hotel with profits from Charles's champagne.'[14]

The dichotomies between Hawtrey's lavish tastes and frugal thriftiness even extended to vegetables, leading to some eccentric escapades.

Paul Denver: 'Sometimes, during show days, or our Saturday off, I'd take Charles into the countryside of North Wales. He spotted this old hotel and I was about to get out of the car, and he said, "Wait a moment. I'm going to check on the peas." So I said, "Shall I come with you?" and he said, "No, because if the peas aren't right, we'll be going somewhere else, so you wait in the car." A couple of minutes later he's back, he'd wanted to know if their peas were fresh garden peas, which luckily they were.'[15]

Aubrey Phillips: 'I was doing *Alice in Wonderland* at the Romiley Forum in Stockport one year and Charles wasn't in it. We were just unloading the set and costumes when a taxi pulled up and Charles, completely pissed, clutching a bottle of champagne, got out and said, "I thought I'd come and see you on the off chance, dear boy!" He came inside and we had a drink. After about an hour I said, "Should we get your taxi driver in? He's been waiting outside all this time." So the driver comes in too and, after a while, I said to him, "Where are you a driver from?" thinking he'd say somewhere local to Stockport. He said, "Deal. Charles flagged me down on the street and asked me to bring him, so I went and told the wife that I'd be away for a few hours." They stayed a bit longer, then set off back to Deal, stopping for Charles to buy some carrots because he reckoned they were cheaper up north.'[16]

Hating the house-cum-block-of-flats he'd hastily bought in Mortlake, Hawtrey's estate-agent friend, Bernard Walsh, had helped sell it to the actor Peter Butterworth and his wife Janet Brown, two of its tenants. After a love at first sight visit to the seaside town of Deal, near Dover, in late 1969, Hawtrey had discovered his next home just as quickly.

Bernard Walsh: 'He said to me, "Bernard, I'd like to leave London altogether. You seem to be so happy when you go to Deal at the weekends, can I come with you?" So we arranged for him to come down for the weekend. I met him off the train on the Saturday morning and we walked along the front and had a lovely lunch. He said, "I love this place already!" He could feel the magic of Deal. I rang Roger Bright, the local estate agent, and said, "Roger, could you bear to work this afternoon? I'd like to see three or four houses." But as soon as we walked into 117 Middle Street, Charles said, "This is it! I don't want to go any further, this is it!" It didn't need anything doing to it. It was in very good condition and Roger had lived in it himself at one time. Charles settled into Deal quite well. I introduced him to two or three friends, such as Roger's mother who used to talk to him about Will Hay. In her company he was always very good; he didn't misbehave himself. Then, slowly, he got his own social life together, and, frankly, I used to try and avoid him at the weekends because I couldn't bear the drinking.'[17]

Aubrey Phillips had begun to experience his own exasperation with Hawtrey's drinking, a problem that, so far, had not affected his performances. When he first played *Babes in the Wood* in 1929, *The Stage* newspaper had described him as "dainty and charming". Now, in Phillips's 1971 version in Telford's town hall, Hawtrey's drunken debut was anything but.

Aubrey Phillips: 'We were going to open on the Tuesday, so I got there on the Sunday and said to Charles, "I've got to go back home, I've been away for weeks, I must go and pick the mail up. I'll be back on Tuesday morning, don't forget there's a matinee at 1.30pm."

"Right-o, dear boy!" So he stayed in the pub opposite. I got back that morning at about eleven, couldn't find Charles, went in the High Street and somebody said, "I think I've just seen him down the bottom of the street, looking for you." Well, it was a one-horse town, only three pubs, so I thought I'd try every pub. Sure enough, he was in the last one and, as I approached the pub, he came out looking for me: "I'm here, dear boy! Hurry, hurry, hurry! I've found a wonderful doubles bar!" I thought, "Oh, God, we've got a matinee and an evening to do and he's on bloody doubles!"

By the time I get into the pub, he's gone to the loo and the barman said, "Are you Aubrey?" I said, "Yes." He said, "Charles said to get you a drink." So I said, "Well, I'll just have a Coke 'cause I've got a matinee to do. What's he drinking?" "Gin and tonic" — which was a very strange drink for Charles. I said, "What, one of each in that glass?"

"No, no," he said, "it's a double." I said, "How many's he had?"

"About five." Well, five times four is twenty. It wasn't even one o'clock. We had a matinee to do! He was almost legless! I got him out of there and into the theatre hall. I went round the cast and said, "They're never going to hear him in this building". He'd had that many years of television and film, he'd lost the art of projecting on stage so we always tried to place microphones strategically, but when he's pissed you'd have no chance at all. He resorted to a mumble. "If you're on stage with him and he's got a comedy line and it hasn't come over, repeat it, so at least the audience get the gag." So we went all afternoon repeating everything he said! The following night, the *Shropshire Star* came out with a write-up of the pantomime, which was quite nice, but the girl who wrote it said, "Why did everybody, except Charles Hawtrey, have all the funny lines?" He went mad and shouted, "I told you this part wasn't funny for me!"'[18]

For the next six years Hawtrey continued to tour exclusively for Phillips as "Muddles the Court Jester" in *Snow White and the Seven Dwarfs* and a couple of other productions both in and out of season ("That sounds peculiar, but I do pantomimes in May and August, as well as October. Believe me, there is an audience"[19]). But, as Phillips himself puts it, "You seemed to have one incident for every town you ever took him to." The pantomime played all the major UK towns and cities including Birmingham, Liverpool, Sunderland (at The Empire, a few months before Sid James died on stage there), Cardiff, Nottingham and Manchester.

As he approached his sixties Hawtrey's irritability with the public began to increase, too. Where once stood a consummate professional, happily signing autograph books and basking in the attention he desperately wanted, now trundled a crude old man, intoxicated and bitter at the world at large.

Aubrey Phillips: 'He had a few stock expressions: "I suppose you think I'm fucking Barbara Windsor" was one of them. One or two people, actually, never knew his name, you know? He'd realise when they didn't know it and say, "Alright then. Well, what's my name?" And if they said something like Kenneth Williams or Kenneth Connor, he'd tear the piece of paper up and tell them to fuck off. But, if it was a young man in his early twenties, he could be ever so polite and sign everything they wanted.'[20]

Backstage with Aubrey Phillips (second from right) for *Snow White and the Seven Dwarfs*.

Bryan Johnson: 'I used to travel from town to town with Charlie. He could be unspeakably rude to people on trains, etc. Many is the time he'd tell some huge bloke where to get off and I would have to step in to stop him from being beaten up. [Visions of "Golightly", Hawtrey's character in *Carry On Sergeant*, come to mind, jabbing his bayonet into a suspended sack of hay: "You beast, peasant, commoner, have at you, varlet!

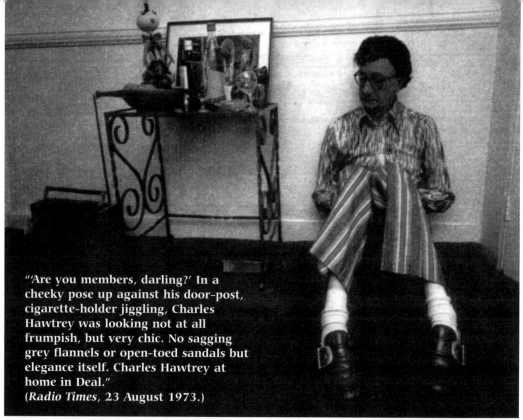

"'Are you members, darling?' In a cheeky pose up against his door-post, cigarette-holder jiggling, Charles Hawtrey was looking not at all frumpish, but very chic. No sagging grey flannels or open-toed sandals but elegance itself. Charles Hawtrey at home in Deal."
(*Radio Times*, 23 August 1973.)

"Heathrow. 20.9.74. Carry On Judge. Veteran film actor Charles Hawtrey, flanked by Dinah May (22) and Suzanne Hilton (19) before they left today for Austria. The girls are among the UK finalists taking part in the final of the Miss Cinema 1974 contest. Mr. Hawtrey is one of the judges." (Publicity picture and accompanying caption.)

Hand back that cup final ticket!"] The tragedy of it was that without the drink he could be thoroughly charming but that was the side that was emerging less and less.'[21]

Aubrey Phillips: 'At The Grand Theatre, Swansea, they had an artist bar backstage and I thought, "Oh God, here we go!" I could see him keep going to the bar and getting these bloody port-wines. By the evening the other comic in the show came to me and said, "I think Charles is a bit gone to the wind." In his last entrance in the first half, he could hardly stand, so this other comic and myself linked arms with him and got him off saying, "Oh, come on, we'll go and find the wicked queen" and got away with it. We got him back to the dressing room and the manager was there, so I said, "John, Charles has had it! The alcohol's taken over, do me a favour, sit with him, distract his attention for a little while, have a drink. He's got a dressing room full of booze." So John goes in, I turn the key in the door in the corridor, locked the pair of them in until the finale, then I opened it and said, "Come on Charles, finale!"
"Oh, already? Oh, that's quick!" We walked him on in the finale. The manager played hell with me every day for the rest of the week. He said, "You bastard, you locked me in with him!"'[22]

For the first time in his career, Hawtrey was about to get a bad review. The *West Sussex County Times* reckoned, "Hawtrey is Hawtrey and that in itself is good enough to make it funny."[23] However, this clemency gradually made way for irritation and sometime later Hawtrey received his first printed attack: "Instead of the usual song sheet the audience were involved in a hand bell act poorly presented by Charles Hawtrey. In an array of brightly coloured costumes, his contribution to the evening was somewhat limited."[24] The longevity and success of *Snow White and the Seven Dwarfs*, which still tours to this day, led Phillips to make a hard decision and he quietly dropped him. Hawtrey never knew.

Aubrey Phillips: 'It'd got to the stage where lots of theatres wouldn't take the shows I had with Charles in. The reputation was going round that he was drunk all the time. They didn't want him. You see, I'd been back to some theatres about six times with the same show. I took Charles there every time and he, virtually, blotted his copy book every time and eventually the managers would say, "Yes, of course we'll have the show back, it always takes money, but put somebody else in it this time."'[25]

Seven years after *Carry On Abroad*, Hawtrey suddenly showed up in two short films. Firstly, on TV in Eric Sykes' silent comedy *The Plank*, which gave cameo roles to a score of comedy actors, Hawtrey was seen sitting alongside Harry H. Corbett and Joanna Lumley in a transit van, his paws on the dashboard like a Dalmatian. Then, in Don Boyd's *The Princess and the Pea*, an 8-minute pilot for a series of fairytales intended for a videodisc release, he played the court jester to Roy Kinnear and Judi Bowker's King and Queen.

Though Hawtrey is only seen for no more than a couple of minutes, he again brings to the screen the only real draw. Kinnear is good but it is Hawtrey who gets the real laughs and memorable moments. Indeed, he is first to enter the film, skipping into shot wearing pixie boots with his scrawny legs encased in red tights. In the opening montage, he tries to make the prince happy with camp dances and shuffles, showing off the long line of potential princesses, each one to no avail. They're brief flashes of his inherent sense of comedy, but the overall film, in terms of Hawtrey's limited contribution, is rather a let-down, an anti-climax to a prolific and remarkable film career.

Don Boyd: 'It was the precursor to the *Storyteller* series and its like. Way ahead of its time. We shot it in the main hall at Burghley House [Stamford, Lincolnshire]. The film wasn't just the princess on her bed and the pea, but it dealt with the court, the prince and how she would fall in love. I thought any court would have a court jester. That's where Charles fitted in. He was fantastic. I met him and he was immediately responsive. He did a brilliant performance; really funny and witty. One of the things that was slightly unusual — because it relied entirely on the voiceover from Michael Hordern — all the performances in it are not dissimilar to the sort you would expect in a silent film. But, unlike his known British film persona, the beauty was he'd done some thinking and he integrated into it a certain flavour that took it away from being a mime.'[26]

Incongruous though it is, Boyd's gushing tribute is not down to the rose-tinting passage of time. Over the two days of filming, Hawtrey, he swears, was back to being utterly professional. Objectively, this may be true; Boyd was in his twenties, respectful and a big fan ("When I first talked to him on the phone I told him how thrilled I was that he wanted to come and do something like this"), he was an up-and-coming director, his passport into a new genre of the cinema, away from the typecasting.

Perhaps Hawtrey saw him as another Hitchcock or Powell, directors he'd worked with at the start of their careers and who'd gone on to hit the big time. He will also have been inspired by Roy Kinnear, proof that worldwide success was attainable for their sort of British character actor.

Hawtrey's ninety-sixth and final film: *The Princess and the Pea* (1979), in which he plays the court jester.

Don Boyd: 'I knew of Charles's reputation. One of the people said, "Are you sure you want this guy? He's apparently a nightmare to work with." But he liked me, I bonded with him. He pitched up at the right time, was totally professional, not difficult or drunk and totally reliable. I wonder if it was because he was doing something where he wasn't expected to be anything other than an actor. The role had no link to any form of comic tradition he'd been connected with. It didn't have a sense of 50s' comedy films or the *Carry Ons*. I think all actors, when they go into films that are slightly out of the mainstream, there's always the thought that maybe it might lead to something else.'[27]

Any starry-eyed thought was wishful thinking. *The Princess and the Pea* was only ever shown on an American cable channel and did nothing to initiate a Charles Hawtrey revival. It would be his last film.

His final stage appearance came soon after, in another company's production of *Jack and the Beanstalk* at the Wyvern Theatre, Swindon, from 19 December 1979 until 26 January 1980. It was directed by Peter Byrne, his fellow Conti student who had also been his replacement in the Will Hay radio series and the newly married husband Pint-Pot had driven to the airport in *Carry On Cabby*.

Peter Byrne: 'I thought, at last, not only will it be a great honour to direct this great comedic actor, but I'll have the opportunity to talk to him about the good old days, Conti and the *Carry Ons*, etc. To my horror, on the very first day, he insulted everybody insight, had a huge brandy and refused to co-operate.'[28]

Spencer K. Gibbons: 'When I was told he was going to be in the pantomime, I was looking forward to it because I thought I would learn a lot from him. I got to the theatre and the stage manager said, "Would you like to meet Charles Hawtrey?" and I said, "Yeah, I would love to!" He said, "You best be aware he's been on the brandy." I went up to the bar. He was sat there by himself, smoking, with his large brandy. The stage manager said, "This is Spencer K. Gibbons, who's going to be playing Jack, and he's just won *New Faces*." He just looked me up and down and said, "Oh, you're one of these mohair-suited comedians, are you? Well, you can fuck off!"'[29]

Considering the theatre, as opposed to film, "was his whole life" and "his interest was entirely of coming into work, going home, making sure his lines were right for the next day", Charles Hawtrey's theatrical career, which had begun 54 years previously, was about to come to a disappointing end. Gone were the marker tapes that he would neurotically place down for the cast to follow. Gone was his obsessive rehearsal of the script. Gone was any remaining scrap of professionalism.

Spencer K. Gibbons: 'We started rehearsals the following day and sadly he couldn't remember his lines, he couldn't remember the princess's name, for example. He wouldn't wear the king's costume. He insisted on wearing one of his own, which was a sort of patchwork, multi-coloured tight pair of trousers and a bright blue silk shirt that didn't look very "kingy" at all. And, if he walked on and didn't get a thundering applause, he used to walk off again and, a minute later, try again!'[30]

Aubrey Phillips: 'They were costumes that he'd taken from me. Wherever he went afterwards he wore the same bloody costumes. The trousers belonged to a set of Spanish costumes we had for Flamenco dancing!'[31]

Peter Byrne: 'In the end, he just couldn't do the dialogue; he'd come on — say "Oh, hello!" — get his applause and that was it. But he gave me nothing but trouble. He tended to lie naked on his bed in his dressing room and I believe he even flashed a WPC in the street …'[32]

Spencer K. Gibbons: 'As the run went on we would regularly have to bail him out of police cells in time for the matinee. He would wander the street very drunk, being obnoxious and get himself arrested for disturbing the peace. It would happen so often that the police eventually used to phone up the company manager to go and collect him.'[33]

As Ernest Maxin, Francis Matthews and others previously recalled, one thing had remained: his mysterious elusiveness.

Spencer K. Gibbons: 'We never ever saw him sign an autograph. I never saw him come out of the theatre. It was as if he disappeared, as if by magic!'

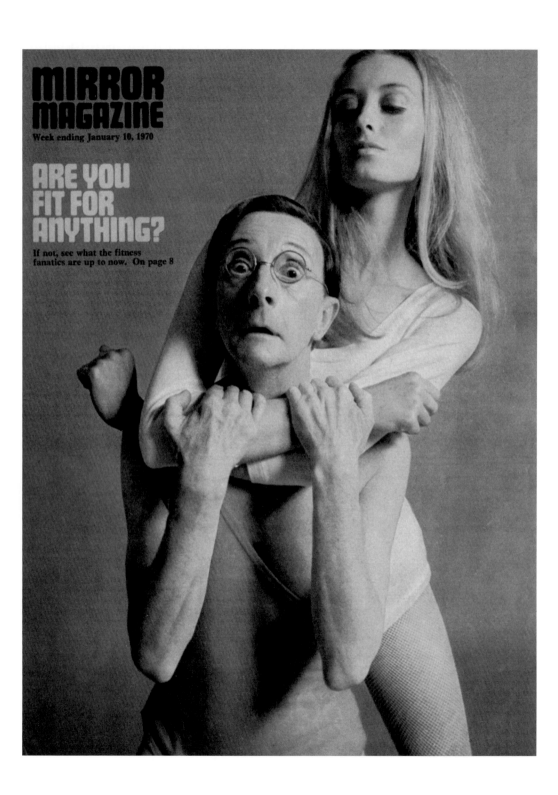

MIRROR MAGAZINE

Week ending January 10, 1970

ARE YOU FIT FOR ANYTHING?

If not, see what the fitness
fanatics are up to now. On page 8

CHAPTER ELEVEN
THE DEAL YEARS

I heard it said that he knocked over a couple's drink in the pub one evening and somebody said to him, "Perhaps you should apologise?" And he turned and said, "I don't apologise to peasants!"

Anonymous Deal Resident

To the townsfolk of Deal, Charles Hawtrey isn't just the "funny fella out of the *Carry Ons.*" From 1969 until his death in 1988 he was their resident drunk, local eccentric and foul-mouthed bogeyman, who lived at 117 Middle Street, an old four-floored smuggler's cottage built in 1760 and not far from the seafront. ("I don't regret it for one moment. I'm completely cut off, there's no noise at night by aeroplanes or traffic."[1])

But it wasn't just the sea air and peace and quiet that Hawtrey found appealing about Deal. Until 1996, seven years after an IRA bomb killed eleven bandsmen, the local barracks was home to the Royal Marines School of Music and it was a popular reason why gay men chose to retire to the area.

Stop anybody over the age of 30 in the street, call in and speak with pub landlords, ask any taxi driver or shop assistant, and each one will have had their own brief encounter with Hawtrey.[2]

Ray Dennis (Pub landlord): 'As a *Carry On* star he brought a lot of laughter into many people's lives. Totally different off the screen: he was a bitter old man. It was very sad. I think it's a shame when people are like that.'

Nancy Dawson (Neighbour): 'We used to go over there and find him lying on the floor, poor man. He hadn't much to live for, quite frankly.'

British Rail Driver: 'Several of the drivers would come in and say, "Oh, we've had Charlie on the last train from Charing Cross last night", and he'd be fast asleep, gone.'

Dennis Senior (Taxi driver): 'The character he portrayed on the screen was different to him in real life. In real life he was a nasty piece of work.'

Elisabeth Bainbridge (Neighbour): 'I have seen him being brought home between two burly Royal Marines, as tight as a tick. He just struck me as a very pathetic person, really.'

Only when his mother passed away and homosexuality was decriminalised two years later was Hawtrey able for the first time to experiment sexually without fear of consequence. When he moved to Mortlake he began frequenting the West End gay scene late at night — clubs such as The Rockingham, The Festival, The Embassy on Bond Street and The Black Cat. But by 1969 Deal was a town already liberally minded and the relaxed attitude encouraged him to go further.

Patrick Newley: 'He was hardly an oil painting. It was so they could say, "I've been to bed with Charles Hawtrey." He was nothing to look at, not a dapper rich old queen. He looked very dishevelled. But if you went to those sorts of dingy clubs, at one o'clock in the morning, then he was always appealing to *someone*.'[3]

Aubrey Phillips: 'Well, I've been in his company in Deal where we met in a pub one day and it was full of Marine Bandsmen. That was hilarious, to begin with. But after about an hour or two I disappeared and went to another pub and left him there with these bandsmen; he was chatting the whole lot up! It got very embarrassing and I gather the next day the landlord asked him never to go in his pub again.'[4]

Ronnè Coyles: 'He would see a fella and he would try to get to talk to them. He would slink his body from side to side. It was a peculiar thing he did, wanting to get recognised.'[5]

Aubrey Phillips: 'Everybody knew he was gay, but you never really saw anybody with him. He liked to talk in gay company but you'd never see him wandering off with anybody — probably was too drunk at the end of the evening to walk off with anyone anyway!'[6]

Most young men, amazed to find themselves in the company of their famous neighbour, laughed off his advances and steered the conversation towards his *Carry On* co-stars.

Patrick Newley: 'What always struck me about Charlie was that he was a very serious person underneath all that clowning about, and if you took him seriously then he would behave seriously. But if you took him as the guy out of the *Carry On* films then the conversation would veer into a different world, like who you're going out with or offers of another drink. He was always looking for trade. He was promiscuous and into rent.'[7]

Hawtrey's friends recall only one boyfriend: a "dark-haired, good looking, nicely spoken"[8] 20-something named Anthony Royal.

Aubrey Phillips: 'He was with him for a number of years, but Charles was really the sugar daddy. We all realised it wasn't *really* his boyfriend, but he liked to think that it was. Anthony would go off and meet a sailor, and Charles would find out he'd gone and get upset. Anthony loved the money. Charles bought a brand new Morris Maxi, so for the first time in his life this lad had four wheels to get around. He bought him suits, he wined and dined him and, in return, he chauffeured him around. Got a wage for it, too. Charles loved him, oh yes. But I don't think he got a lot in return, sure he didn't. I was never friendly with the boy myself, because I just thought he was taking him for a ride. From what I could see, in the background, Anthony's choice of male friend had to be about 16 or 18, so obviously Charles wasn't the right person for him, was he?'[9]

Bernard Walsh: 'Anthony rather took over Charles's life, but I thought "Thank God someone's taking him off our backs!" When the boy moved on, the car went with him. I knew that whatever affection was there was Charles's affection for him only. There was quite obviously none coming towards him.'[10]

Turning to Freud, as one can't help but do with Hawtrey, the death of Alice will have increased his need to love men as she had loved him. By showering Royal with expensive gifts and love, he could take over his mother's role and recreate their special bond. But it was a script that had been wrongly cast. Some friends suggest Royal would beat Hawtrey when he refused to increase his allowance or have exclusive use of the house.

Paul Denver: 'I remember having dinner with him, which was OK, but suddenly he announced to Anthony: "Anthony! We're going to open … the pears! We've got special guests here … open the tin of pears!"'[11]

Joy Leonard: 'I shall never forget when Hattie Jacques came to tea. [Anthony] made a trifle, and he's walking up and down, beating this thing and I thought, "Oh my God! Hattie Jacques is going to *love* that!" And there are those ghastly silver balls on the top — you know? Tooth breakers! Anyway, we were all talking about somebody or other, who was having an affair, and Charles said, "Don't talk like that while the boy's in the room," as though he was purer than pure — and this boy's an out-and-out homosexual! Well, Hattie Jacques got into this corner chair to eat the trifle and she couldn't get out of it! Charles and I were pulling either side of her, trying to pull her out of this chair, but ended up on the floor with her on top of us, with her bottom still stuck inside it!'[12]

Joan Sims: 'If Kenneth Williams' flat was remarkable for his sparseness, Charlie's was quite the opposite. It was chaos, with pieces of furniture stacked halfway up each wall.'[13]

Hattie Jacques and Joan Sims weren't the only colleagues who tried to keep in touch with Hawtrey when he moved to Deal. Williams also paid a visit in 1970 as he recorded in his diary and a letter to friend Jeffery Kemp:

Kenneth Williams: 'When he first retired to Deal I went down there with some friends. Banged and banged on the door, to no avail. Eventually a window on the opposite side screeched open and a woman with the hair in curlers shouted, rudely, "You after Charlie?"
"Mister Hawtrey," I returned haughtily. "We were seeking Mister Hawtrey!"
"Try the Saracen's Head," she bawled and shut the window. Well, we must have visited half the pubs in the neighbourhood, but eventually CH was found. Rather the worse for wear. Insisted on taking us to tea with these "wonderful friends of mine that have a little café where they make everything with their own home stoneground flour." After eating one of their own cakes, I just think I got the stone. Felt like a foundation stone. Just sank into the stomach relentlessly. Took a lot of bicarb and farting to shift it. Oh never again. As we walked along the front, fisherman eyed us wearily. Charlie was in orange trousers, blue shirt and silk scarf at the neck. He was carrying an umbrella as a parasol. The day was quite fine. The rest of us were trying to look anonymous. "Hello lads!" he kept calling out to men painting their boats. "They all adore me here," he told us. "Brings a bit of glamour into their dull lives." They smiled back uneasily and certainly some returned his salutations, but I didn't get the impression of universal adoration. The house was awful. Everywhere you went there were these huge brass beds. "They'll come back into fashion one day and I'll make a fortune!" he declared as he rubbed them affectionately. Then he recited an endless saga about some boys from the Royal Marines School of

Music carousing with him round the local hostelries and all piling back to his place to stay the night. "And just look at what they gave me to show their appreciation," he cried thrusting a huge portfolio in front of us. Somebody asked nervously, "What is it?" and with extraordinary triumph CH announced, "The original score of the Bohemian Girl." He kept on about this being an original and repeating that it had "the Vienna stamp on it." But the whole thing smacked of fraudulence. What on Earth has Balfe to do with Vienna one asks oneself?'[14]

… 'T[om] and C[live] arrived at 9.15 and we left for Deal. We called at Middle Street and Charlie came to the door in his undervest, unshaven. On entering, we saw his lunch steaming on the table, so we went off for more drinks 'til he was ready. He was still unshaven but showed us all over the house which is rambling and incredibly tat — like a lodging house which all the boarders have suddenly deserted and that revolting smell of rising damp and cat's fish everywhere. She [sic] produced male physique magazines with a great flourish and meaningful remarks, but they were all quite innocuous. I was horrified to learn then that Charles was travelling back with us! 'cos Tom had foolishly offered him a lift to London and Miss Cadge jumped at it. So we had her all the way! A nightmare journey of three hours and she *had* to lose her cigarette holder and search the car at Victoria (where we dumped her) to find the wretched thing. She pressed us all to come again and "please regard it as your second home." Before I do that, I'll need the rest home.'[15]

Paul Denver: 'Me and my partner Danny stayed there for two nights, but it was very strange, very naval; it had ropes going up the stairs. What struck me was the lack of furniture. There was garden furniture inside the house, patio stuff. It was very uncomfortable. The bedroom that Charles had given us had a very small single bed in it, so it was a tight squeeze. Then, in the morning, knock on the door, and Charles, being the perfect host, comes in, not wearing a dressing gown but a raincoat, and he says, "Breakfast, boys!" He puts it down and leaves us. We poured the tea, which was cold (a Chinese tea that he liked — an acquired taste). Likewise with the boiled eggs, when we opened those they weren't cooked.'[16]

Aubrey Phillips: 'It was never warm; it was always bloody cold! I stayed there numerous times and you were frightened to take your shirt off in the winter when you went to bed. You wanted everything to stay on, including your socks. I'd once let him stay at my place on the seafront in Rhyl, and when I got back one night the kitchen was in a *hell* of a state. He'd decided to have beans on toast. He'd got a tin of beans out of the cupboard, put it in a pan of water to boil, with the beans still in the fucking can; couldn't find the tin opener. The thing exploded and the beans were all over the fucking ceiling and down the walls. He was fast asleep and didn't know what he'd done.'[17]

Eventually, Hawtrey's relationship with Anthony Royal came to its predictable end. Hawtrey replaced his company with a cat, named after his mother, and Royal went on to marry "for convenience", but in the end died of an AIDS-related illness. [18]

Joy Leonard: 'When his cat died, and it died on the bed, he got hold of the little body and he got one of his favourite scarves and put it on the chair. He was talking to it all the time and was crying like mad. It was a very wild, black little cat. When I used to go to the house it would scurry behind a chair. When it died it broke his heart. I could tell that he was so lonely, because he'd say, "Give Charlie a cuddle." And I'd put my arms around him and it was like putting your arms around a seagull. It was all little bones and nothing there.'[19]

With Hawtrey still devastated over Alice's death, Leonard quickly found herself Hawtrey's new female companion. He liked her because she was a performer too, enjoying her cabaret shows on the end of Deal Pier, a typical show business darling but not insincere and, most of all, willing to play mother.

Joy Leonard: 'I'd say, "Charles, you're being naughty! Now stop that!" Like once when he phoned me and said, "I want you to come round." So I said, "I can't, I'm busy. I've got a lot to do."
"Well, I'll come round to you?"
"No, no, you can't," I said.
"Oh, oh, there you are then! You come round to my house and drink all my drink, but I mustn't go to yours and drink yours ..."
So I said, "Don't be naughty. That's very, very naughty, isn't it Charles?"
"I don't care, I've said it now ... Goodbye!" And off he went.'[20]

Leonard had what Peter Rogers has been credited with when it comes to Hawtrey: "the patience of a saint and the diplomatic skills of the highest order."[21] She endured many embarrassing nights at The Pink Panther ('There was a bloke singing and Charles was shouting, "Shurrup, shurrup! Oh my God! To think, Charlie's got to listen to this!'), his bizarre dress sense ('He bought a woman's hat from this little junk shop on the corner of the High Street. He looked like Old Mother Riley') and, of course, his drinking.

Joy Leonard: 'He'd say, "I know what Charlie's got for you, how about some champers?" Then he'd go into the corner, crouch down and while he's pouring mine out, he's swigging it on the floor round the corner. He'd give me a little drop and then he'd fill up the glass for himself. Then he'd keep filling his up and wouldn't ask about me having some more! Afterwards, he'd say, "Do you know, we've got through a bottle? We soon got through that!"'[22]

The elfin boy into which Hawtrey would regress only presented himself in the company of Leonard. To anybody else he was the enigmatic movie star, reclusive and unapproachable. Those who tried — usually children, faced a Terrier with Tourette's.

Joy Leonard: 'A little boy came up: "Oh, Mr. Hawtrey, can I have your autograph please?" He said, "Why?"
"Well, I'd like it."
"Well, do you *know* me?" The little boy said, "No."
"Well, you don't need my autograph then. I don't give it to people who don't know me. Go away!"'[23]

Leonard has toned down the profane language that Hawtrey now fearlessly used with local people "coming up to him with all that inane talk." When he first moved to Deal he was happy to oblige but, as pointed out by Roger Lewis, since being "rejected by movie moguls and impresarios he took the only revenge possible which was to reject his own public."[24]

Ray Dennis: 'I mostly think of him lying on my bar floor with his legs in the air, absolutely plastered and incapable of speech. Adults and children used to try and get his autograph. He rarely gave one and if he had been drinking they also got a great deal of nastiness for asking. Everybody locally stopped asking a long time ago.'[25]

Young men were an exception to the rule and if willing, or for hire, were invited to 117 Middle Street with strict instructions to use the back door rather than the front (**Peter Stephens**: "They always had to come via the garage and most of his guests were entertained in the cellar, where he kept his train set."[26]). Invariably, once Hawtrey had had his way, their payments were refused; not an unusual characteristic of the man who was insisting taxis ferry him from the Ship Inn to his house, doors away.

Ray Dennis: 'He'd shout, "I want to go home, I want a taxi!" I offered to walk him home but he'd say, "No, I want a taxi!" So we'd have to phone for a taxi, the taxi would come, he'd get in and it'd reverse back.'[27]

Basil Kidd: 'Another landlord would call a taxi, put him in it and bid him farewell. But he'd get out the other side and by the time the landlord got back to the bar, he was back in there!'[28]

Dennis Senior: 'First, you went there and had to try and persuade him to come out, which was about ten minutes, then eventually you got him into the car. Then you took him to his house. Then you'd have to get him out of the car, which took another ten minutes. And, if you were lucky, you might get paid! So consequently we didn't like doing the job, because it was time-consuming and nothing but aggravation. It got to the stage where we refused to pick him up because he was obnoxious, he refused to pay the bill and he was most arrogant and most rude. Totally he was a bad fare.'[29]

As dawn broke at around 6am on Sunday 5 August 1984, the Kent Fire Brigade received the first in a series of frantic telephone calls made by Hawtrey. The night before, he had taken "16-year-old" rent boy Courtney Hills back home to Middle Street. When the youth came to leave, Hawtrey, in typical style, refused to pay and in an effort to scare the old man, Hills had set fire to his cherished settee.

Joy Leonard: 'He bought that settee after a show he did. He saw it somewhere or other and he adored it. It was all right, but he thought it was wonderful. "You can sit on it," he said, "but be careful, don't smoke on it …" And it was he who burnt it in the finish!'[30]

In the time it took Hawtrey to haggle with the boy and find his chequebook, the blaze had engulfed the first and second floors of his

Angered by the gathering crowd and the lens of local photographer Basil Kidd, Hawtrey pictured with Fire Fighter Barry Bullock moments after being rescued from his burning home in August 1984.

cottage. Hills had managed to get out and made the first call to 999 at a nearby payphone. This was quickly followed by Hawtrey, trapped on the second floor, desperately redialling the operator on a telephone that was melting in his hand because of the intense heat from the fire that raged below. His neighbour, Gary McLellan, recalled to the press what happened next.

Gary McLellan: 'Hawtrey was standing at the window without a stitch on. The lad was just wearing trousers and was shouting for help. Smoke and flames were everywhere.'[31]

Marcus Gidman: 'At the time I was the Station Commander of Deal Fire Station and was summoned by telephone to a fire at Charles's address. During my short journey I was informed by radio that several telephone calls had been made to Fire Brigade Control which generally indicated a severe fire situation. I turned my car into Middle Street and it was immediately apparent that there was indeed a severe fire with someone shouting for help from the second floor window area. A builder's ladder had been pitched to the window but due to the smoke issuing I was unable to see anyone. I quickly dressed in my fire kit and made my way up the ladder and into the front bedroom where I located Charles, in a state of shock, suffering from smoke inhalation. He was sitting on a bed. He was in a state of complete undress. As the situation in the room was deteriorating very rapidly, with fire appearing from below the bedroom door, and the likelihood of a flashover imminent, I made my way to the window with him, rather than wait for assistance from the oncoming crews. There was no time to cover him up to save embarrassment, as the situation had become one of urgency. As I stood at the head of the ladder and told Charles to climb out between my arms he misunderstood or was confused as to what was expected of him. He decided to climb backwards out of the window and over my head and down my back, at the same time clinging to me like a limpet! This usual method of bringing someone down a ladder may have been all right for one of his *Carry On* films,[32] but not one generally practised by the fire brigade! However, I successfully brought him to the ground where he was received by a fireman who covered him in his own fire tunic as, by this time, a crowd had gathered.'[33]

The fireman was Barry Bullock, who also gave Hawtrey his helmet to protect his baldhead from the lens of the local press. As a thank you

Hawtrey gave Bullock his passport saying, "This'll be worth something one day."

Barry Bullock: 'Charles was distraught. He was a very tragic character and was five minutes away from death. I particularly remember he was very angry to see the photographer Basil Kidd outside his house.'[34]

Basil Kidd: 'If I remember rightly he didn't have anything on. He must have had something wrapped round him. I know he was starkers, but the firemen must have slopped something on him. I remember he wasn't impressed and he didn't want any pictures taken. Once I went to take his picture opening the hospital fête and the wind took his wig off — he wasn't very happy about that, either.'[35]

David Reid: 'He was up on the podium, about to open the fête, when there was this sudden gust of wind and his toupée flew off. He screamed, "Don't you dare take any photos!"'[36]

Aubrey Phillips: 'He wore a toupée all the time. He was bald. He had two. He'd take one off, put the other one on and then thoroughly clean the first one with acetone and put it in the box. It was a toupée more than a wig, but it was a bloody big toupée! That'd be funny, when he'd had a few drinks, falling off the bar and the bloody thing would twist a bit!'[37]

Basil Kidd: 'He wasn't very happy at all and certainly didn't want pictures taken. I sympathised with him, I wouldn't have taken anything to upset him. It's a local town. It's all right for the nationals. When you do stuff locally, and you've got to live with them, it's a different kettle of fish.'[38]

But evidently Kidd's photographs *were* upsetting to Hawtrey. His picture on the front page of the *East Kent Mercury*, sardonically captioned "Comedy actor Charles Hawtrey thanks firemen for saving his life," shows Hawtrey mid-rant, eyebrows raised, mouth snarled, right hand raised in sheer anger, semi-naked and clutching two packets of cigarettes and a rain Mac.

According to the paper: "Mr. Hawtrey (69) raised the alarm himself when the smell of smoke awoke him … Fire investigators are examining the theory that the fire was caused by a cigarette left burning on a settee in a ground floor room." [39]

"Eastry firemen mop up in the room where the fire started, causing thousands of pounds of damage." (East Kent Mercury, 8 August 1984.)

"What a Carry On," reported *The Sun*, the next day. "Last night it was boarded up and Hawtrey was staying with friends. Hawtrey, who had a heart attack three months[40] [sic] ago, said: 'The smell of smoke woke me up and there were flames coming up the stairway. I've lost a lot of valuable antiques and sentimental keepsakes, but I am all right. It was all very frightening.'"[41]

No mention was made directly about the rent boy until four years later, when *The Sun*, presumably fearing legal action beforehand, ran their article just before Hawtrey's death: "Firemen wearing breathing gear plucked him to safety after neighbours spotted him without a stitch on, screaming for help from his window. After the blaze the star had to face embarrassing questions about his private life. For a lad in his 20s also had to be rescued from the blazing building. A neighbour said: "Hawtrey was naked but the young lad had his trousers on. All Hawtrey said as the firemen reached him was 'But I've got not clothes on.' He didn't panic."[42]

The Chinese whispers continued with Kenneth Williams claiming to know what really happened. In a letter to his friend Jeffery Kemp he wrote, "When the firemen brought him down the ladder wrapped in a blanket, they said, 'You're all right now' and he told them, 'No I'm not. My fags are upstairs by the bed, and my boyfriend's in it. And it was true."[43]

But not according to Fire Fighter Knight ("As my engine drew close to the scene I saw this lad running up the road, wearing nothing but blue velvet trousers"[44]) and the man who rescued Hawtrey from the blaze, Marcus Gidman.

Marcus Gidman: 'I can confirm that there was a young man in the street, naked except for a pair of trousers. This person remained within the vicinity until it was clear that Charles had been brought out of the house safely. He then left the scene and was unable for comment or to provide information as to the cause of the fire. I have never seen this person since. The ladder placed up to Charles' bedroom window was not a fire brigade ladder, but one that could be described as being a wooden builder's ladder. Who placed this ladder up to the open window? If this young man had been in Charles's bedroom, how did he make his escape, by dropping from the window? It would be impossible to escape from the fire without sustaining severe burns. Who was this young man? Each answer seems to give rise to more questions!'[45]

After his rescue Hawtrey adamantly refused to be taken to hospital saying he was "self-healing" and he insisted on waiting with a neighbour until the fire had been extinguished. Once he was sure it was out, Gidman took Hawtrey to stay at an "elderly friend of his" in nearby Grosvenor Mansions.

Lucy Windsor: 'I did see him very shortly after he had this terrible fire, because he wasn't insured, you know? So it was a pretty horrendous thing for him.'[46]

The People's expose of "The star who gets no laughs as a sad drunk" in May 1988 featured one of the workmen whom Hawtrey had hired to rebuild his home. "We hardly saw him at all," the anonymous builder told the tabloid. "He stayed right out of our way and never came down to see how we were getting on with the work. His house is fabulous inside. Everything is neat and tidy and kept very clean. It's as though he spends most of his time doing the housework."[47]

It's a sceptical quotation. (Just how can one do housework in a burnt out shell or on a building site?) On the other hand, having plunged further into reclusion after the restoration was complete, Hawtrey was said to have told *The Sun*: "Getting drunk and dusting are all I do now. It's a funny life but not inappropriate."[48]

21/8/87

Dear Mr. Alan Coles,

Thank you for your letter addressed
to Mr. Charles Hawtrey.
Mr. Hawtrey is no longer available,
his whereabouts are private, and no
letters are forwarded to him.

Yours truly

Alice Dunne

Alice Dunne

An example of the sort of letters Hawtrey sent to fans using his mother-inspired
pseudonym of Alice Dunne.

In the years leading up to his death, Hawtrey worked on the radio just once more. Exactly a year after the fire, he was heard in his third and final comedy for a Radio 4 series that also featured *Carry On* tall man Bernard Bresslaw.

Martin Jenkins: 'There was this demeanour of a rather frail, camp, elderly gentleman, with a very sharp sense of humour and a very good sense of timing. Although we didn't really know whether he was with it or not; I think he was under the influence. At one point, Bernard literally picked him up and plonked him down in front of the microphone. But when the red light came on, his delivery, his timing, and his sense of character were very good. I suspect by instinct not through doing a scrap of homework. I very much doubt that he'd even read it.'[49]

The anxiety Hawtrey once felt over his ambitious career mutated into agoraphobia. He began to barricade himself into his house, reluctantly opening his door and developing an *alter ego* — a character named "Alice Dunne", to deflect telephone calls or correspondence from the outside world.

"Dear Mr. Alan Coles," begins one of 'her' letters dated 21 August 1987. "Thank you for your letter addressed to Mr. Charles Hawtrey. Mr. Hawtrey is no longer available, his whereabouts are private, and no letters are forwarded to him." Any amateur sleuth can see it's the same typewriter he'd used for all those begging letters stored in the BBC's Written Archive. Alice's signature is in the same precise, thin hand of Hawtrey's, and her very name is his mother's.

Ms Dunne wasn't exclusive to strangers or a new experience for some. Patrick Newley says he spoke to her in as early as 1973.

Patrick Newley: 'I tried, unsuccessfully, to get him to do an autobiography about a year or two after we'd first met. We were vaguely getting somewhere with the idea. I had sold Ann Todd's autobiography to the publisher William Kimber and that had done very well. So I went to see Kimber and said, "How would you like the autobiography of Charles Hawtrey?[50] He said, "Absolutely, this is a wonderful idea." I rang Charlie about it and initially he was interested and I said, "You're going to have do a synopsis." He got very iffy about that, very huffy and refused. So I came back to him, again he said no. Then I went down to see him in Deal and he wanted to know how much. I gave him the publisher's name and number.

234   Whatshisname

They called him two days later and offered him £6000 — £3000 advance and £3000 on delivery. It was a lot of money back then, for somebody who was not a huge star. Even that didn't work. I pleaded with him on the phone. But as the months went by he got more difficult and eventually it got to the stage where, when you phoned up, he would do this rather strange act, saying "Mr. Hawtrey doesn't live here anymore" or, "Mr. Hawtrey's abroad at the moment". It was very bizarre. I'd say, "Don't do this to me, you know perfectly well who I am!" But he'd slam the phone down.'[51]

The distinction between Hawtrey and his "housekeeper" gradually disappeared entirely when the telephone calls he would make to his remaining friends became incoherent and nonsensical.

Joan Sims: 'His convoluted telephone calls became a regular feature of Sunday afternoons. The phone would ring, I'd pick it up, and there would be that unforgettable voice: "Aaah … Hello darling … Aaah …"
"What are you up to, Charles?"
"Aaah … Darling girl … Aaah …" He'd go on in this vein for about half an hour, and then his conversation (if you can call it that) would peter out altogether and he'd hang up — probably to go and get himself a refill.'[52]

Aubrey Phillips: 'If he was alive today, it would be nothing for that phone to go now, at quarter past ten at night, and you'd get that kind of call about three times a week.'[53]

Bryn Hawkins: 'I used to be his milkman. He used to peer round the door; he'd never open the door fully to you. He wouldn't like anything left on the doorstep to advertise the fact that he wasn't in.'[54]

Joy Leonard: 'He used to lock the door from the inside. He said, "These hooligans could come breaking in while we're here." He'd put the key down his neck and I'd think, "Oh my God, I'm trapped!" Then he'd drink and drink and drink and his head would be … I'd think, "He's gone to sleep and I'm trapped! I can't put my hand down his neck to get the key out!" Then, suddenly, without warning, his little face would come up and he'd say, "Oh, hello!"'[55]

Local children, who Hawtrey had told to "Piss off" when asking for his autograph, had grown into teenagers and sought their revenge.

Chris Burrows: 'I'm now an attendant on Deal Pier, but when I was about 15 years old he used to come to the Pier Café and sit in the corner, the same table, drinking double whiskeys. We always used to poke fun at him through the windows. We'd go round knocking on his door, shouting different things, hoping that he would look out the window. Sometimes he'd come down to the door and we'd just run off, wait for him to go back in and do the same thing again!'[56]

Joy Leonard: 'If he went out at all, he'd sidle along the wall so that people wouldn't notice him — but they'd notice him all the more! They'd think, "What's he walking all funny like that for?" Plus, he'd wear a floppy white sun hat and this ghastly black coat. He looked like a bat out of hell! It went right down to his ankles and from the collar to the hem there were buttons

Hawtrey's final role, April 1987: providing aristocratic aid to *Supergran*, as Clarence, Duke of Claridge.

right down the back, the size of old pennies. I'd say to him sometimes, if we were going out for a drink, "Charles, do you have to have that hat on?" "Yes! Yes I do!"
"OK, please yourself, you look funny."
"I do *not* look funny."
"OK then, you look ordinary."
"I do *not* look ordinary — I'm Charles Hawtrey and I do not look ordinary!"'[57]

Leonard was right the first time. He had always looked funny and that, so he assumed, was the problem. Instead of embracing his unique looks and enjoying his distinct and varied career, Hawtrey had pompously believed he was owed one better.

It is ironic (and no doubt would have been deeply galling to Hawtrey, had he realised) that his final appearance was on children's television, playing Clarence, Duke of Claridge in an episode of *Supergran*, broadcast 12 April 1987.

After a few short minutes of feigning disgust with having to abandon a game of Trivial Pursuit with his stuffed Corgi and go to the aid of his Duchess wife, the last ever shot of Charles Hawtrey occurs at Tynemouth Railway Station. As a Union Jack-waving crowd cheer goodbye, he waves regally from the window while the train makes its way into the distance. Looking closely at the screen, he's neither looking nor waving at the crowd, but straight ahead. In acting terms, he isn't in the zone. For the first and last noticeable time on screen, he was going through the motions.

Nevertheless, this quintessential Hawtrey performance, whether we view it as good or bad, epitomised all those wasted years of irrational anxiety over "fulfilling his expectations of stardom".[58] He desperately tried to avoid such typecast supporting roles, but continually had to accept them to bring in a wage. He hated being famous for such "rubbish" but to his consternation realised that without Norman Bones, The Professor, Private Widdle, Muddles the Court Jester and the rest, he had achieved nothing. He wanted better from life, when all along he was doing better than most.

Twenty-two years after his death and, though the majority of us may not have known his name, we still love him. Can there be any greater legacy?

CHAPTER TWELVE

HEAVEN KNOWS I'M MISERABLE NOW

Poor boy! Poor boy!
Down-hearted and depressed and in a spin
Poor boy! Poor boy!
Oh, youth can really do a fellow in!

'I'm Glad I'm Not Young Anymore',
from Hawtrey's favourite musical,
Gigi (1958)

"**L**a commedia è finita!" the broken-hearted clown Pagliacci cries out after he stabs his wife and her lover, on stage, in front of an audience who think it's all part of the show. Ever since that opera by Leoncavallo in 1892, we have been fascinated with this contradiction in terms: comedians who shed tears of anguish and heartache, who through their misery turn to alcohol and drugs and who, sometimes, end up committing suicide. It is what drove millions of us to tune into the BBC4 dramatisations about the lives of Tony Hancock, Frankie Howerd and Kenneth Williams, giving the digital channel its best ever viewing figures. It could well be the reason you are reading this book.

Yet Charles Hawtrey's character predates the late nineteenth century. You can bet your life Shakespeare was thinking of someone like him when he created Sir Andrew Ague-Cheek for *Twelfth Night* in the early 1600s. That is not to say the slowness and cowardice of Ague-Cheek were Hawtrey's attributes too, because they're not, far from it. But he was (using Wikipedia as a source) "entertaining" and cared for "singing" and playing "musical instruments". He was "poked fun at", "often drunk", "ageless", possessing "a blank look on his face", and, "by the end of his [life] was friendless."

In the third scene of the second act, Ague-Cheek[1] famously murmurs: "I was adored once too." Which is such a Hawtrey-ism. And a line he surely remembered. Indeed, in his 1929 copy of *The Works of Shakespeare*, one of the items salvaged after his death during the house-clearance, this entire play has faint pencil annotations and where that very quote appears, a thick scribble has crossed out the rest of the scene. Hawtrey, it seems, had thought it a perfect line to end with.

After his death, his most public adoration came from the singer-songwriter Morrissey. Back in early 1984 he had written to Hawtrey asking if he would sing on The Smiths' new version of their debut, 'Hand In Glove', but having failed to generate a response, even from Alice Dunne, the band's second choice, Sandie Shaw, was invited and the song reached number 27.[2]

The normally publicity-shy Morrissey would go on to eulogise Hawtrey in the *NME* as "the very last comic genius. [He was] sixty per cent of *Carry On*'s appeal. By never giving press interviews and, by all accounts being unfriendly and friendless, Hawtrey's mystique surpasses Garbo. I personally loved him."[3]

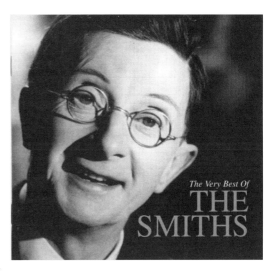

But the extent of his fascination didn't end with their mutual enigma.[4] Any time you play The Smiths' 'Stop Me If You Think You've Heard This One Before' from 1987 or, for that matter, Mark Ronson's 2007 reworking, know that it's based on Hawtrey's throwaway line in *Carry On Cleo* ("Stop me if you've heard it before …"), or log on to YouTube and watch Tim Broad's video for Morrissey's 1988 solo classic 'Everyday Is Like Sunday' and there is Eustace Tuttle, popping up in *Carry On Abroad*, carrying his blow-up ball and lilo and then knocking himself out on sun lotion.

When Hawtrey died later that year, Morrissey had images of him printed on to the backstage passes for his December show in Wolverhampton. The following spring he set his music video 'Interesting Drug' in a school named "Hawtrey High — School for Boys". He also revealed that towards the end of The Smiths he had "whittled down several potential sleeve images of Hawtrey to one contender", though the group's acrimonious split meant it would never be used.[5] Hawtrey's face finally appeared on Warner's hastily compiled 2001 release 'The Very Best of the Smiths', but it had little chance of getting to number one. Because of quality issues, the press first condemned it as a money-grabbing exercise, followed by both Morrissey and Johnny Marr, who went so far as to post on a fan messageboard, "It has the worst cover I've ever seen. I believe Morrissey is less than pleased about this album but I can only speak for myself when I say that it should be ignored by fans."[6] The music magazine *Mojo* described it as "an adman's approximation of a Smiths' cover." Its highest chart position was number 30.

However, where Morrissey and Hawtrey differ is where most people think they would connect. "I think I'm a realist, which people who don't like me consider to be pessimism," Morrissey admitted. "It isn't pessimism

at all. If I was a pessimist I wouldn't get up, I wouldn't shave, I wouldn't watch *Batman* at 7:30am. Pessimists just don't do that sort of thing."[7]

In that case, Hawtrey, who didn't own a television, was unkempt and hermitic, the very definition of a pessimist. And that's hard to equate with a man we've spent our lives watching and laughing at. In that respect, for those of us who never met him, Hawtrey hardly seems real, like a leprechaun or a fairy, only appearing to us on Bank Holiday afternoon television. But what Morrissey loves about Hawtrey is what draws us all to him as a human being. We want to understand why one of the cinema's most cheerful faces, having given us so much joy, endured a life filled with terrible anxiety and depression, utterly convinced that it'd gone wrong somewhere down the line. We can't comprehend why he felt the way he did and yet we also feel a tremendous amount of empathy towards him because we've all experienced failure, disappointment and isolation ourselves. We can appreciate that if it were us who'd appeared in nearly a hundred films and 50 West End shows, taught ourselves to play the piano as a child, directed films, produced plays and rubbed shoulders with the *hoi polloi*, then ended up branded as the country's number one wimp, we'd be pretty miffed too.

"One is apt to be labelled," he said in 1980, "and I do object to that — 'Oh, he's the funny man.' But I've discovered that all funny men, so called, are really very serious people."[8]

In other words, he's anything but a funny man. Because what the "peasants" are forgetting is that he was once the leading boy soprano in the country, had worked with the greatest actors of the twentieth century, and wasn't just limited to playing the "odd-man-out"[9].

Hawtrey's foremost loves, so say the majority of people interviewed for this book, were his mother, the theatre and his cat. They are equally unanimous in their description of how "he was just the same as he was in the *Carry Ons*." Admittedly, these are references to his ageless looks ("They called Charles Hawtrey the Ageless One and much else"[10]), but his 23 roles in the series are also entrenched in reality: there's the alcoholism of Big Heap, the mother domination of Eustace Tuttle, the mental health issues of Mr. Barron, the haughtiness of the Duke de Pomfrit, the indomitable eagerness of Pint-Pot, and, of course, the loneliness of Charlie Muggins (which was, perhaps, his primary emotion).

At the wedding of Ernest Maxin and Leigh Maddison, *Carry On* writer Norman Hudis caught sight of Hawtrey as the couple walked down the aisle on their way out. Hawtrey had sat forward, leaning with both arms on the pew in front, intent on them, unblinking, his head a little to one side. He'd turned up in his usual bizarre attire: an Anthony Eden hat and long dark coat. But in his eyes, luminous and melancholy, Hudis saw his tenderness. It wasn't envy; it was childlike wonder. It wasn't sadness; it was joy for the two people in love, or for all who ever loved or will love. "Then he caught me looking at him and dropped the expression as if it was scorching his face with the intolerable flame of truth. It was, I think, the last time I saw him. It was a fitting, human image."[11]

We will never truly understand Hawtrey. That much is true. He was too secretive, reliably erratic and, in the end, utterly disinterested in leaving any accurate account of his life. But, over the years, in cards and letters, he did send snapshots of his private world to Ann Ashwell, an old friend in Hounslow, and this is probably as good as it gets.

Behind the bolted bright red door of 117 Middle Street, he regularly bashed away at his typewriter, providing us now with an unrivalled firsthand glimpse into his mind. This correspondence shows a side to Hawtrey that is hitherto unknown, increasingly buried by bitterness and booze. It is moving, therefore, to read such concern and love.

"Hope you enjoyed your holiday. This is second day of mine. Waiting for sunshine! It's all fiesta and no siesta. Love from Carlos Hawtrey." (23 March 1973 – Palma-de-Mallorca).

"My dear Ann, Whatever I did and said to upset you – I much regret and apologise. Hope your cold has cleared away – Love from Charles." (8 November 1977)

"Dear Ann, Thinking of you – do hope all is under control. Try and get along here when you can – the sea air and being waited on can't be bad for

you. No news – am only offered rubbish. Am keeping my own company. Love from Charles." (18 August 1983)

"You are never far from my thoughts and hope you spent a restful and less worried Birthday on 6th December, and wish you many healthier and less worried Birthdays. All my love, Charles." (12 December 1983)

Just under a year before he died, he typed to her his last letter. At two pages (naturally on notepaper he'd long ago scavenged from a hotel) it was also his longest, and it's all there: the fear of leaving his house, the teenage vandals and his deteriorating health, Alice Dunne and the unwanted fan mail, the aborted autobiographies, penny pinching at the local charity shop, and his doomed effort to tame his back garden (which Joy Leonard described as "weird. It was sort of like a deep well, cut right down and covered with trees and bushes. 'I sunbathe down there,' he said. 'I sunbathe with no clothes on, because nobody can see me!' And I thought, 'Little skinny Charles, surely his neighbours think, 'What's that peculiar insect down there?'"[12])

Above all, though not entirely surprisingly, his ambition remains. He talks of a new entry in *Spotlight* to promote him across the world and reaffirms his unfaltering belief that "I think it high time that I was supported".[13]

He was still waiting for his stardom, yet still saw himself as a boy actor. That demon he couldn't let go.

3 November 1987

Dear Ann,

Thank you for your information. Hope you are having less back trouble. L.P.T.B. [London Passenger Transport Board] help in your travelling must have been very welcome. Without seeming self indulgent, here is my health news. The two following incidents were in no way related to my periodic visits to the specialist, who is wonderful. Gives me tests and questioning, prescribing four kinds of tablets, which I take regularly. Some little time ago I could only crawl, phoned the local doctor at his home, give him symptoms, he quickly arrived and prescribed the tablets, four daily, and I was cured. In trying to clear up my garden, I slid over in the slush, falling over on my left side. My arm became useless and painful. After three days an X-ray showed a fracture in the left arm. Am having therapy twice weekly, and practise daily. Still with a sense of humour and keeping cheerful, with many other problems: do not leave the house but for groceries and newspapers and helping others; dismantled doorbell ages ago because of vandals; door knocking I ignore. The house is still upside down. I tire very quickly. Have noted that my railcard expired last May 7th, will replace when required. Today reported that my electric white meter is out of alignment. Front room chimney needs new pot and cowl. Roof, generally, requires new slates. Purchased various items from Oxfam at give away prices. Fan mail delivered daily, which is a confounded bore, particularly when one husband and wife wrote that they and their child would be coming to stay with me, after reading that I lived alone. A boy of sixteen wrote three similar letters. I wrote replies to these letters signed Alice Dunne, stating that "Mr. Hawtrey is not available, his whereabouts strictly private and no letters were forwarded." Will they never leave me alone? I am thinking of renewing the Spotlight half page. It is very expensive, but free copies are sent worldwide to studios and managers and agents. This is my first typing since the fracture. The therapist said I should try. Aided by my trolly, took a mountain of washing to the Wishee-Washee this morning. Not before time. Last week I had a fifth proposal of compiling a biography. I always say no, but they are so insistent and impertinent that I have to restrain myself from saying, "Oh, sod off!" and putting the receiver down. Work wise, I am offered rubbish, particularly from Aubrey, all of which could do more harm than good, hence my Spotlight renewal in the section leading "Formerly Character". There are so many character actors who support, I think it high time that I was supported! Bernard, now retired except for advisory roles, is again selling up at a profit and moving, this time somewhat nearer. Friends in Bromley permanently write and phone and were very comforting when I had the house disaster, which you have refused to refer to. Well, let me know if LPTB offer transport near Deal. Though older, we have to be more beautiful! Why not!

Good wishes from elderly boy actor,

Charles

AFTERWORD

Charles Hawtrey was always known to the public as the little chap in glasses.

I cast him in films long before the advent of the *Carry On* series which made him famous; he must have thought it strange after being in so many films as mere support. However, he was a star in his way and as important as any of the other members of the *Carry On* cast.

In spite of the odd drinking bouts for which he became equally famous he was a true professional and one you could rely on to turn in a good performance. He was a gentleman and behaved on the set as George Arliss might have done with his pot of tea at four o'clock. In fact, when we had an end of picture party, he was always the one sitting at a table on his own with a pot of tea! But he *was* a pot of tea; you could say Charlie Hawtrey was a pot of tea!

We all loved him and appreciated the problem emanating from his particular kind of loneliness. He was not one to take part in the high jinks practised by other members of the cast but remained somewhat aloof and austere in complete contradiction to the part he happened to be playing.

He is a gentleman to be missed.

PETER ROGERS

APPENDICES

NOTES

PROLOGUE

[1] This scene is a figment of the author's imagination, the combination of numerous anecdotes, including those of Aubrey Phillips, Patrick Newley and Ronnè Coyles.
[2] The Carry On Companion, p.18: *"Carry On Nurse* independently saved the independent American distribution company, Grosvenor Films. The Crest Cinema in Westwood, Los Angeles, ran the film for over a year and the visual gag that closed *Nurse* struck such a chord with American audiences that millions of plastic daffodils were especially manufactured for sale at theatres screening the film."
[3] See The East Kent Mercury, *Lasting Tribute to the Man Who Brought Laughter* by Sue Briggs, 19 November 1998.
[4] Michael Medwin, letter to Louise Dillon and Catrina Margette.
[5] Michael Whittaker, interview with the author, 17 November 2008.
[6] *Fallen Stars, Tragic Lives and Lost Careers*, p.71.
[7] Robert Ross, *Carry On Darkly*, Channel 4, 1999.
[8] Bernard Walsh, Daily Star, 28 October 1988.
[9] Transcribed from Terry Scott's copy of the script for *Carry On Camping* by Talbot Rothwell (author's collection).

CHAPTER ONE

[1] *The Truth At Last*, p333.
[2] *The Pain of Laughter – The Last Days of Kenneth Williams*, BBC Radio 4, April 2008.
[3] *Middlesex Chronicle*, 27 May 1933.
[4] *The Sun*, 29 September 1988.
[5] *The Daily Telegraph*, 28 October 1988.
[6] *What a Carry On*, p.33.
[7] *Carry On Columbus*, the thirty-first, didn't set sail until four years after Hawtrey's death.
[8] *What a Carry On*, p.9 and Peter Rogers, interview with the author, August 1997.
[9] http://en.wikipedia.org/wiki/Carry_On_(series)
[10] *Film Review*, September 1972, p.41 and *What a Carry On*, p.33.
[11] *The Sun*, 15 August 1987.
[12] *The People*, 29 May 1988.
[13] Bernard Walsh, interview with the author, September 2000.
[14] *The Sun*, 29 September 1988.
[15] *The Sun*, 30 September 1988.
[16] *Ibid.*
[17] Patrick Newley, interview with the author, 6 April 2000.
[18] *The Sun*, 29 September 1988.
[19] Hawtrey in a Christmas card to Ann Ashwell, 12 December 1983: "… a secondary ailment increased over the years affecting mobility – saw the local Doctor [sic] who prescribed a capsule three times daily – which made it worse and very painful – so a different capsule – and like you battling on!"
[20] *The Man Who Was Private Widdle*, p. 92.
[21] Cockney rhyming slang: iron hoof = puff.
[22] Chris Clear, interview with the author, August 1997.
[23] Bernard Walsh, *op.cit.*
[24] Fire Fighter Knight, interview with the author, August 1997.
[25] Bernard Walsh, *op.cit.*
[26] Hawtrey had only ever made one will, in 1946, which left everything to his mother. The lack of a revised copy meant he died intestate.
[27] Bernard Walsh, *op.cit.*
[28] *The Man Who Was Private Widdle*, p. 92.
[29] *The Sun*, 28 October 1988.
[30] Aubrey Phillips, *Carry On Darkly*, Channel 4, 1999.
[31] Re-told by Aubrey Phillips to the author, April 2009.
[32] Aubrey Phillips, interview with the author, April 2009.

33 *The Sun*, 28 October 1988.
34 *Ibid.*
35 Taken from unattributed newspaper article by David Rose.
36 *The Sun*, 28 October 1988.
37 *Daily Mail*, 28 October 1988.
38 *The Sun*, 28 October 1988.
39 Kenneth Williams (26), Joan Sims (24), Hawtrey (23), Sid James (19), Kenneth Connor (17), Hattie Jacques (14) and Bernard Bresslaw (14).
40 *The People*, 29 May 1988.
41 Bernard Walsh, *op.cit.*
42 *The East Kent Mercury*, 2 November 1988.
43 Carole Ellison, interview with the author, 30 September 2008.
44 Bernard Walsh, *op.cit.*
45 *The Sun*, 3 November 1988.
46 Peter Willis, interview with the author, 1999.
47 *The Sun*, 3 November 1988.
48 Peter Willis, *op.cit.*
49 *The Sun*, 3 November 1988.
50 *Doncaster Star*, 29 October 1988.
51 Bernard Walsh, *op.cit.*
52 Carole Ellison, *op.cit.*
53 *Evening Standard*, 25 January 1989.
54 *Meridian Tonight*, 30 November 1998.
55 *Ibid.*
56 *The Carry-On Book*, p.37.
57 *The Times*, 28 October 1988.
58 Joy Leonard, interview with the author, August 1997.
59 *Daily Mirror*, 28 October 1988.
60 *The Sun*, 16 August 1972.

CHAPTER TWO

1 *Radio Times*, 25-31 August 1973, p.8.
2 *Radio Times* article, c.1952.
3 John Hartree, letter to the author, 28 October 2008.
4 Peter Rogers, *op.cit.*
5 Alice Hartree's case papers, taken from the Royal Albert Orphanage files held at Worcestershire Record Office (record reference 705:686), which includes her nomination papers, medical certificate and related papers. (Alice Hartree's entry is not indexed, however.) The nomination form gives the date as 7 Jan 1889 and the election date as 6 March 1889.
6 *Ibid.*
7 *Ibid.*
8 Joy Leonard, *op.cit.*
9 Maureen Hartree, interview with the author, 19 January 2010.
10 John Hartree, interview with the author, 20 January 2010.
11 *The Interpretation of Dreams.*
12 Doris Poccock, interview with the author, April 2004.
13 Joy Leonard, *op.cit.*
14 Violet Humphries, interview with the author, April 2004.
15 Doris Pocock, *op.cit.*
16 Hawtrey to Brian Matthew, BBC Radio 2, 28 November 1980.
17 William John Hartree died 6 December 1952 in Heston, Isleworth. He was 67 years old. The cause of death was registered as "Chronic Bronchitis and Emphysema, Hyperpiesis Myocardial Degeneration".
18 Sid Filbrey, letter to the author, 21 April 2000.
19 Violet Humphries, *op.cit.*
20 Joan Hanson, letter to the author, 22 April 2000.

[21] John Hartree, Hawtrey's nephew, says the "shed" was, in fact, his grandfather's pigeon coop which Hawtrey had commandeered.
[22] Doris Pocock, *op.cit.*
[23] Hawtrey to Brian Matthew, BBC Radio 2, 28 November 1980.
[24] http://www.youtube.com/watch?v=SM6p7xQ3_t4
[25] *Cor!* magazine, p22.
[26] *Movie Memories*, p.67.
[27] Roy Hudd, letter to Louise Dillon and Catrina Margette.
[28] A British actor who had left for Hollywood and ended up working for D. W. Griffith, before having a go behind the camera himself. He assisted Buster Keaton on the direction of *The Navigator* and won an Oscar for his role in *How Green Was My Valley*.
[29] Taken from a synopsis held by the British Film Institute.
[30] *Kinematoraph Weekly*, 26 April 1923.
[31] Joan Woodley, letter to the author, 28 August 1997.
[32] Cynthia Hayes, interview with the author, August 2000.
[33] John Hartree, letter to the author, 28 October 2008.
[34] *Middlesex Chronicle*, 27 May 1933.
[35] *Bournemouth Times & Directory*, 25 December 1926, p.3.
[36] *The Stage*, 20 January 1927.
[37] Hawtrey to Brian Matthew, BBC Radio 2, 28 November 1980.

CHAPTER THREE

[1] Noël Coward, p.4.
[2] Cynthia Hayes, *op.cit.*
[3] Peter Byrne, interview with the author, 2004.
[4] *The Play Pictorial*, No. 370, p.iii.
[5] *The Conti Story*, p.129.
[6] Cynthia Hayes, *op.cit.*
[7] Hawtrey to Brian Matthew, BBC Radio 2, 28 November 1980.
[8] Bernard Walsh, telephone conversation with the author, 1997.
[9] *What a Carry On*, p.32-3.
[10] Hawtrey to Brian Matthew, BBC Radio 2, 28 November 1980.
[11] Peter Byrne, *op.cit.*
[12] Theatre programme, held in The Raymond Mander and Joe Mitchenson Theatre Collection.
[13] It may have been his suit but, contrary to legend, and even the Conti website, Coward was never a "Conti chick".
[14] Hawtrey to Brian Matthew, BBC Radio 2, 28 November 1980.
[15] Peter Byrne, *op.cit.*
[16] Cynthia Hayes, *op.cit.*
[17] *The Play Pictorial*, No. 370, p.ii.
[18] Cynthia Hayes, *op.cit.*
[19] *Ibid.*
[20] Peter Byrne, *op.cit.*
[21] Cynthia Hayes, *op.cit.*
[22] *The Man Who Was Private Widdle*, p.9-10.
[23] Cynthia Hayes, *op.cit.*
[24] *Ibid.*
[25] *Ibid.*
[26] *The Guardian*, 31 October 1988.
[27] *Ralph Richardson, An Actor's Life*, p.42.
[28] *The Man Who Was Private Widdle*, p.11.
[29] *The Stage*, 2 January 1930.
[30] *The Stage*, 30 January 1930.
[31] *The Stage*, 20 March 1930.
[32] Hawtrey had kept copies of the first two. Griffiths, luckily, has cherished them all.
[33] Evelyn Griffiths, interview with the author, 8 June 2004.
[34] *The Sun*, 16 August 1972.
[35] Denis Wright, interview with the author, 2008.

[36] *Radio Times* article, c.1952.
[37] *Radio Times* 25-31 August 1973, p.8.

CHAPTER FOUR

[1] *Radio Times* article, c.1952.
[2] Richard O' Callaghan, interview with the author, 1999.
[3] *Film Weekly*, 1 July 1932, p.12.
[4] *Monthly Film Bulletin*, c.1937.
[5] Peter Byrne, *op.cit.*
[6] *Good Morning Boys*, p.126.
[7] Peter Byrne, *op.cit.*
[8] *The Times*, 8 November 1988.
[9] *The Sun*, 16 August 1972.
[10] Peter Byrne, *op.cit.*
[11] There are two actors, actually.
[12] *Good Morning Boys*, p.126.
[13] Peter Byrne, *op.cit.*
[14] *Funny You Should Ask*

CHAPTER FIVE

[1] Stephen Fry, *Carry On Darkly*, Channel 4, 1999.
[2] Dinah Sheridan, letter to Louise Dillon and Catrina Margette.
[3] Hawtrey to Brian Matthew, BBC Radio 2, 28 November 1980.
[4] *The Daily Telegraph*, c.1936.
[5] *The Kenneth Williams Diaries*, 1 November 1985.
[6] Leigh's win for Best Actress in *Gone With The Wind* would come in 1939.
[7] *The Stage*, 23 December 1937.
[8] The play was the first one to use the 'Kinema', a revolving stage that many productions have used since —- most notably *Les Misérables*.
[9] *The Daily Telegraph*, 16 August 1939.
[10] *The Daily Express*, 16 August 1939.
[11] *The Stage*, 17 August 1939.
[12] *The Times*, 16 August 1939.
[13] *Brixton Free Press*, 1 September 1939.
[14] *Sporting Life*, 18 August 1939.
[15] *The Observer*, 20 August 1939.
[16] *The Star*, 16 August 1939.
[17] *An Audience with Kenneth Williams*, LWT, 1983.
[18] *The Daily Sketch*, 16 August 1939.
[19] Released in late 1940, it was the second film he was to make for Butcher's Film Service. After his success with *Well Done Henry*, producers had promoted Hawtrey to his first starring role in the cinema. It did well at the box office, apparently.
[20] *The Stage*, 2 January 1941.
[21] *Dancing Times*, c.1940.
[22] *The Man Who Was Private Widdle*, p.26-7.
[23] Richard O' Callaghan, *op.cit.*
[24] *Brief Encounters*, p.132-3.
[25] Stephen Dixon in *The Irish Times*, 6 April 2002: 'Hawtrey was a feisty and courageous little actor who was always defiantly his own man and couldn't care less what people thought of him. As a flamboyantly gay man, he attracted the kind of attention that was fraught with danger in the 1950s. But unlike many homosexual public figures, he never pretended to be anything other than his true self. "No, bring me a nice gentleman," he insisted when photographers wanted him to pose with starlets.'

CHAPTER SIX

1   20 January 1947.
2   31 May 1955.
3   Did this end under a cloud, too? Letter from Hawtrey, dated 30 September 1946, held in the BBC Written Archive: "My dear Charles, May I remind you of my anxiety to broadcast, particularly after my episode with the *Just William* series, which I decided not to accept. Bless you, Yours very sincerely, Charles Hawtrey." (A letter had been sent to Hawtrey seeing if he would continue to play the same part in the second series. Producer Alick Hayes even offered to pre-record the show on days to suit Hawtrey, so why did he turn it down?)
4   Richard O'Callaghan, *op.cit.*
5   *Ibid.*
6   To watch this film for free, visit the BFI Southbank's Mediatheque.
7   *The Stage*, 26 October 1944.
8   *The Stage*, 25 February 1943.
9   Hawtrey to Brian Matthew, BBC Radio 2, 28 November 1980.
10 Peggy Cummins, interview with the author, November 2008.
11 *The Stage*, 24 May 1945.
12 *The Stage*, 28 June 1945.
13 *The Stage*, 11 June 1953.
14 Hawtrey to Brian Matthew, BBC Radio 2, 28 November 1980.
15 *Monthly Film Bulletin*, 30 September 1947.
16 *Kinematograph Weekly*, 17 January 1946.
17 *Today's Cinema*, 11 January 1946.
18 Jill Summers (1910-1997), best-known for her role as Phyllis Pierce in *Coronation Street*.
19 *Kinematograph Weekly*, *op.cit.*
20 *Today's Cinema*, 11 January 1946.
21 *Today's Cinema*, 15 January 1946.
22 *Kinematograph Weekly*, *op.cit.*
23 *Monthly Film Bulletin*, 31 January 1946.
24 *Kinematograph Weekly*, *op.cit.*
25 *Kinematograph Weekly*, *op.cit.*
26 *Kinematograph Weekly*, 21 August 1947.
27 Aubrey Phillips, *op.cit.*
28 Patrick Newley, *op.cit.*
29 Letter from Hawtrey to Graeme Muir at the BBC, 7 January 1955.
30 Letter from Al Parker to the BBC, 15 June 1948.
31 *Chain Male* was Hawtrey's fifth outing on television and he hadn't once been the star.
32 Burton then wrote to the BBC on 22 July 1949, conveying Hawtrey's message: "You will remember some months ago that we had a discussion about our client's fee and you said that you felt that he would get more broadcasting in the future if he reduced his fee which was excessive. He finally agreed to take a cut of 25% for a trial period of six months which has just expired and during this time I think you have been dealing with him direct. I have now received a letter from the artist, from which I quote …"
33 15 May 1950.
34 *The Man Who Played Private Widdle*, p.66.
35 Letter from Hawtrey to Mike Meehan at the BBC, 1 December 1954.
36 Letter from Hawtrey to Michael Barry at the BBC, 16 September 1952. Two of those included *Room To Let*, a Jack the Ripper thriller set in Victorian London, and *The Smart Aleck*, a curious tale of a bounder who, with a watertight alibi, kills his rich uncle. Once acquitted, knowing the double jeopardy law, the man holds a press conference and smugly explains how he did it.
37 Group 3 Limited, set up "encourage young film makers of talent and promise".
38 Written by R.F. Delderfield, whose book *The Bull Boys* became the basis for *Carry On Sergeant*.
39 Letter from Hawtrey to Norman Rutherford at the BBC, 22 November 1955.

CHAPTER SEVEN

[1] The full four-page treatment is held in Granada Television's Archive, Manchester.
[2] *Daily Telegraph*, 8 April 1957.
[3] *Cor!* magazine, p.14.
[4] Frank Williams, interview with the author, 1999.
[5] Ernest Maxin, interview with the author, 2000.
[6] Francis Matthews, interview with the author, 2008.
[7] Frank Williams, *op.cit.*
[8] *Ibid.*
[9] Francis Matthews, *op.cit.*
[10] Frank Williams, *op.cit.*
[11] Peter Rogers, *op.cit.*
[12] See *The Carry-On Book*, p.21.
[13] Peter Rogers, *op.cit.*
[14] Hawtrey to Roy Hudd, *Movie Memories*, Anglia Television, 1980.
[15] Peter Rogers, *op.cit.*
[16] Norman Hudis, letter to the author, 17 November 2000.
[17] Hawtrey to Roy Hudd, *Movie Memories*, Anglia Television, 1980.
[18] Peter Rogers, *op.cit.*
[19] *What a Carry On*, p.34.
[20] Joy Leonard: 'I used to get to the house and the door would be slightly open and he'd be conducting to the hi-fi system; he'd be throwing his arms around like mad!'
[21] Aubrey Phillips, *op.cit.*
[22] *The Culture of Queers*, p.153-4.
[23] *Cor!* magazine, p.17.
[24] *The Sun*, 29 September 1988.
[25] Michael Medwin, letter to Louise Dillon and Catrina Margette.
[26] Norman Rossington, letter to Louise Dillon and Catrina Margette.
[27] *Ibid.*
[28] Michael Medwin, *op.cit.*
[29] January 1960.
[30] 13 September 1960.

CHAPTER EIGHT

[1] *The Pink Paper*, c. October 1988.
[2] Ernest Maxin, *op.cit.*
[3] *Ibid.*
[4] *High Spirits*, p.102.
[5] Ernest Maxin, *op.cit.*
[6] *Ibid.*
[7] *Ibid.*
[8] Peter Rogers, op.cit.
[9] Norman Hudis, letter to the author, 17 November 2000.
[10] *Ibid.*
[11] *The Stage*, 3 January 1963.
[12] Brad Ashton, interview with the author, 2008.
[13] Ernest Maxin, *op.cit.*
[14] Doris Pocock, letter to author, 24 April 2000.
[15] Joy Leonard, *op.cit.*
[16] Brad Ashton, *op.cit.*
[17] Ernest Maxin, *op.cit.*
[18] Barbara Windsor, *Carry On Carrying On*, BBC Radio 2, 1994.
[19] Aubrey Phillips, *op.cit.*
[20] Peter Rogers, *op.cit.*
[21] Barbara Windsor, telephone conversation with the author, 1997.
[22] Ernest Maxin, *op.cit.*
[23] Hawtrey to Brian Matthew, BBC Radio 2, 28 November 1980.

[24] Aubrey Phillips: 'Charlie never called them just Woodbines, it was always "Wild Woodbines". His mother used to smoke them too.'

[25] Jon Pertwee, *Carry On Carrying On*, BBC Radio 2, 1994.

[26] Jack Douglas, letter to Louise Dillon and Catrina Margette.

[27] *Stop It Nurse!* also featured Barry Howard from the TV's *Hi-De-Hi*: 'Charlie's drinking was undoubtedly playing havoc with his career. When he came on stage there would be huge cheers and applause for this great comic actor, but by the end of his first scene people would be talking among themselves because he would be so awful. He often couldn't remember his lines or his moves and sometimes his speech would be slurred.' (*Cor!* magazine, p.48.) Hawtrey played "picturesque psychiatrist Dimple Simple with pops of brandy balls, sleep-inducing metronome and Charlie says ..." (*The Stage*, 17 August 1972)

[28] Aubrey Phillips, *op.cit.* Hawtrey couldn't even say his name, as illustrated in an episode of the BBC's radio comedy quiz show called *Funny You Should Ask* broadcast on 19 May 1981. ("Is it K. Connor?")

[29] Joy Leonard, *op.cit.*

[30] A linguistic term for describing the way in which newspaper headlines are constructed. *"Telegraphese"* is characterised by its terseness, meaning the messages are brief and effectively concise.

[31] *An Audience with Kenneth Williams*, LWT, 1983.

[32] *The Carry On Companion*, p.31.

[33] Norman Hudis, email to the author, 2008.

[34] *The Carry-On Book*, p.105-6.

[35] Hawtrey to Vincent Frith on the set of *Carry On Regardless* (filmed between 28 November 1960 and 17 January 1961) for *ABC Film Review*.

[36] Ernest Maxin, *op.cit.*

[37] Peter Rogers, *op.cit.* and interview with the author, 14 May 2004.

[38] Brad Ashton, *op.cit.*

[39] *The Carry-On Book*, p.35.

[40] *Ibid* and Peter Rogers, *op.cit.*

[41] Peter Rogers, *op.cit.*

[42] John Hartree, letter to author, 28 October 2008.

[43] Richard O' Callaghan, *op.cit.*

[44] He was actually 48, once saying, "I'm allergic to dates. Whose business is it anyway, dear?" (*Radio Times*, 25-31 August 1973)

[45] John Hartree, interview with the author, 20 January 2010.

[46] Jack Douglas, letter to Louise Dillon and Catrina Margette.

[47] *Barbara: The Laughter and Tears of a Cockney Sparrow*, p.74-5.

[48] *The Carry-On Book*, p.84-5.

[49] Southern Evening Echo, 18 June 1965.

[50] Peter Rogers, *op.cit.*

[51] Marlene Hargrave, interview with the author, 15 November 1998.

[52] *Ibid.*

[53] *Barbara: The Laughter and Tears of a Cockney Sparrow*, p.75.

[54] Aubrey Phillips, *op.cit.*

[55] Jack Douglas, *op.cit.*

[56] John Hartree, letter to the author, 28 October 2008.

CHAPTER NINE

[1] *The Carry-On Book*, p.34-5.

[2] Peggy Mount: 'A Night of A Thousand Stars: the other performers being Sir Ralph Richardson and Jack Hawkins. Charles played a clumsy and rather rude butler and his timing was absolutely perfect.' In July 1964 the Palladium event was staged again with a mesmerising cast including Gloria Swanson, Judy Garland and Merle Oberon.

[3] Violet Humphries, *op.cit.*

[4] Typed letter from Hawtrey to Ann Ashwell, 12 September 1986: "Dear Ann, Am writing, since it is not possible to reach you by phone – I learned politely that your neighbour works at night and sleeps daytime. I have experienced the long physical and mental upset you have endured – hence my writing to you. Deal has undergone many changes – some of the best and the worst

people have sold up and moved away. Shops close and re-open under new owners, so there are give away sales of old stock – I have made several purchases while the going was good. My work at 117 [Middle Street, Deal] is endless, I tire very quickly, one job done creates many others. In recent years I have lost many friends and acquaintances who have 'passed on' – some without obituary in the Press [sic]. Most of all, of course, I miss Alice, I am comforted knowing that she is happy in that 'better place'! My fan mail now extends to Germany. My trip to Newcastle was unforgettable and improved morale. Charles."

5   Maureen Hartree, interview with the author, 19 January 2010.
6   Letter to Michael Sullivan, Hawtrey's agent, from BBC Artist's Book Department, 14 May 1965.
7   *The Carry On Companion*, p.58.
8   Jack Douglas, letter to Louise Dillon and Catrina Margette.
9   *Radio Times*, 25-31 August 1973.
10 *Ibid.*
11 *High Spirits*, p.152. Gerald Thomas's editing wasn't so refined that this is missed. For a split second when she says the line, we hear Hawtrey snort with laughter and see Sims about to lose it.
12 *Ibid.*
13 *The Man Who Was Private Widdle*, p.32.
14 Aubrey Phillips, *op.cit.*
15 Aubrey Phillips, *op.cit.*
16 *The Man Who Was Private Widdle*, p.88.
17 Aubrey Phillips, *op.cit.*
18 *The Stage*, 15 June 1995: 'Michael Sullivan, who for many years was one of the country's leading agents, died with his wife, the film actress Dany Robin, following a fire in their Paris flat on May 25. He was 74, his wife 68.'
19 Aubrey Phillips, *op.cit.*
20 Ronnè Coyles, interview with the author, 2000.
21 *Ibid.*
22 *Ibid.*
23 Jack Douglas, letter to Louise Dillon and Catrina Margette.
24 *The Stage*, 8 January 1970.
25 Ronnè Coyles, *op.cit.*
26 Patrick Newley, *op.cit.* and *The Man Who Was Private Widdle*, p.83.
27 *The Man Who Was Private Widdle*, p.77.
28 Peggy Mount, letter to Louise Dillon and Catrina Margette.
29 *Just Williams*, p.198.
30 *Evening News*, 24 May 1969.
31 DVD sleeve.
32 Patrick Newley, *op.cit.*
33 Aubrey Phillips, *op.cit.*
34 As told by Kenneth Williams in *Back Drops*, p.54.
35 Patrick Newley, *op.cit.*
36 *The Times*, 23 September 2000.
37 *The Carry-On Book*, p.36-7.
38 Hawtrey to Brian Matthew, BBC Radio 2, 28 November 1980.
39 *The Carry-On Book*, p.37.
40 Aubrey Phillips, *op.cit.*

CHAPTER TEN

1   *Cor!* magazine, p.48.
2   John Hartree, letter to the author, 28 October 2008.
3   Aubrey Phillips, *op.cit.*
4   Paul Denver, interview with the author, June 2001.
5   *Ibid.*
6   Aubrey Phillips, *op.cit.*
7   Paul Denver, *op.cit.*
8   Aubrey Phillips, *op.cit.*

[9] Paul Denver, *op.cit.*
[10] Aubrey Phillips, *op.cit.*
[11] *The Stage*, 13 August 1970.
[12] *Carry On Regardless: The Genius of Charles Hawtrey* by Richard Dyer at the National Film Theatre (as part of the fourth London Lesbian and Gay Festival), 24 October 1989
[13] *The Culture of Queers*, p.154-6.
[14] Paul Denver, *op.cit.*
[15] *Ibid.*
[16] Aubrey Phillips, *op.cit.*
[17] Bernard Walsh, *op.cit.*
[18] Aubrey Phillips, *op.cit.*
[19] Hawtrey to Brian Matthew, BBC Radio 2, 28 November 1980.
[20] Aubrey Phillips, *op.cit.*
[21] *Cor!* magazine, p.48-9.
[22] Aubrey Phillips, *op.cit.*
[23] *The West Sussex County Times*, c.1973.
[24] *The Stage*, 10 January 1974
[25] *Ibid.*
[26] Don Boyd, interview with the author, 9 October 2009.
[27] *Ibid.*
[28] Peter Byrne, *op.cit.*
[29] Spencer K. Gibbons, interview with the author, June 2001.
[30] *Ibid.*
[31] Aubrey Phillips, *op.cit.*
[32] Peter Byrne, Spencer K. Gibbons.
[33] Spencer K. Gibbons, *op.cit.*
[34] *Ibid.*

CHAPTER ELEVEN

[1] Hawtrey to Brian Matthew, BBC Radio 2, 28 November 1980.
[2] Deal residents, interviewed August 1997.
[3] Patrick Newley, *op.cit.*
[4] Aubrey Phillips, *Carry On Darkly*, Channel 4, 1999.
[5] Ronnè Coyles, *op.cit.*
[6] Aubrey Phillips, *op.cit.*
[7] Patrick Newley, *op.cit.*
[8] *Ibid.*
[9] Aubrey Phillips, *op.cit.*
[10] Bernard Walsh, *op.cit.*
[11] Paul Denver, *op.cit.*
[12] Joy Leonard, *op.cit.*
[13] *High Spirits*, p.152.
[14] *The Kenneth Williams Letters*, 9 September 1987.
[15] *The Kenneth Williams Diaries*, 10 May 1970.
[16] Paul Denver, *op.cit.*
[17] Aubrey Phillips, *op.cit.*
[18] *Ibid.*
[19] Joy Leonard, *op.cit.*
[20] *Ibid.*
[21] *Cor!* magazine, p.32.
[22] Joy Leonard, *op.cit.*
[23] *Ibid.*
[24] *The Man Who Was Private Widdle*, p.86.
[25] Ray Dennis, interview with the author, August 1997.
[26] Peter Stephens, interview with the author, August 1997.
[27] Ray Dennis, *op.cit.*
[28] Basil Kidd, interview with the author, 1998.

[29] Dennis Senior, interview with the author, August 1997.

[30] Joy Leonard, *op.cit.*

[31] *The Sun*, 6 August 1984.

[32] Fire Fighter Knight has similar comedic memories: wading through the cellar, shin deep in empty wine bottles, whilst his colleague became entangled in a pair of curtains.

[33] Marcus Gidman, letter to the author, 1997.

[34] Barry Bullock, conversation with the author, August 1997.

[35] Basil Kidd, *op.cit.*

[36] David Reid, interview with the author, August 1997.

[37] Aubrey Phillips, *op.cit.*

[38] Basil Kidd, *op.cit.*

[39] *East Kent Mercury*, 8 August 1984, p.1.

[40] *The News of the World*, 7 June 1981: 'Veteran *Carry On* comedy star Charles Hawtrey was recovering in hospital in Deal, Kent, yesterday after a heart attack at his home.'

[41] *The Sun*, 6 August 1984.

[42] *The Sun*, 29 September 1988.

[43] *The Kenneth Williams Letters*, 17 July 1987.

[44] Fire Fighter Knight, interview with the author, August 1997.

[45] Marcus Gidman, *op.cit.*

[46] Lucy Windsor, interview with the author, August 1997.

[47] *The People*, 29 May 1988.

[48] *The Sun*, 29 September 1988.

[49] Martin Jenkins, interview with the author, 18 December 2009.

[50] Newley continues: 'The publisher wanted to call it "Carry On Charlie", and Charlie wasn't happy about that. I think he wanted to call it "My Autobiography by Charles Hawtrey"'.

[51] Patrick Newley, *op.cit.*

[52] *High Spirits*, p.152.

[53] Aubrey Phillips, op.cit.

[54] Bryn Hawkins, interview with the author, August 1997.

[55] Joy Leonard, *op.cit.*

[56] Chris Burrows, interview with the author, August 1997.

[57] Joy Leonard, *op.cit.*

[58] *Doncaster Star*, 29 October 1988.

CHAPTER TWELVE

[1] As well as "Natasha" and a "Vivanidère" in the *New Faces* show of 1940, Hawtrey had also played Ague-Cheek, in a quick song taken from that very scene ("O Mistress Mine").

[2] *New Statesman*, 1 October 2001.

[3] *NME*, September 1989.

[4] Morrissey, of course, wasn't the only musical fan of Hawtrey's. In 1969, John Lennon preceded the recording of The Beatles' track 'Dig A Pony' with, "I dig a pygmy by Charles Hawtrey and the Deaf Aids. Phase one: in which Doris gets her oats!" (The Deaf Aids was the nickname The Beatles gave to their Vox amplifiers and the adlib was later edited to the start of 'Two of Us'). Another name-check occurs on the B-side of Adam Ant's number three record 'Ant Rap' (1981). Entitled 'Friends', his lyrics include the line "I'm an old friend of Charles Hawtrey" amongst a long list of quirky names he claims to have befriended.

[5] *Mozipedia, The Encyclopedia of Morrissey and The Smiths*, p.63-4.

[6] http://www.morrissey-solo.com/article.pl?sid=01/06/19/0617211

[7] See *The Guardian*'s article entitled Unhappy Birthday? 22 May 2009.

[8] Hawtrey to Brian Matthew, BBC Radio 2, 28 November 1980.

[9] *The Guardian*, 31 October 1988.

[10] *Ibid.*

[11] Norman Hudis, letter to the author, 17 November 2000.

[12] Joy Leonard, *op.cit.*

[13] Even Peter Rogers could sense Hawtrey's unhappiness saying, "From the early days of Gainsborough Films he was always in support of something or other." Peter Rogers, interview with the author, 14 May 2004.

Theatre

The majority were listed by Hawtrey in his typed résumé, enclosed with his letter of 1 December 1954 to Mike Meehan at the BBC. The Raymond Mander and Joe Mitchenson Theatre Collection supplied the early dates, the rest remain unknown.

As performer:

Dec. 1925 The Windmill Man
           Hippodrome Boscombe,
           Bournemouth
Dec. 1927 Bluebell in Fairyland
           Scala Theatre, London
Dec. 1928 Where the Rainbow Ends
           Holborn Empire, London
Dec. 1929 Quality Street
           Haymarket, London
?   House That Jack Built
           Touring
Dec. 1929 Babes in the Wood
           Theatre Royal, Exeter
? 1930   Loves Labour Lost
           Haymarket, London
Sep. 1930 Street Scene
           The Globe, London
? 1931   Cavalcade
           Drury Lane, London
Dec. 1931 Peter Pan
           Palladium, London
? 1931   Evergreen
           Adelphi Theatre, London
? 1934   The Maitlands
           Leeds
Dec. 1936 Your Number's Up
           The Gate Theatre Studio, London
Dec. 1936 Peter Pan
           Palladium, London
Mar. 1937 Bats in the Belfry
           Ambassadors Theatre, London
Dec. 1937 Members Only
           The Gate Theatre Studio, London
? 1938   Strange Family
           Q Theatre, Richmond
? 1938   Chain Male
           Richmond Theatre
May 1938   Happy Returns
           Adelphi Theatre
Aug. 1938 A Midsummer Night's Dream
           Open Air Theatre
Nov. 1938 Strange Family
           Q Theatre, Richmond

Mar. 1939 The Taming of the Shrew
           The Old Vic, London
Jul. 1939 Printer's Devil
           Embassy Theatre, Swiss Cottage
Aug. 1939 Counterfeit
           Duke of York's Theatre, London
Feb. 1940 Without the Prince
           Richmond Theatre, Surrey
Apr. 1940 New Faces
           Comedy Theatre, Mayfair
Jul. 1941 New Ambassadors Review
           Ambassadors Theatre, London
Apr. 1942 Scoop
           Vaudeville Theatre, London
Feb. 1943 Old Chelsea
           Prince's Theatre, London (and tour)
? 1943   Housemaster
           Q Theatre, Richmond
Dec. 1943 Claudius the Bee
           Q Theatre, Richmond
Oct. 1944 Merrie England
           The Winter Garden, London
           (and tour from Feb. 1945)
Mar. 1945 Salute to Variety
           Victoria Palace, London
? 1946   Variety
           Q Theatre, Richmond
Jan. 1947 Vice Versa
           Q Theatre, Richmond
Oct. 1949 Who's Your Lady Friend?
Jan. 1951 Frou Frou
           New Lindsay Theatre,
           Notting Hill Gate
Mar. 1951 Husbands Don't Count
           New Lindsay Theatre,
           Notting Hill Gate
Oct. 1952 Husbands Don't Count
           Winter Garden Theatre, London
May 1952   Bless You!
           Q Theatre
Jan. 1966 Dick Whittington
           King's Theatre, Southsea
           (with Dick Emery)
May 1966   Second Honeymoon
           Grand, Blackpool
           (with Arthur Askey)
Dec. 1966 Babes in the Wood
           ABC Theatre, Stockton-on-Tees
Jun. 1967 Carry On Laughing
           King's Theatre, Southsea
           (with Kenneth Connor)
Dec. 1968 Sleeping Beauty
           ABC Theatre, Peterborough

Jun. 1969 The Mating Game
           Yvonne Arnaud, Guilford
           (with Terry Scott)
Jun. 1972 Stop It Nurse!
           Pavillion Theatre, Torquay
           (with Kenneth Connor)
Jun. 1974 No Sex Please We're British
           Dreamland Theatre, Margate
Dec. 1979 Jack and the Beanstalk
           Wyvern Theatre, Swindon

As producer:

May 1945   Temporary Ladies   Peggy Cummins
Jun. 1945 Oflag 3   Julian Dallas
May 1946   Guest in the House   Rene Ray
Sep. 1946 Mother of Men   Barbara Mullen
Nov. 1948?Happy Birthday   Mary Clare
           By Candlelight   Magda Kun
           Trial of Mary Dugan   Alice Gachet
           Peg of My Heart   Eileen Thorndike
           Trouble in the House
           Gus McNaughton
           Chinese Bungalow Joan Greenwood
           Other People's Business Irene Handl
           and Helen Goss
Oct. 1949 Who's Your Lady Friend?
Apr. 1950 Happiest Days of Your Life
                                  Viola Lyel
           Uncle Harry   Wally Patch
           Murder in MayfairTonie Edgar Bruce
           How Are They At Home
                       Mignon O'Doherty and
                            Anthony Nicols
Jan. 1950 The Perfect Woman
                 John Blythe and Violet Loxley
Oct. 1951 Young Men's Fancy
            John Blythe and Violet Farebrother
           Czechmate   Joan Greenwood
           You Can't Take It With You
           Bessie Love
Apr.1952   Many Happy Returns   Irene Handl
Jun. 1953 The Blue Lamp   Fred Kitchen

As performer for Aubrey Phillips: (incomplete)

Jack and the Beanstalk
22 Dec. 1967 Victoria Theatre, Salford
             (until 3 February 1968)
26 Dec. 1969 Arcadia Theatre, Llandudno
             (for two weeks)
5 Jan. 1970 Palace, Morecambe
             (for one week)

12 Jan. 1970 Memorial Hall, Northwich?
             (for one week)
19 Jan. 1970 Opera House, Buxton
             (for one week)
26 Jan. 1970 Grand Theatre, Leek
             (for one week)
9 Feb. 1970 Victoria Theatre, Salford
             (for one week)

Carry On Holiday Startime starring
Charles Hawtrey
29 Jun. 1970 Gaiety Theatre, Rhyl
             (for the summer season)

Dick Whittington
26 Dec. 1972 Romiley Forum, Cheshire
             (for six weeks)

Snow White and the Seven Dwarfs (Aubrey
Phillips: "We also played Alfred Beck Theatre
Hayes, Playhouse Weston-super-Mare, Town
Hall Theatre Oakengates, Royal Opera House
Scarborough, Theatre Royal Bury St. Edmonds,
Civic Theatre Barnsley, Theatre Royal St.
Helens, Key Theatre Peterborough, Kings
Theatre Southsea, Pavilion Bournemouth,
Princes Theatre Torquay, Theatre Royal Lincoln,
Palace Theatre Manchester, Pavilion Theatre
Glasgow, Lyceum Theatre Crewe, Grand Theatre
Wolverhampton, Grand Pavilion Porthcawl and
Gaiety Theatre Ayr. In all cases he was court
jester — Muddles — and I was Dame
Martha.")

? Dec. 1973   The Arts Centre, Basildon
              (for three weeks)
? Jan. 1974   Capitol Theatre, Horsham
              (for one week)
? Apr.1974   Southampton Guildhall
8 Apr.1974   Theatre Royal, Nottingham
              (for one week)
22 Apr. 1974 Festival Hall, Malvern
              (for two days)
25 Apr. 1974 Empire Theatre, Liverpool
              (for three days)
? Nov, 1974   Grand Theatre, Swansea
18 Dec. 1974 Civic Theatre, Bow, London
              (for four weeks)
24 Mar. 1975 Birmingham Hippodrome
              (for one week)
13 Oct. 1975 Alhambra Theatre, Bradford
              (for one week)
? Nov. 1975   Empire Theatre, Sunderland

26 Dec. 1975 Pavilion Theatre, Weymouth
(until 10 January 1976)
31 Mar. 1976 New Theatre, Cardiff
(for one week)
? Mar. 1976 Birmingham Hippodrome
3 Apr. 1976 Princes Hall, Aldershot
(for three days)
12 Apr. 1976 Theatre Royal, Norwich
(for one week)
19 Apr. 1976 Southampton Guildhall
(for six days)
17 May 1976 Wyvern Theatre, Swindon
(for one week)
31 May 1976 Wimbledon Theatre
(for one week)

23 Nov. 1976? Bristol Hippodrome
(for one week)
27 Dec. 1976 Royal Spa Centre,
Leamington Spa (for one week)
10 Jan. 1977 Civic Theatre, Corby
(for one week)
17 Jan 1977 The Polar Cinema, Welshpool
(for one week)
31 Oct. 1977 New Theatre, Cardiff
(until 5 November)

The Old Woman Who Live in a Shoe
29 Nov. 1976? The King's Theatre, Southsea
(for one week)

Filmography

1922
Tell Your Children (5532ft) Cert A, B/W, Silent
International Artists

p ....Martin Sabine
d ....Donald Crisp
s ....(Novel) Rachel McNamara (*Lark's Gate*)
sc ....Leslie Howard Gordon
Doris Eaton ....Rosny Edwards
Walter Tennyson............................John Haslar
Margaret Halstan................Lady Sybil Edwards
Gertrude McCoy ....Maudie
Warwick Ward ....Lord Belhurst
Mary Rorke...................................Susan Haslar
Cecil Morton York ....Reuben Haslar
Adeline Hayden Coffin ....Nanny Dyson
A. Harding Steerman................................Vicar

1923
This Freedom (7220ft) Cert A, B/W, Silent
Ideal Film Company

d/sc ....Denison Clift
s ....(Novel) A. S. M. Hutchinson
Fay Compton............................Rosalie Aubyn
Clive Brook................................Harry Occleve
John Stuart ....Huggo Occleve
Athene Seyler ....Miss Keggs
Nancy Kenyon ....Doda Occleve
Gladys Hamer.....................................Gertrude
Fewlass Llewellyn ....Rev. Aubyn
Adeline Hayden Coffin ....Mrs. Aubyn
Mickey Brantford ....Robert
Bunty Fosse................................Rosalie (child)
Joan Maud..Hilda
Charles Vane ....Uncle Pyke

Gladys Hamilton ....Aunt Belle
Robert English.....................................Mr. Field

1932
Marry Me (85m) Cert U, B/W, Sound
Gainsborough Pictures (Ideal)

p ....Michael Balcon
d ....William Thiele
s ....Stephen Zador, Franz Schulz, Ernst Angel
sc Angus MacPhail, Anthony Asquith, Desmond Carter

Renate Müller ....Ann Linden
Harry Green............................Sigurd Bernstein
George Robey ....Aloysius Novak
Ian Hunter ....Robert Hart
Maurice Evans ....Paul Hart
Billy Caryll..Meyer
Charles Hawtrey Jr ....Billy Hart
Charles Carson ....Korten
Viola Lyel.....................................Frau Krause
Sunday Wilshin ....Ida Brun
Roland Carter..Tailor
Bryan Lawrance ....Singer

1933
The Melody Maker (56m) Cert U, B/W
Warner Brothers/First National Productions

p ....Irving Asher
d ....Leslie Hiscott
Lester Matthews ....Tony Borrodaile
Joan Marion...Mary
Evelyn Roberts ....Reggie Bumblethorpe
Wallace Lupino ....Clamart
A. Bromley Davenport............................Jenks
Vera Gerald ....Grandma

Joan White ....Jerry
Charles Hawtrey...Tom
Tonie Edgar Bruce ....Donna Lola

1933
Case Hardened (No record)
Devil To Pay (No record)
Good As New (No record)

High Finance (67m) Cert A, B/W
Warner Brothers/First National Productions
p ....Irving Asher
d..George King
Gibb McLaughlin ....Sir Grant Rayburn
Ida Lupino ....Jill
John Batten..Tom
John H. Roberts ....Ladcock
D. A. Clarke-Smith..............................Dodman
Abraham Sofaer ....Myers

Mayfair Girl (67m) Cert A, B/W
Warner Brothers/First National Productions
p ....Irving Asher
d..George King
s ....Brandon Fleming
Sally Blane ....Brenda Mason
John Stuart....................................Robert Blair
D. A. Clarke-Smith ....Capt. Merrow
Glen Alyn ....Santa
Roland Culver..................................Dick Porter
James Carew
Charles Hickman
Winifred Oughton
Philip Strange
Lawrence Anderson

Smithy (53m) Cert A, B/W
Warner Brothers/First National Productions
p ....Irving Asher
d..George King
Edmund Gwenn ....John Smith
Peggy Novack..Jane
D. A. Clarke-Smith ....Boyd
Clifford Heatherley ....Sir Olds
Viola Compton ....Lucy
Charles Hickman ....Son
Eve Gray...Daughter

The Office Wife (43m) Cert A, B/W
Warner Brothers/First National Productions
p ....Irving Asher
d..George King
s ....(Novel) Faith Baldwin

sc..Randall Faye
Nora Swinburne.......................................Anne
Dorothy Bouchier ....Linda
Cecil Parker ....Lawrence Bradley
Percy Walsh ....Simms
Violet Farebrother.........................Aunt Cynthia
Hamilton Keene.....................................Gregory

1934
Man With a Million (No record)

Trouble in Store (39m) Cert U, B/W
Warner Brothers/First National Productions
p ....Irving Asher
d..Clyde Cook
James Finlayson ....The Watchman
Jack Hobbs...Jack
Glen Alyn ....Gloria
Anthony Hankey.......................................Tony
Clifford Heatherley....................................Potts
Margaret Yarde...................................Landlady
Charles Carson ....Sanderson
Millicent Wolf ....Mabel

Little Stranger (51m) Cert A, B/W
MGM
(Reissued 1943, 100ft cut)
d...George King
Nigel Playfair ....Sam Collins
Eva Moore ....Jessie Collins
Norah Baring ....Millie Dent
Hamilton Keene..................................Tom Hale

Murder at Monte Carlo (70m) Cert A, B/W
Warner Brothers/First National Productions
p ....Irving Asher
d...Ralph Ince
s..(Novel) Tom Van Dyke
sc ....John Hastings Turner, Michael Barringer
Errol Flynn...Dyter
Eve Gray ....Gillian
Paul Graetz ....Dr. Heinrich Becker
Molly Lamont ....Margaret Becker
Ellis Irving ....Marc Orton
Lawrence Hanray ....Collum
Henry Victor...Major
Brian Buchel...Yates
Peter Gawthorne ....Duprez

Guest of Honour (53m) B/W
Warner Brothers/First National Productions
p ....Irving Asher
d ....George King
s .....(Play) *The Man From Blankley's* by F. Anstey
sc ....W. Scott Darling
Henry Kendall ....Lord Strathpeffer
Edward Chapman ....Montague Tidmarsh
Miki Hood..Marjorie
Margaret Yarde ....Emma Tidmarsh
Eve Gray ....Cissie Poffley
Joan Playfair ....Mrs. Bodfish
Hay Plumb...............................Mr. Bodfish
Helen Ferrers ....Mrs. Gilwattle
Cecil Humphreys ....Mr. Gilwattle
Louis Goodrich...Butler

Hyde Park (48m) Cert U, B/W
Warner Brothers/First National Productions
p ....Irving Asher
d/s ....Randall Faye
George Carney ....Joe Smith
Eve Lister......................................Mary Smith
Barry Clifton ....Bill Lenbridge
Wallace Lupino ....Alf Turner
Charles Carson ....Lord Lenbridge
Phyllis Morris...............................Mrs. Smith

1935
Kiddies On Parade (22m) Cert U, B/W
Majestic Enterprises
p ....Burt Hyams
d ....Stewart B. Moss
s ....Fay Glenn
Charles Hawtrey, Tommie Hayes, Rosie
Youngman, Dan Rowles, Peter Yorke, Italia Conti's
Juveniles, Pat Rose and his Majestic Orchestra

Windfall (65m) Cert U, B/W
Embassy/RKO
p...............................George King, Randall Faye
d..George King
s...(Play) R. C. Sherriff
sc ....Randall Faye, Jack Celestine
Edward Rigby ....Sam Spooner
Marie Ault ....Maggie Spooner
George Carney ....Syd
Marjorie Corbett ....Mary
Derrick de Marney ....Tom Spooner
Googie Withers...Dodie

Man of the Moment (81m) Cert A, B/W
Warner Brothers/First National Productions
p ....Irving Asher
d ....Monty Banks
s ....(Play) Yves Mirande (*Water Nymph*)
sc.Roland Pertwee, Guy Bolton, A. R. Rawlinson
Douglas Fairbank Jr ....Tony
Lara La Plante..Mary
Claude Hulbert ....Rufus
Margaret Lockwood ....Vera Barton
Donald Calthrop ....Godfrey
Peter Gawthorne............................Mr. Barton
Monty Banks...Doctor
Morland Graham ....Runcorn
Eve Gray ....Miss Maddern
Wyndham Goldie ....Randall
Martita Hunt ....Gambler
Hal Gordon ....Sergeant
Charles Hawtrey...Tom
Tony Hankey/Margaret Yarde

Get Off My Foot (82m) Cert A, B/W
Warner Brothers/First National Productions
p ....Irving Asher
d ....William Beaudine
s.............(Play) Edward Paulton (*Money By Wire*)
sc ....Frank Launder and Robert Edmunds
Max Miller ....Herbert Cronk
Jane Carr ....Helen Rawlingcourt
Chili Bouchier...Marie
Norma Varden ....Mrs. Rawlingcourt
Morland Graham.................Maj. Rawlingcourt
Anthony Hankey ....Algy
Reginald Purdell...Joe
Vera Boggetti ....Matilda
Wally Patch ....Tramp

1936
Cheer Up! (72m) Cert U, B/W
Stanley Lupino (Associated British Film
Distributors)
d..Leo Mittler
s...Stanley Lupino
sc ....Michael Barringer
Stanley Lupino ....Tom Denham
Sally Gray..Sally Gray
Roddy Hughes ....Dick Dirk
Gerald Barry ....John Harman
Kenneth Kove ....Wilfred Harman
Wyn Weaver ....Mr. Carter
Marjorie Chard ....Mrs. Carter
Ernest Sefton ....Tom Page
Syd Crossley ....Waiter

Sabotage (76m) Cert A, B/W
USA: *The Woman Alone*
Gaumont-British Picture Corporation
p ....Michael Balcon
ap ....Ivor Montagu
d..Alfred Hitchcock
s..........(Novel) Joseph Conrad (*The Secret Agent*)
sc.Charles Bennett, Ian Hay, Alma Reville, Helen Simpson, E. V. H. Emmett
Sylvia Sidney..................................Sylvia Verloc
Oscar Homolka..............................Carl Verloc
John Loder ....Ted Spencer
Desmond Tester ....Steve
Joyce Barbour...Renée
Matthew Boulton ....Supt. Talbot
S. J. Warmington.......................Hollingshead
William Dewhurst ....A. S. Chatman
Austin Trevor....................................Vladimir
Torin Thatcher...Yunct
Aubrey Mather ....Greengrocer
Peter Bull ....Michaelis
Charles Hawtrey ....Youth
Martita Hunt ....Miss Chatman
Hal Walters...Father

The Brown Wallet (68m) Cert A, B/W
Warner Brothers/First National Productions
p ....Irving Asher
d..Michael Powell
s....................................(Story) Stacy Aumonier
sc..Ian Dalrymple
Patric Knowles.............................John Gillespie
Nancy O'Neil ....Eleanor
Henry Caine.....................................Simmonds
Henrietta Watson ....Aunt Mary
Charlotte Leigh ....Miss Barton
Shayle Gardner.............................Witherspoon
Edward Dalby ....Minting
Eliot Makeham ....Hobday

1937
Well Done, Henry (86m) Cert A, B/W
Neville Clarke Productions (Butcher's Film Service)
d ....Wilfred Noy
s ....Selwyn Jepson
sc.............................Wilfred Noy, A. Barr-Smith
Will Fyffe ....Henry McNab
Cathleen Nesbitt............................Mrs. McNab
Charles Hawtrey ....Rupert McNab
Iris March....................................Mary McNab
Donald Gray...................................Jimmy Dale
Marjorie Taylor............................Celia Canford

Torin Thatcher..........................George Camford
Hugh McDermott....................................Sevier
Paul Sheridan..Leroux

Good Morning, Boys! (79m) Cert A, B/W
USA: *Where There's a Will*
Gainsborough Pictures
p..Edward Black
d ....Marcel Varnel
s ....Anthony Kimmins
sc............Marriott Edgar, Val Guest, Leslie Arliss
Will Hay ....Dr. Benjamin Twist
Lilli Palmer..Yvette
Martita Hunt...............................Lady Bagshot
Peter Gawthorne..............Col. Wiloughby-Gore
Graham Moffatt ....Albert
Fewlass Llewellyn ....Dean
Mark Daly...Arty Jones
Peter Godfrey ....Cliquot
C. Denier Warren..........................Henri Duval
Charles Hawtrey ....Septimus
Will Hay Jr ....Clarence
Basil McGrail ....Watson
Jacques Brown ....Manager

The Gap (38m) Cert A, B/W
Gaumont-British Instructional (General Film Distributors)
(Made in co-operation with Army Council and Air Council)
d...Donald Carter
G. H. Mulcaster.......................Air Vice-Marshal
Patrick Curwen............................Major General
Carlton Hobbs..........................Cabinet Minister
Jack Vyvyan ....Butcher
Charles Denville ....Baker
Norman Wooland ....Candlestick Maker
Foster Carlin....................................Apothecary
Arthur Metcalfe ....Rich man
Peter Cozens ....Poor man
Michael Rennie ......The Chemist/Radio Operator

East of Ludgate Hill (47m) Cert U, B/W
Fox-British Pictures
d ....Manning Haynes
s...(Play) Arnold Ridley
sc ....Edward Dryhurst, Stanley Jackson
Robert Cochran.................................Derek Holt
Nancy O'Neil ....Norah Applin
Eliot Makeham.........................Mr. Tallweather
Hal Gordon ....Bert Bickley
Aubrey Mallalieu ....James McIntyre
Pamela Wood ....Minnie Hazell

Vernon Harris ....Martin Bland
Paul Blake................................Hilary McIntyre
Charles Hawtrey ....Edwin Tallweather
Annie Esmond ....Miss Monkton

Melody and Romance (71m) Cert U, B/W
(Reissued 1946)
British Lion Film Corporation
p...Herbert Smith
d..Maurice Elvey
s...............Leslie Howard Gordon, Maurice Elvey
sc..L. DuGarde Peach
Hughie Green ....Hughie Hawkins
Margaret Lockwood..............Margaret Williams
Jane Carr.......................................Kay Williams
Alastair Sim ....Prof. Williams
Garry Marsh ....Warwick Mortimer
C. Denier Warren......................Capt. Hawkins
Julien Vedey ....Jacob
Margaret Scudamore ....Mrs. Hawkins
Rex Roper and Maisie, Hughie Green's Gang

1939
Where's That Fire? (73m) Cert U, B/W
Twentieth Century Productions
p...Edward Black
d ....Marcel Varnel
s ....Maurice Braddell
sc............Marriott Edgar, Val Guest, John Orton
Will Hay.......................Capt. Benjamin Viking
Moore Marriott ....Jerry Harbottle
Graham Moffatt...........................Albert Brown
Peter Gawthorne ....Chief Officer
Eric Clavering.............................Hank Sullivan
Hugh McDermott ....Jim Baker
Charles Hawtrey ....Youth
George Carney..................................Councillor
Sebastian Smith ....Major
Frank Atkinson ....Clerk
Dave O'Toole......................................Postman
Charles Victor....................................Proprietor
Wilson Coleman ....Doctor

1940
Jailbirds (73m) Cert U, B/W
(Reissued 1943, 591ft cut)
Butcher's Film Service
p..F. W. Baker
d ....Oswald Mitchell
s...(Sketch) Fred Karno
sc...Con West
Albert Burdon ....Bill Smith
Shaun Glenville ....Col. Pepper

Charles Farrell...............................Spike Nelson
Charles Hawtrey ....Nick
Lorraine Clewes...........................Mary Smith
Sylvia Coleridge ....Mrs. Smith
Harry Terry ....Narky
Cyril Chamberlain ....Bob
Nat Mills and Bobbie....................Mr. and Mrs.
Popodopulous

1941
The Warning (No record)

The Ghost of St. Michael's (82m) Cert A, B/W
(Reissued 1944, 1947, 1955)
Ealing Studios (Associated British Film
Distributors)
p ....Michael Balcon
ap ....Basil Dearden
d ....Marcel Varnel
s........................Angus MacPhail, John Dighton
Will Hay.....................................William Lamb
Claude Hulbert ....Hilary Teasdale
Charles Hawtrey ....Percy Thorne
Raymond Huntley ....Mr. Humphries
Felix Aylmer...................................Dr. Winter
Elliot Mason ....Mrs. Wigmore
John Laurie..Jamie
Hay Petrie...............................Procurator Fiscal
Roddy Hughes ....Amberley
Manning Whiley......................................Stock
Derek Blomfield..................................Sunshine
Brefni O'Rorke ....Sgt. MacFarlane

1942
Let the People Sing (105m) Cert U, B/W
(Reissued 1948, 1162ft cut)
British National Films
p/d ....John Baxter
s..(Novel) J. B. Priestley
sc........John Baxter, Barbara K. Emary, Geoffrey
Orme
Alastair Sim...........................Prof. Ernst Kronak
Fred Emney............Sir George Denberry-Baxter
Edward Rigby ....Timmy Tiverton
Oliver Wakefield ....Sir Reginald Foxfield
Patricia Roc ....Hope Ollerton
Olive Sloane..................................Daisy Barley
Gus McNaughton ....Ketley
Robert Atkins.......................................Hassock
Richard George ....Tom Largs
Annie Esmond..............................Lady Foxfield
Peter Gawthorne.................Maj. Shiptonthorpe
Marian Spencer ....Lady Shepshod

Aubrey Mallalieu ....Cdr. Spofforth
Ian Fleming......................................Spokesman
Peter Ustinov.....................................Dr. Bentika
Eliot Makeham ....Clerk
Maire O'Neill ....Mrs. Mitterley
Charles Hawtrey ....Orton
A. Bromley Davenport ....Agent
Michael Martin-Harvey ....Candover
Mignon O'Doherty..........................Dr. Buckley
Ida Barr...Katy
Stan Paskin ....Attendant
Wally Patch ....Sam
Horace Kenney...........................Walter Shepton
Morris Harvey ....Jim Flagg
George Merritt.....................................Sergeant
Syd Crossley.................................Uncle Alfred
Diana Beaumont ....Secretary
G. H. Mulcaster.................................Inspector
James Knight, Billy Merson

Much Too Shy (92m) Cert U, B/W
(Reissued 1947, 1950)
Columbia (British) Productions
p ....Ben Henry
d ....Marcel Varnel
s ....Ronald Frankau
sc ...Walter Greenwood, Michael Vaughan, John
Arthur, Jack Marks
George Formby.............................George Andy
Kathleen Harrison ....Amelia Peabody
Hilda Bayley ....Lady Driscoll
Eileen Bennett ....Jackie Somers
Joss Ambler ....Sir George Driscoll
Jimmy Clitheroe ....Jimmy
Frederick Bertwell ....Mr. Harefield
Brefni O'Rorke ....Mr. Somers
Eric Clavering ....Robert Latimer
Glib McLaughlin ....Rev. Sheepshanks
Peter Gawthorne ....Counsel
Gus McNaughton ....Manager
D. J. Williams ....Judge
Valentine Dyall.................................Counsel
Percy Walsh...................................Art Master
Wally Patch ....Constable
Alf Goddard ....Pavement Artist
Charles Hawtrey ....Osbert
Frank Atkinson................................Constable

The Goose Steps Out (79m) Cert U, B/W
(Reissued 1946, 1955, 1961)
Ealing Studios
p ....Michael Balcon
ap...S. C. Balcon

d ....Will Hay, Basil Dearden
s ....Bernard Miles, Reginald Groves
sc........................Angus McPhail, John Dighton
Will Hay ....William Henry Potts/Müller
Frank Pettingell ....Prof. Hoffman
Julien Mitchell ....Gen. von Glotz
Charles Hawtrey ....Max
Peter Croft ....Hans
Anne Firth...Lena
Leslie Harcourt ....Vogel
Jeremy Hawk.............................Aide-de-camp
Raymond Lovell..................................Schmidt
Aubrey Mallalieu ....Rector
Barry Morse...Curt
Lawrence O'Madden ....Col. Truscott
Peter Ustinov ....Krauss
John Williams...............................Maj. Bishop
Leslie Dwyer ....Soldier
Richard George ....Pilot
Billy Russell ....Adolf Hitler
William Hartnell ....Officer

1943

Bell-Bottom George (97m) Cert U, B/W
Columbia (British) Productions
p ....Ben Henry
d ....Marcel Varnel
s ....Richard Fisher, Peter Cresswell
*sc*Peter Fraser, Edward Dryhurst, John I. Arthur
George Formby ....George
Anne Firth ....Pat
Reginald Purdell ....Birdie Edwards
Peter Murray Hill ....Shapley
Manning Whiley ....Church
Hugh Dempster ....White
Dennis Wyndham ....Black
Charles Farrell.............................Jim Benson
Eliot Makeham ....Johnson
Jane Welsh ....Rita
Peter Gawthorne ....Adm. Coltham
Harry Fowler ....Errand Boy
Frank Atkinson ....Harry
Ian Fleming...Carter
Charles Hawtrey ....Producer

1944

A Canterbury Tale (124m) Cert U, B/W
(Reissued 1948, Eros; cut)
Independent Producers/Archers Film
Productions
p/d/s ....Michael Powell, Emeric Pressburger
Eric Portman..........................Thomas Colpeper
Sheila Sim ....Alison Smith

Dennis Price..............................Sgt. Peter Gibbs
Sgt. John Sweet ....Sgt. Bob Johnson
Esmond Knight ....Narrator/Soldier/Idiot
Charles Hawtrey.....................Thomas Duckett
Hay Petry ....Woodcock
George Merritt ....Ned Horton
Edward Rigby..................................Jim Horton
Freda Jackson ....Prudence Honeywood
Betty Jardine.......................................Fee Baker
Eliot Makeham......................................Organist
Anthony Holles.....................Sgt. Berty Bassett
Wally Bosco..ARP Man
Charles Patten....................................Ernie Brooks
Jane Millican...Woman
John Slater...Sergeant
Graham Moffatt.......................................Stuffy
Esma Cannon ....Maid
Michael Howard ....Archie
Margaret Scudamore...................Mrs. Colpeper
Joss Ambler ....Inspector
H. F. Maltby ....Portal

1945
The Ten Year Plan (17m) Cert U, B/W
Gaumont-British Instructional
d ....Lewis Gilbert
Charles Hawtrey ....Charles Martin
Megs Jenkins ....Housewife

What Do We Do Now? (74m) Cert A, B/W
(Reissued 1947, 906ft cut)
Grand National Film Productions
p ....Maurice J. Wilson
d ....Charles Hawtrey
s ....George A. Cooper
George Moon..Wesley
Burton Brown...Lesley
Gloria Brent..Diana
Jill Summers ....Birdie Maudin
Ronald Frankau..Drunk
Leslie Fuller..Cabby
Barry Lupino ....Jeff
Harry Parry's Swing Band, Edmundo Ros'
Conga Band, Steffani and his Silver Songsters,
Monte Crick, Gail Page

Dumb Dora Discovers Tobacco (42m) Cert U, B/W
(Reissued 1947 as *Fag End*, 5m cut)
Hurley Productions (Grand National Film
Productions)
p ....Victor Katona
d ....Charles Hawtrey
s..............................J. Szenas, Robin Robinson

sc................................Victor Katona, Henry King
Henry Kendall....................................Mackenzie
Pamela Stirling..Dora
Gene Gerrard.............................Smoking Tutor
Claud Allister.....................................Sir Percival
Hugh Dempster ....Peter Pottlebury
Phillip King ....Justice Hare
Wally Patch...Heckler

1947
Meet Me At Dawn (99m) Cert A, B/W
(Reissued 1953, *The Gay Duellist*)
Excelsior Film Productions Limited
p ....Marcel Hellman
d ....Thornton Freeland
s..(Film Story) Anatol Litvak, Marcel Achard (*Le Tueur*)
sc..........James Seymour, Lesley Storm, Maurice Cowan
William Eythe ....Charles Morton
Hazel Court...........................Gabrielle Vermorel
Margaret Rutherford..................Mme. Vermorel
Stanley Holloway ....Emile
Basil Sydney ....George Vermorel
Irene Browne ....Mme. Renault
George Thorpe.........................Senator Renault
Ada Reeve ....Concierge
Graham Muir ....Count de Brissac
Beatrice Campbell....................................Margot
John Salew...Gaston
Charles Victor...Client
Katy Johnson ....Harriette
Percy Walsh ....Showman
Hy Hazell..Suzette
Wilfrid Hyde-White ....Garin
James Harcourt ....Henri
Diana Decker ....Germaine
Charles Hawtrey ....Reporter
Jack Melford......................................Husband
William Kendall..Friend
Guy Rolfe ....Gentleman
Lind Joyce ....Yvonne Jadin

The End of the River (83m) Cert A, B/W
Independent Producers/Archers Film
Productions
p ....Michael Powell, Emeric Pressburger
d ....Derek Twist
s ....(Novel) Desmond Holdridge
sc..........Wolfgang Wilhelm, Emeric Pressburger,
Michael Powell, Robert Westerby, ...Derek Twist
Sabu ....Manoel
Bibi Ferreira...Teresa

Esmond Knight......................................Dantos
Robert Douglas..................................Mr. Jones
Antoinette Cellier..............................Conceicão
Torin Thatcher..Lisboa
Orlando Martins.................................Harrigan
Raymond Lovell..............................Col. Porpino
James Hayter...Chico
Nicolette Bernard ....Dona Serafina
Maurice Denham ....Defence
Alan Wheatley ....Irygoyen
Charles Hawtrey ....Raphael
Zena Marshall...Sante
Dennis Arundell ....Contínho
Milton Rosmer ....Judge

1948

The Story of Shirley Yorke (92m) Cert A, B/W
Nettlefold Productions
p ....Ernest G. Roy
d ....Maclean Rogers
s........................(Play) Horace Annesley Vachell
sc ....A. R. Rawlinson, Maclean Rogers, Kathleen
Butler
Derek Farr ....Gerald Ryton
Dinah Sheridan ....Shirley Yorke
Margaretta Scott........................Alison Gwynne
John Robinson........................Dr. Bruce Napier
Barbara Couper ....Muriel Peach
Beatrix Thomson ....Lady Camber
Ian McLean ....Dr. Harris
Jack Raine................................Stansfield Yorke
Lesley Osmond...........................Jennifer Ware
Valentine Dyall ....Edward Holt
Eleanor Summerfield ....Doris
Bruce Seton ....Captain Sharp

1949

Passport To Pimlico (84m) Cert U, B/W
Ealing Studios (General Film Distributors)
p ....Michael Balcon
ap ....E. V. H. Emmett
d ....Henry Cornelius
s ....Henry Cornelius, T. E. B. Clarke
sc ....T. E. B. Clarke
Stanley Holloway.................Arthur Pemberton
Hermione Baddeley ....Edie Randall
Margaret Rutherford ....Prof. Hatton–Jones
Paul Dupuis ....Duke of Burgandy
Basil Radford ....Gregg
Naunton Wayne....................................Straker
Raymond Huntley....................................P. J. Wix
John Slater ....Frank Huggins
Jane Hylton ....Molly

Betty Warren......................Connie Pemberton
Barbara Murray ....Shirley Pemberton
Sydney Tafler ....Fred Cowan
Frederick Piper ....Jim Garland
Philip Stainton ....PC Ted Spiller
Charles Hawtrey...............................Bert Fitch
James Hayter ....Commissionaire
Michael Hordern ....Insp. Bashford
Richard Hearne......................................Drunk
Masoni ....Conjuror

The Lost People (88m) Cert A, B/W
Gainsborough Pictures
p ....Gordon Wellesley
d ....Bernard Knowles, Muriel Box
s......................(Play) Bridget Bowland (*Cockpit*)
sc ....Bridget Bowland, Muriel Box
Dennis Price ....Capt. Ridley
Mai Zetterling...Lili
Richard Attenborough..................................Jan
Siobhan McKenna ....Marie
Maxwell Reed...Peter
William Hartnell ....Sgt. Barnes
Gerard Hines ....Professor
Zena Marshall...Anna
Olaf Pooley ....Milosh
Harcourt Williams ....Priest
Philo Houser ....Draja
Jill Balcon ....Rebecca
Gray Blake ....Capt. Saunders
Marcel Poncin...Duval
Peter Bull ....Wolf
Charles Hawtrey...................Prisoner (role cut)

Dark Secret (85m) Cert A, B/W
(Reissued 1952, 10m cut)
Nettlefold Productions
p ....Ernest G. Roy
d ....Maclean Rogers
s......(Play) Mordaunt Shairp (*Crime at Blossoms*)
sc ....A. R. Rawlinson, Moie Charles
Dinah Sheridan......................Valerie Merryman
Emys Jones ....Chris Merryman
Irene Handl ....'Woody' Woodman
Hugh Pryse.........................A Very Late Visitor
Barbara Couper ....Mrs. Barrington
Percy Marmont ....Vicar
Geoffrey Sumner...........................Jack Farrell
Mackenzie Ward ....Artist
Charles Hawtrey........................Arthur Figson
John Salew ....Mr. Barrington
George Merritt...............................Mr. Lumley
Stanley Vilven...........................Mr. Woodman

1950

Room To Let (68m) Cert A, B/W
Hammer Film Productions

p	Anthony Hinds
d	Godfrey Grayson
s	(Radio Play) Margery Allingham
sc	John Gilling, Godfrey Grayson
Jimmy Handley	Curley Minter
Valentine Dyall	Dr. Fell
Christine Silver	Mrs. Musgrave
Merle Tottenham	Alice
Charles Hawtrey	Mike Atkinson
Constance Smith	Molly Musgrave
J. Anthony La Penna	James Jasper
Reginald Dyson	Sgt. Cranbourne
Laurence Naismith	Editor

1951

Smart Alec (58m) Cert A, B/W
Vandyke Picture Corporation

p	Roger Proudlock
d	John Guillermin
s	Alec Coppel
Peter Reynolds	Alec Albion
Mercy Haystead	Judith
Leslie Dwyer	Gossage
Edward Lexy	Inspector
Kynaston Reeves	Uncle Edward
Charles Hawtrey	Farr
David Hurst	Poppi
David Keir	Mr. Guppy
Annette Simmonds	Sylvia
Frederick Morant	Edward Hall
Vernon Smyth	Judge
Peter Bull	Prosecuting Counsel
Basil Dignam	Defending Counsel

The Galloping Major (82m) Cert U, B/W
(Reissued 1955)
Danischewsky-Cornelius Productions (Romulus Films/Sirius Productions)

p	Monja Danischewsky
d	Henry Cornelius
s	Basil Radford
sc	Monja Danischewsky, Henry Cornelius
Basil Radford	Maj. Arthur Hill
Jimmy Handley	Bill Collins
Janette Scott	Susan Hill
A. E. Matthews	Sir Robert Medleigh
Rène Ray	Pam Riley
Charles Victor	Sam Fisher
Joyce Grenfell	Maggie

Hugh Griffith	Harold Temple
Julien Mitchell	Sgt. Adair
Sydney Tafler	Mr. Leon
Charles Hawtrey	Lew Rimmel
Sidney James	Bookie
Alfie Bass	Newsboy

Charlie Smirk, Raymond Glendenning, Bruce Belfrage, Marion Harris Jr

1952

Brandy For The Parson (78m) Cert U, B/W
Group 3 (Associated British Film Distributors)

p	John Grierson, Alfred O'Shaughnessy
d	John Eldridge
s	(Novel) Geoffrey Household
sc	John Dighton, Walter Mead, Alfred O'Shaughnessy
James Donald	Bill Harper
Kenneth More	Tony Rackham
Jean Lodge	Petronella Brand
Frederick Piper	Insp. Marle
Charles Hawtrey	George Crumb
Michael Trubshawe	Redworth
Alfie Bass	Dallyn
Wilfrid Caithness	Minch
Reginald Beckwith	Scoutmaster
Arthur Wontner	Maj. Glokleigh
Brian Weske	Jackie

Hammer the Toff (71m) Cert U, B/W
Nettlefold Productions

p	Ernest G. Roy
d	Maclean Rogers
s	(Novel) John Creasey
John Bentley	Hon. Richard Rollison
Patricia Dainton	Susan Lancaster
Valentine Dyall	Insp. Grice
John Robinson	Linnett
Wally Patch	Bert Ebbutt
Katherine Blake	Janet Lord
Roddy Hughes	Jolly
Basil Dignam	Superintendent
Lockwood West	Kennedy
Charles Hawtrey	Cashier

You're Only Young Twice (81m) Cert U, B/W
Group 3 (Associated British Film Distributors)

xp	John Grierson
p	John Baxter
d	Terry Bishop
s	(Play) James Bridie (*What Say They?*)
sc	Reginald Beckwith, Lindsay Galloway, Terry Bishop

Duncan MacRae............................Prof. Hayman
Joseph Tomelty ....Carroll O'Grady
Patrick Barr ....Sir Archibald Asher
Charles Hawtrey ....Adolphus Hayman
Diane Hart...Ada Shore
Robert Urquhart.....................................Sheltie
Edward Lexy ....Lord Carshennie
Jacqueline Mackenzie ....Nellie Kelly
Eric Woodburn..............................The Bedellus
Molly Urquhart..............................Lady Duffy
Reginald Beckwith ....BBC Commentator
Ronnie Corbett ....Mather
Roddy McMillan.................................Mulligan
Russell Waters..................................Prof. Baikie

1954
Five Days (72m) Cert A, B/W
USA: *Paid To Kill*
Hammer Film Productions
p..Anthony Hinds
d..Montgomery Tully
s..Paul Tabori
Dane Clark......................................James Nevill
Thea Gregory ....Andrea Nevill
Paul Carpenter...................................Paul Kirby
Cécile Chevreau ....Joan
Anthony Forwood ....Glanville
Howard Marion Crawford.................McGowan
Avis Scott ....Eileen
Peter Gawthorne.................................Bowman
Charles Hawtrey ....Bill

To Dorothy, a Son (84m) Cert U, B/W
USA: *Cash On Delivery*
Welbeck Films Limited
p.................................Ben Schrift, Sydney Box
d ....Muriel Box
s ....(Play) Roger MacDougall
sc...Peter Rogers
Shelley Winters ....Myrtle 'La Mar' Robinson
Peggy Cummins.....................Dorothy Rapallo
John Gregson ....Tony Rapallo
Wilfrid Hyde-White...........................Mr. Starke
Mona Washbourne......................Nurse Appleby
Hartley Power ....Cy Daniel
Martin Miller ....Brodcynsky
Anthony Oliver ....Reporter
Joan Sims ....Telephonist
Hal Osmond.........................Livingstone Potts
Aubrey Mather ....Dr. Cameron
Ronald Adam ....Parsons
Charles Hawtrey....................................Potman
Alfie Bass...Taxi-driver

Meredith Edwards ....Owner
Marjorie Rhodes ....Landlady

1955
As Long As They're Happy (91m) Cert U,
Eastmancolor
Group Film Productions
p..Raymond Stross
d ....J. Lee Thompson
s ....(Play) Vernon Sylvain
sc..Alan Melville
Jack Buchanan.............................John Bentley
Jean Carson ....Pat Delaney
Janette Scott ....Gwen Bentley
Brenda de Banzie...........................Stella Bentley
Susan Stephen.......................................Corinne
Jerry Wayne..............................Bobby Denver
Diana Dors ....Pearl Delaney
Hugh McDermott...............................Barnaby
Nigel Greene..................................Peter Pember
David Hurst ....Dr. Schneider
Athene Seyler...........................Mrs. Arbuthnot
Joan Sims ....Linda
Dora Bryan..Mavis
Charles Hawtrey...............................Teddyboy
Gilbert Harding....................................Himself
John Blythe ....Conductor
Ronnie Stevens ....Frankie
Hattie Jacques..Woman
Norman Wisdom.................................Himself

Man of the Moment (88m) Cert U, B/W
Group Film Productions (Rank Film
Distributors)
p ....Hugh Stewart
d..John Paddy Carstairs
s...Maurice Cowan
sc ....John Paddy Carstairs, Vernon Sylvaine
Norman Wisdom ....Norman
Lana Morris..Penny
Belinda Lee ....Sonia
Jerry Desmonde ....Jackson
Karel Stepanek ....Lom
Garry Marsh ....Delegate
Inia Te Wiata...Toki
Evelyn Roberts.................................Sir Horace
Violet Farebrother ....Queen Tawaki
Martin Miller ....Tailor
Lisa Gastoni...............................Chambermaid
Charles Hawtrey ....Producer
Man Mountain Dean.......................Bodyguard
Eugene Deckers ....Liftman
Michael Ward ....Photographer

Hugh Morton ....Mitchell
Cyril Chamberlain ....Delegate
The Beverley Sisters, McDonald Hobley, Phillip
Harben, Ronald Waldman, 'The Grove Family',
Bruce Seton

Timeslip (93m) Cert A, B/W
USA: *The Atomic Man*
Anglo-Guild Productions
p..Alec Snowden
d/sc ....Ken Hughes
s..........................(TV Play) Charles Eric Maine
Gene Nelson ....Mike Delaney
Faith Domergue............................Jill Friday
Joseph Tomelty..............................Insp. Cleary
Donald Gray..Maitland
Vic Perry ....Vasquo
Peter Arne.............................Stephen Maitland
Launce Maraschal ....Editor
Charles Hawtrey..Scruffy
Martin Wyldeck ....Dr. Preston
Carl Jaffé..Dr. Marks
Barry Mackay ....Insp. Hammond

Simon and Laura (91m) Cert U, Eastmancolor,
Vistavision
Group Film Productions (Rank Film
Distributors)
p ....Teddy Baird
d ....Muriel Box
s............................(Play) Alan Melville
sc ....Peter Blackmore
Peter Finch.....................................Simon Foster
Kay Kendall ....Laura Foster
Muriel Pavlow.........................Janet Honeyman
Hubert Gregg..............................Bertie Burton
Maurice Denham....................................Wilson
Ian Carmichael ....David Prentice
Richard Wattis ....Controller
Thora Hird..Jessie
Terrence Longdon ....Barney
Clive Parritt...Timothy
Alan Wheatley ....Adrian Lee
Joan Hickson..Barmaid
Cyril Chamberlain..Bert
Marianne Stone ....Elsie
Muriel George ....Grandma
Charles Hawtrey ....Porter
Esma Cannon...............................Mrs. Foster
Julia Arnall ....Make-up Girl
Gilbert Harding, Lady Isobel Barnet, John
Ellison, George Cansdale, Peter Haigh,
Raymonde

An Alligator Named Daisy (88m) Cert U, B/W
Group (Rank Film Distributors)
p..Raymond Stross
d ....J. Lee Thompson
s..(Novel) Charles Terror
sc ....Jack Davies
Donald Sinden ....Peter Weston
Diana Dors ....Vanessa Colebrook
Jean Carson..........................Moira O'Shannon
James Robertson Justice.....Sir James Colebrook
Stanley Holloway ....Gen. Weston
Roland Culver ....Col. Weston
Margaret Rutherford ....Prudence Croquet
Avice Landone................................Mrs. Weston
Stephen Boyd ....Albert O'Shannon
Richard Wattis ....Hoskins
Michael Shepley ....Judge
Henry Kendall..John
Charles Victor ....Sergeant
Ernest Theisger ....Notcher
Wilfrid Lawson ....Irishman
George Moon ....Al
Harry Green.....................Irving Rosenbloom
Patrick Cargill ....Steward
George Woodbridge ....PC Jorkins
Joan Young...Owner
Ronnie Stevens.....................................Crooner
Jimmy Edwards, Gilbert Harding, Frankie
Howerd, Ken Mackintosh and his Band, Ras
Prince, Monolulu, Nicholas Parsons

1956
Jumping For Joy (88m) Cert U, B/W
J. Arthur Rank Film Productions (Rank Film
Distributors)
p..Raymond Stross
d................................John Paddy Carstairs
s..Jack Davies
sc................................Henry E. Blyth
Frankie Howerd ....Willie Joy
Stanley Holloway ....Jack Montague
A. E. Matthews ....Lord Cranfield
Tony Wright................................Vincent
Susan Beaumont ....Susan
Alfie Bass ....Blagg
Joan Hickson ....Lady Cranfield
Lionel Jeffries ....Bert Benton
Terrence Longdon.....................................John
Colin Gordon..Max
Richard Wattis ....Carruthers
Danny Green ....Plugugly
William Kendall ....Blenkinsop
Ewen Solon ....Haines

Reginald Beckwith ....Smithers
Michael Ward ....Pertwee
Charles Hawtrey ....Punter

Who Done It? (85m) Cert U, B/W
(Reissued 1961)
Ealing Studios (Rank Film Distributors)
xp....................................Michael Balcon
p.....................................Michael Relph
d....................................Basil Dearden
s.....................................T. E. B. Clarke
Benny Hill ....Hugo Dill
Belinda Lee..................................Frankie Mayne
David Kossoff ....Zacco
Garry Marsh ....Insp. Hancock
George Margo ....Barakov
Ernest Theisger ....Sir Walter Finch
Denis Shaw...................................Otto Stumpf
Frederick Schiller.......................................Gruber
Thorley Walters ....Raymond Courtney
Nicholas Phipps ....Scientist
Gibb McLaughlin ....Scientist
Irene Handl.......................................Customer
Charles Hawtrey ....Disk Jockey
Stratford Johns.............................PC Coleman

Norah Blaney ....Actress
Peter Bull...Bunbury
Cyril Smith ....Man
Arthur Lowe..............................Demonstrator
Arthur Rigby.......................................Sergeant
Jeremy Hawk, Robert McDermott, Dagenham
Girl Pipers

The March Hare (85m) Cert U, Eastmancolor,
Cinemascope
Achilles Productions (B and A Productions)
p.........................Bertram Ostrer, Albert Fennell
d..George More O'Ferrall
s .....(Novel) T. H. Bird (*Gamblers Sometimes Win*)
sc ....Gordon Wellesley, Allan Mackinnon, Paul
Vincent Carroll
Peggy Cummins ....Pat Maguire
Terrence Morgan......................Sir Charles Hare
Wilfrid Hyde-White ....Col. Keene
Martita Hunt ....Lady Anne
Cyril Cusack ....Lazy Mangan
Derrick de Marney......................Capt. Marlow
Charles Hawtrey ....Fisher
Maureen Delany....................................Bridget
Ivan Samson ....Hardwicke
Macdonald Parke ....Maguire
Reginald Beckwith ....Broker

Peter Swanwick ....Nils Svenson
Fred Johnson....................................Joe Duffy
Stringer Davis.......................................Doctor
Harry Taub...Dooley
Edward Lexy ....Bookie
Raymond Glendenning

1958
Carry On Sergeant (83m) Cert U, B/W
Insignia Films (Anglo Amalgamated Film
Distributors)
p.......................................Peter Rogers
d ....Gerald Thomas
s ....(Story) R. F. Delderfield (*The Bull Boys*)
sc ....Norman Hudis, John Antrobus
William Hartnell ....Sgt. Grimshaw
Bob Monkhouse ....Charlie Sage
Shirley Eaton ....Mary Sage
Eric Barker.....................................Capt. Potts
Dora Bryan ....Nora
Bill Owen ....Cpl. Copping
Charles Hawtrey........................Peter Golightly
Terrence Longdon ....Miles Haywood
Kenneth Connor ....Horace Strong
Norman Rossington ....Herbert Brown
Gerald Campion ....Andy Galloway
Hattie Jacques..................................Capt. Clark
Kenneth Williams ....James Bailey
Cyril Chamberlain ....Instructor
Terry Scott ....Sgt. Paddy
Edward Judd..Soldier

I Only Arsked! (82m) Cert U, B/W
Hammer Film Productions/Granada Productions
p ....Anthony Hinds
d ....Montgomery Tully
s..............(TV Series) Sid Colin (*The Army Game*)
sc.......................................Sid Colin, Jack Davies
Bernard Bresslaw ....Popeye Popplewell
Michael Medwin.........................Cpl. Springer
Alfie Bass.........................Excused Boots Bisley
Geoffrey Sumner...............Maj. Upshott-Bagley
Charles Hawtrey ....Professor
Norman Rossington ....Cupcake Cook
David Lodge ....Sgt. Potty Chamber
Michael Bentine..Fred
Arthur Howard ....Sir Redvers
Francis Matthews............................Mahmoud
Marne Maitland ....King Fazim
Marie Deveraux...............................Harem Girl

1959

Carry On Nurse (86m) Cert U, B/W
Beaconsfield (Anglo Amalgamated Film
Distributors)

p..Peter Rogers
d ....Gerald Thomas
s........(Play) Patrick Cargill, Jack Beale (*Ring For Catty*)
sc..Norman Hudis
Shirley Eaton ....Dorothy Denton
Kenneth Connor ....Bernie Bishop
Charles Hawtrey ....Mr. Hinton
Hattie Jacques ....Matron
Wilfrid Hyde-White ....Colonel
Terrence Longdon ....Ted York
Bill Owen....................................Percy Hickson
Leslie Phillips....................................Jack Bell
Joan Sims....................................Stella Dawson
Susan Stephen............................Georgie Axwell
Kenneth Williams....................Oliver Reckitt
Michael Medwin ....Ginger
Susan Beaumont ....Frances James
Ann Firbank....................................Helen Lloyd
Joan Hickson ....Sister
Cyril Chamberlain............................Bert Able
Harry Locke..Mick
Irene Handl ....Marge Hickson
Susan Shaw ....Jane Bishop
Jill Ireland ....Jill Thompson
June Whitfield..Maisie

Carry On Teacher (86m) Cert U, B/W
Beaconsfield (Anglo Amalgamated Film
Distributors)

p..Peter Rogers
d ....Gerald Thomas
s ....Norman Hudis
Ted Ray ....William Wakefield
Kenneth Connor ....Gregory Adams
Charles Hawtrey ....Michael Bean
Leslie Phillips ....Alistair Crigg
Joan Sims ....Sarah Allcock
Kenneth Williams ....Edwin Milton
Hattie Jacques....................................Grace Short
Rosalind Knight........................Felicity Wheeler
Cyril Chamberlain ....Alf
Richard O'Sullivan ....Robin Stevens
Carol White ....Sheila Dale

Please Turn Over (87m) Cert A, B/W
Beaconsfield (Anglo Amalgamated Film
Distributors)

p..Peter Rogers

d ....Gerald Thomas
s............(Play) Basil Thomas (*Book of the Month*)
sc..Norman Hudis
Ted Ray ....Edward Halliday
Jean Kent ....Janet Halliday
Leslie Phillips ....Dr. Henry Manners
Joan Sims ....Beryl
Julia Lockwood..............................Jo Halliday
Tim Seely....................................Robert Hughes
Charles Hawtrey ....Jeweller
Dilys Laye ....Millicent Jones
June Jago ....Gladys Worth
Colin Gordon ....Maurice
Ronald Adam..Appleton
Joan Hickson ....Saleswoman
Victor Maddern..Smith
Lee Patterson ....Man

1960

Carry On Constable (86m) Cert U, B/W
G. H. W. Productions (Anglo Amalgamated Film
Distributors)

p..Peter Rogers
d ....Gerald Thomas
s..Brock Williams
sc..Norman Hudis
Sidney James........................Sgt. Frank Wilkins
Eric Barker ....Insp. Mills
Kenneth Connor....................Charlie Constable
Charles Hawtrey ....Timothy Gorse
Kenneth Williams....................Stanley Benson
Leslie Phillips ....Tom Potter
Joan Sims ....Gloria Passworthy
Hattie Jacques ....Laura Moon
Shirley Eaton ....Sally Barry
Cyril Chamberlain ....PC Thurston
Joan Hickson ....Mrs. May
Irene Handl........................Distraught Woman
Terrence Longdon ....Herbert Hall
Jill Adams..................................WPC Harrison
Freddie Mills..Crook
Victor Maddern ....Detective
Joan Young ....Mayoress
Esma Cannon......................................Woman
Robin Ray ....Manager
Michael Balfour....................................Crook

Inn For Trouble (90m) Cert U, B/W
Film Locations (Eros)

p....................Norman J. Hyams, Edward Lloyd
d ....C. M. Pennington-Richards
s............(TV Series) Fred Robinson (*The Larkins*)
sc..Fred Robinson

Peggy Mount ....Ada Larkins
David Kosoff ....Alf Larkins
Leslie Phillips ....John Belcher
Glyn Owen...........................Lord Bill Osborne
Yvonne Monlaur ....Yvette
Charles Hawtrey ....Silas
A. E. Matthews ....Sir Hector Gore-Blandish
Shaun O'Riordan ....Eddie Larkins
Ronan O'Casey ....Jeff Rogers
Alan Wheatley ....Harold Gaskin
Graham Moffatt ....Jumbo Gudge
Willoughby Goddard ....Sgt. Saunders
Gerald Campion ....George
Stanley Unwin ....Farmer
Irene Handl..Lily
Fred Robinson...Red
Esma Cannon...Dolly

1961
Carry On Regardless (93m) Cert U, B/W
G. H. W. Productions (Anglo Amalgamated Film
Distributors)
p...Peter Rogers
d ....Gerald Thomas
s ....Norman Hudis
Sidney James.....................................Bert Handy
Kenneth Connor ....Sam Twist
Charles Hawtrey ....Gabriel Dimple
Joan Sims ....Lilly Duveen
Kenneth Williams ....Francis Courtenay
Bill Owen ....Mike Western
Liz Fraser...Delia King
Terrence Longdon.Montgomery Infield-Hopping
Hattie Jacques...Sister
Esma Cannon...............................Miss Cooling
Sydney Tafler..Manager
Julia Arnall.............................Trudi Trelawney
Terrence Alexander...................Trevor Trelawney
Stanley Unwin ....Himself
Joan Hickson...Matron
Fenella Fielding ....Penny Panting
Jerry Desmonde............................Martin Paul
Eric Pohlmann ....Sinister Man
Freddie Mills ....Lefty Vincent

What a Whopper! (89m) Cert U, B/W
Viscount Films
p..Teddy Joseph
d ....Gilbert Gunn
s...........................Trevor Peacock, Jeremy Lloyd
sc ....Terry Nation
Adam Faith..Tony Blake
Sidney James ....Harry

Carole Lesley...............................Charlie Pinner
Terence Longdon......................................Vernon
Marie France...Marie
Clive Dunn ....Mr. Slate
Freddie Frinton ....Gilbert Pinner
Charles Hawtrey.......................................Arnold
Spike Milligan ....Tramp
Wilfrid Brambell ....Postie
Fabia Drake ....Mrs. Pinner
Harold Berens...Sammy
Terry Scott ....Policeman
Fyfe Roberston......................................Himself

Dentist on the Job (88m) Cert U, B/W
USA: Get On With It!
Bertram Ostrer Productions (Anglo
Amalgamated Film Distributors)
p...Bertram M. Ostrer
d ....C. M. Pennington-Richards
s.................Hazel Adair, Hugh Woodhouse, Bob
Monkhouse
Bob Monkhouse ....David Cookson
Kenneth Connor.................................Sam Field
Shirley Eaton ....Jill Venner
Eric Barker.................Col. Proudfoot/The Dean
Richard Wattis ....Macreedy
Ronnie Stevens ....Brian Dexter
Reginald Beckwith ....Duff
Charles Hawtrey..Roper
Graham Stark ....Man
Charlotte Mitchell ....Mrs. Burke
Jeremy Hawk ....Prof. Lovitt
David Horne.................................Southbound
Ian Whittaker ....Fuller
Patrick Holt ....Newsreader
Michael Miles ....Himself
Keith Fordyce ....Himself

1963
Carry On Cabby (91m) Cert U, B/W
Adder Productions (Anglo Amalgamated Film
Distributors)
p..Peter Rogers
d ....Gerald Thomas
s...............................Sidney Green, Richard Hills
sc...................................Talbot Rothwell
Sidney James..........................Charlie Hawkins
Hattie Jacques ....Peggy Hawkins
Kenneth Connor.............................Ted Watson
Charles Hawtrey.....................Pint-Pot Tankard
Esma Cannon....................................Flo Simms
Liz Fraser ....Sally
Bill Owen ....Smiley Sims

Milo O'Shea ....Len
Judith Furse ....Battleaxe
Ambrosine Phillpotts................................Lady
Renée Houston ....Molly
Jim Dale ....Father
Cyril Chamberlain................................Sarge
Amanda Barrie ....Anthea
Norman Chappell ....Albright

Carry On Jack (91m) Cert A, Technicolor
Anglo-Amalgamated Film Distributors
p...Peter Rogers
d ....Gerald Thomas
s ....Talbot Rothwell
Kenneth Williams ....Capt. Fearless
Bernard Cribbins ....Albert Poop-Decker
Juliet Mills...Sally
Charles Hawtrey....................Walter Sweetley
Donald Houston...............Lt. Jonathan Howett
Cecil Parker..................................First Sea Lord
Percy Herbert ....Bosun Angel
Jim Dale ....Carrier
Patrick Cargill ....Don Luis
Ed Devereaux ....Hook
Peter Gilmore.................................Roger Patch
Jimmy Thompson ....Lord Nelson
Anton Rodgers ....Hardy

1964
Carry On Spying (87m) Cert A, B/W
Adder Productions (Anglo Amalgamated Film
Distributors)
p...Peter Rogers
d ....Gerald Thomas
s..................................Sid Colin, Talbot Rothwell
Kenneth Williams ....Desmond Simkins
Barbara Windsor................Daphne Honeybutt
Bernard Cribbins ....Harold Crump
Charles Hawtrey..........................Charlie Bind
Eric Barker...Chief
Dilys Laye..Lila
Jim Dale ....Carstairs
Richard Wattis ....Cobbley
Eric Pohlmann............................Emile Fauzak
Victor Maddern ....Milchmann
Judith Furse ....Dr. Crow
John Bluthal................................Head Waiter
Renée Houston....................................Madam

Carry On Cleo (92m) Cert A, Eastmancolor
Adder Productions (Anglo Amalgamated Film
Distributors)
p...Peter Rogers

d ....Gerald Thomas
s.......(Plays) William Shakespeare (*Julius Caesar,
Antony and Cleopatra*)
sc..Talbot Rothwell
n.....................................E. V. H. Emmett
Sidney James...............................Marc Antony
Kenneth Williams.........................Julius Caesar
Kenneth Connor ....Hengist Pod
Charles Hawtrey ....Seneca
Joan Sims ....Calpurnia
Jim Dale...Horsa
Amanda Barrie................................Cleopatra
Victor Maddern ....Sergeant-Major
Sheila Hancock..............................Senna Pod
Francis de Wolff ....Agripper
Brian Oulton ....Brutus
Julie Stevens ....Gloria
Jon Pertwee...................................Soothsayer
Michael Ward ....Archimedes
Warren Mitchell ....Spencius

1965

Carry On Cowboy (95m) Cert A, Eastmancolor
Adder Productions (Anglo Amalgamated Film
Distributors)
p...Peter Rogers
d ....Gerald Thomas
s ....Talbot Rothwell
Sidney James....................................Rumpo Kid
Kenneth Williams ....Judge Burke
Jim Dale ....Marshal P. Knutt
Charles Hawtrey...............................Big Heap
Joan Sims...Belle
Angela Douglas ....Annie Oakley
Bernard Bresslaw ....Little Heap
Peter Butterworth......................................Doc
Percy Herbert ....Charlie
Jon Pertwee ....Sheriff Albert Earp
Sydney Bromley.........................Sam Houston
Edina Ronay ....Dolores
Davy Kaye ....Josh Moses
Cal McCord..Outlaw
Ballet Montparnasse

1966

Carry On Screaming (97m) Cert A, Eastmancolor
Ethiro Productions (Anglo Amalgamated Film
Distributors)
p...Peter Rogers
d ....Gerald Thomas
s ....Talbot Rothwell

Harry H. Corbett ....Sgt. Sidney Bung
Kenneth Williams ....Dr. Watt
Jim Dale ....Albert Potter
Charles Hawtrey...............................Dan Dann
Fenella Fielding.............................Valerie Watt
Joan Sims ....Emily Bung
Angela Douglas.............................Doris Mann
Peter Butterworth ....Slowbotham
Bernard Bresslaw....................................Sockett
Jon Pertwee...Fettle
Tom Clegg ....Odbodd
Billy Cornelius ....Odbodd Jr.
Denis Blake...Rubbatiti

Don't Lose Your Head (90m) Cert A, Eastmancolor
(Reissued *Carry On Don't Lose Your Head*)
Adder Productions (Rank Film Distributors)
p..Peter Rogers
d ....Gerald Thomas
s ....Talbot Rothwell
n..Patrick Allen
Sidney James.......................Sir Rodney Ffing
Kenneth Williams................Citizen Camembert
Jim Dale...Lord Darcy
Charles Hawtrey ....Duke de Pomfrit
Joan Sims ....Désirée Dubarry
Dany Robin ....Jacqueline
Peter Butterworth ....Citizen Bidet
Peter Gilmore ....Robespierre
Michael Ward...Henri
Leon Greene ....Malabonce
Diana Macnamara.................Princess Stephanie

1967

The Terrornauts (75m) Cert U, Pathécolor
Anglo-Embassy/Amicus (Avco Embassy)
p......................Milton Subotsky, Max Rosenberg
d ....Montgomery Tully
s.(Novel) Murray Leinster (*The Wailing Asteroid*)
sc...John Brunner
Simon Oates ....Dr. Joe Burke
Zena Marshall..................................Sandy Lund
Charles Hawtrey ....Yellowlees
Patricia Hayes...................................Mrs. Jones
Stanley Meadows ....Ben Keller
Max Adrian............................Dr. Henry Shore
Frank Barry....................................Burke (child)
Richard Carpenter ....Danny
Leonard Cracknell..Nick
Frank Forsyth..Uncle
Robert Jewell ....Robot Operator

Follow That Camel (95m) Cert A, Eastmancolor
(Reissued *Carry On Follow That Camel*)
Adder Productions (Rank Film Distributors)
p..Peter Rogers
d ....Gerald Thomas
s ....Talbot Rothwell
Phil Silvers.......................................Sgt. Nocker
Kenneth Williams.............Commandant Burger
Jim Dale ....Bertram O. West
Charles Hawtrey ....Cap. Le Pice
Joan Sims ....Zigzag
Angela Douglas.................Lady Jane Ponsonby
Peter Butterworth ....Simpson
Bernard Bresslaw ....Abdul Abulbul
Anita Harries ....Corktip
John Bluthal.................................Cpl. Clotski
William Mervin.......................Lord Ponsonby
Peter Gilmore......................................Bagshaw
Vincent Ball ....Officer

Carry On Doctor (94m) Cert A, Eastmancolor
Adder Productions (Rank Film Distributors)
p..Peter Rogers
d ....Gerald Thomas
s ....Talbot Rothwell
n..Patrick Allen
Frankie Howerd ....Francis Bigger
Sidney James.................................Charlie Roper
Kenneth Williams ....Doctor Tinkle
Charles Hawtrey ....Mr. Barron
Jim Dale ....Dr. Kilmore
Barbara Windsor ....Sandra May
Joan Sims ....Chloe Gibson
Hattie Jacques ....Matron
Anita Harries................................Nurse Clarke
Bernard Bresslaw ....Ken Biddle
Peter Butterworth ....Mr. Smith
Dilys Laye ....Mavis Winkle
Derek Francis ....Sir Edmund Burke
Peter Jones..Chaplain
Dandy Nichols ....Mrs. Roper

1968

Carry On … Up the Khyber (88m) Cert A, Eastmancolor
Adder Productions (Rank Film Distributors)
p..Peter Rogers
d ....Gerald Thomas
s ....Talbot Rothwell
n..Patrick Allen
Sidney James.............Sir Sidney Ruff-Diamond
Kenneth Williams ....Khasi of Kalabar
Charles Hawtrey..................Pte. James Widdle

Roy Castle..Capt. Keene
Joan Sims.........................Lady Ruff-Diamond
Bernard Bresslaw...........................Bungdit Din
Peter Butterworth...........................Rev. Belcher
Terry Scott.......................Sgt – Maj. MacNutt
Angela Douglas.............................Princess Jelhi
Cardew Robinson.......................................Fakir
Julian Holloway.....................Maj. Shorthouse
Leon Thau...Stinghi
Alexandra Dane..Busti
Jeremy Spenser...Indian

1969
Carry On Camping (88m) Cert A, Eastmancolor
Adder Productions (Rank Film Distributors)
p...Peter Rogers
d..Gerald Thomas
s...Talbot Rothwell
Sidney James.....................................Sid Boggle
Kenneth Williams...............................Dr. Soper
Charles Hawtrey.......................Charlie Muggins
Terry Scott.....................................Peter Potter
Joan Sims.......................................Joan Fussey
Barbara Windsor......................................Babs
Hattie Jacques...............................Miss Hagard
Dilys Laye....................................Anthea Marks
Bernard Bresslaw............................Bernie Lugg
Peter Butterworth.......................Joshua Fiddler
Julian Holloway............................Jim Tanner
Betty Marsden...........................Harriet Potter
Trisha Nobble..Sally

Carry On Again, Doctor (89m) Cert A,
Eastmancolor
Adder/Ethiro (Rank Film Distributors)
p...Peter Rogers
d..Gerald Thomas
s...Talbot Rothwell
Sidney James.......................Gladstone Screwer
Kenneth Williams....................Frederick Carver
Charles Hawtrey................Dr. Ernest Stoppidge
Jim Dale.............................Dr. James Nookey
Joan Sims....................................Ellen Madder
Barbara Windsor.........................Goldie Locks
Hattie Jacques...........................Matron Soper
Patsy Rowlands............................Miss Fosdick
Peter Butterworth.................................Patient
Patricia Hayes............................Mrs. Beasley
William Mervin..................................Chairman
Harry Locke...Porter
Valerie Leon...Deidre
Elspeth March..Woman
Wilfrid Brambell..................................Pullen

Zeta One (82m) Cert X, Eastmancolor
Tigon British Film Productions
p...........................Tony Tenser, George Maynard
d...Michael Cort
s.......................Michael Cort, Alastair McKenzie
James Robertson Justice...............Maj. Bourdon
Charles Hawtrey......................................Swyne
Robin Hawdon..............................James Word
Anna Gael..Clotho
Brigitte Skay....................................Lachesis
Dawn Addams...Zeta
Yutte Stensgaard..............................Ann Olsen
Lionel Murton..W
Valerie Leon.......................................Atropos
Carol-Ann Hawkins...................................Zara
Wendy Lingham.........................Edwina Strain
Yolande Del Mar.................................Stripper

1970
Carry On Up the Jungle (89m) Cert A,
Eastmancolor
Adder/Ethiro (Rank Film Distributors)
p...Peter Rogers
d..Gerald Thomas
s...Talbot Rothwell
Frankie Howerd.......................Prof. Ingo Tinkle
Sidney James.....................................Bill Boosey
Charles Hawtrey........Tonka (Sir Walter Bagley)
Joan Sims..........................Lady Evelyn Bagley
Terry Scott......................................Jungle Boy
Kenneth Connor.......................Claude Chumley
Bernard Bresslaw...............................Upsidasi
Jacki Piper...June
Reuben Martin.....................................Gorilla
Valerie Leon...Leda

Carry On Loving (88m) Cert A, Eastmancolor
Adder Productions (Rank Film Distributors)
p...Peter Rogers
d..Gerald Thomas
s...Talbot Rothwell
Sidney James.................................Sidney Bliss
Kenneth Williams.....................Percival Snooper
Charles Hawtrey..........................James Bedsop
Joan Sims..................................Esme Crowfoot
Hattie Jacques..Sophie
Terry Scott................................Terrence Philpot
Richard O'Callaghan.....................Bertie Muffet
Bernard Bresslaw.........................Gripper Burke
Jacki Piper.....................................Sally Martin
Imogen Hassall............................Jenny Grubb
Patsy Rowlands....................Miss Dempsey
Bill Maynard....................................Mr. Dreery

Sonny Farrar ....Violinist
Lauri Lupino Lane.............................Husband
Kenny Lynch ....Conductor
Peter Butterworth ....Dr. Crippen

Carry On Henry (89m) Cert A, Eastmancolor
Adder Productions (Rank Film Distributors)
p..Peter Rogers
d ....Gerald Thomas
s ....Talbot Rothwell
Sidney James...................................Henry VIII
Kenneth Williams ....Sir Thomas Cromwell
Joan Sims ....Marie of Normandy
Charles Hawtrey ....Sir Roger de Lodgerley
Terry Scott ....Cardinal Wolsey
Barbara Windsor ....Bettina
Kenneth Connor...........................Lord Hampton
Julian Holloway ....Sir Thomas
Peter Gilmore ....King Francis
Julian Orchard ....Duc de Pincenay
Gertan Klauber...Bidet
David Davenport ....Major – Domo
William Mervyn ....Physician
Bill Maynard ....Guy Fawkes
Patsy Rowlands ....Jane Seymour
Monica Dietrich....................Katherine Howard
Peter Butterworth ....Earl of Bristol
David Essex ....Man

1971
Carry On at Your Convenience (90m) Cert A,
Eastmancolor
Peter Rogers Productions (Rank Film
Distributors)
p..Peter Rogers
d ....Gerald Thomas
s ....Talbot Rothwell
Sidney James..................................Sid Plummer
Kenneth Williams............................W. C. Boggs
Charles Hawtrey ....Charles Coote
Joan Sims ....Chloe Moore
Hattie Jacques..........................Beattie Plummer
Bernard Bresslaw ....Bernie Hulke
Kenneth Cope ....Vic Spanner
Jacki Piper ....Myrtle Plummer
Richard O'Callaghan......................Lewis Boggs
Patsy Rowlands ....Miss Withering
Bill Maynard...............................Fred Moore
Davy Kaye...Benny
Margaret Nolan......................................Popsy
Dilys Laye ....Anthea Marks
Bernard Bresslaw ....Bernie Lugg
Peter Butterworth ....Joshua Fiddler

Julian Holloway ....Jim Tanner
Betty Marsden.............................Harriet Potter
Trisha Nobble.......................................Sally
Renée Houston.........................Agatha Spanner
Harry Towb ....Doctor
Hugh Futcher ....Ernie
Marianne Stone ....Maud
Philip Stone.......................................Bulstrode
Leon Greene...Chef
Julian Holloway ....Roger

1972
Carry On Matron (87m) Cert A, Eastmancolor
Peter Rogers Productions (Rank Film
Distributors)
p..Peter Rogers
d ....Gerald Thomas
s ....Talbot Rothwell
Sidney James..Sid
Kenneth Williams ....Sir Bernard Cutting
Charles Hawtrey ....Dr. Goode
Joan Sims..Mrs. Tidey
Hattie Jacques ....Matron
Bernard Bresslaw.....................................Ernie
Kenneth Cope..Cyril
Terry Scott ....Dr. Prodd
Barbara Windsor ....Susan Ball
Kenneth Connor.................................Mr. Tidey
Jacki Piper ....Sister
Bill Maynard..Freddy
Patsy Rowlands ....Evelyn Banks
Derek Francis ....Arthur
Amelia Bayntun ....Mrs. Jenkins
Valerie Leon ....Jane Darling
Gwendoline Watts ....Frances Kemp
Wendy Richards ....Miss Willing
Jack Douglas..Himself
Marianne Stone ....Mrs. Putzova
Margaret Nolan ....Mrs. Tucker
Valerie Shute ....Mrs. Smethurst
Michael Nightingale............................Pearson

Carry On Abroad (88m) Cert A, Eastmancolor
Peter Rogers Productions (Fox-Rank)
p..Peter Rogers
d ....Gerald Thomas
s ....Talbot Rothwell
Sidney James....................................Vic Flange
Kenneth Williams.....................Stuart Farquhar
Charles Hawtrey ....Eustace Tuttle
Joan Sims ....Cora Flange
Bernard Bresslaw ....Brother Bernard
Barbara Windsor ....Sadie

Kenneth Connor ....Stanley Blunt
Peter Butterworth ....Pepe
Jimmy Logan ....Bert Conway
June Whitfield...............................Evelyn Blunt
Hattie Jacques ....Floella
Derek Francis ....Brother Martin
Sally Geeson....................................Lily White
Ray Brooks ....Giorgio
Carol Hawkins.........................Marge Plunkett
John Clive ....Robin
Jack Douglas ....Harry
Patsy Rowlands ....Miss Dobbs
David Kernan ....Nicholas
Alan Curtis ....Police Chief
Gertan Klauber ....Vendor

1979

The Princess and the Pea (8m) Cert U, Colour
Boyd's Co./Kendon Films (Bordeaux
International)
p...Don Boyd
d..Keith Goddard
s.......................(Story) Hans Christian Andersen
Judy Bowker...Princess
Roy Kinnear ....King
Charles Hawtrey............................Court Jester
Michael Hordern.................................Narrator

TV & Radio

CP	Comedy Playhouse	
SNT	Saturday Night Theatre	
NB	Norman and Henry Bones	
WFS	Writing For Sound	
RX	Date of recording	
GF	General Forces	
LP	BBC Light Programme	
HS	BBC Home Service	
MHS	BBC Midlands Home Service	
SHS	BBC Scottish Home Service	
CH	BBC Children's Hour	
PS	BBC Pacific Service	
AS	BBC African	
TS	BBC Transcription Service (Overseas)	

* plus one return fare Southsea/London at £2.0.6.
** plus two nights' subsistence at 20/- a night and third class return voucher London/Birmingham
*** plus three nights' subsistence @ £1 per night and third class return voucher London/Glasgow
**** plus four nights' subsistence @ £1 per night and third class return voucher London/Glasgow
***** plus two nights' subsistence allowance @ 27/6 per night and third class return travel warrant London/Manchester

BBC Radio

List compiled from contracts held at the BBC's Written Archive, Caversham. Shows pre-1944 have no record but his first *Norman and Henry Bones* episode, *Mystery at Ditchmoor*, was broadcast on 17 July 1943. Hawtrey also appeared in a shortened version of *Doctor Faustus* with Robert Donat on 8 September 1940 (Prod. Barbara Burnham).

1944

21/7	The Diary of a Dominie (with Will Hay)	GF
18/8	The Will Hay Programme	GF
25/8	The Will Hay Programme	GF
1/9	The Will Hay Programme	GF
8/9	The Will Hay Programme	GF
15/9	The Will Hay Programme	GF
22/9	The Will Hay Programme	GF
29/9	The Will Hay Programme	GF
6/10	The Will Hay Programme	GF
11/11	The Will Hay Programme	HS
20/12	The Will Hay Programme	HS
26/12	The Will Hay Programme	HS

1945

3/1	The Will Hay Programme	HS
10/1	The Will Hay Programme	HS
17/1	The Will Hay Programme	HS
24/1	The Will Hay Programme	HS
10/3	Music Hall Programme (with Will Hay)	HS
11/5	Will Hay celebrates Victory at St. Michael's	HS
21/12	Just William (Ep.8) Prod. Alick Hayes, LP	20gns

1946

17/1	Linton Abbey (NB) Prod. Josephine Plummer, CH	18gns
25/1	If You Were A Child in Australia Prod. Mr. Dixon, HS	12gns
29/1	Just William (Ep.14) Prod. Alick Hayes, LP	20gns
5/2	Just William (Ep.15) Prod. Alick Hayes, LP	20gns
12/2	Just William (Ep.16) Prod. Alick Hayes, LP	20gns
19/2	Just William (Ep.17) Prod. Alick Hayes, LP	20gns
20/2	Postman's Knock (NB) Prod. Josephine Plummer, CH	18gns
21/2	Treasure Island (Part 1) (Role of Jim Hawkins, boy) Prod. Derek McCulloch, CH	18gns
24/2	Nottingham Castle (Role of Montacute and "Voice") Prod. Derek McCulloch, CH	18gns
28/2	Treasure Island (Part 2) (Role of Jim Hawkins, boy) Prod. Derek McCulloch, CH	18gns
19/3	Just William (Ep.21) Prod. Alick Hayes, LP	20gns
26/3	Just William (Ep.22) Prod. Alick Hayes, LP	20gns
2/4	Just William (Ep.23) Prod. Alick Hayes, LP	20gns
6/4	The White Owl (NB) Prod. Josephine Plummer, CH	18gns
9/4	Just William (Ep.24) Prod. Alick Hayes, LP	20gns

16/4	Just William (Ep.25)	20gns
	Prod. Alick Hayes, LP	
23/4	Just William (Ep.26)	20gns
	Prod. Alick Hayes, LP	
30/4	Just William (Ep.27)	20gns
	Prod. Alick Hayes, LP	
7/5	Just William (Ep.28)	20gns
	Prod. Alick Hayes, LP	
14/5	Just William (Ep.29)	20gns
	Prod. Alick Hayes, LP	
21/5	Just William (Ep.30)	20gns
	Prod. Alick Hayes, LP	
28/5	Just William (Ep.31)	20gns
	Prod. Alick Hayes, LP	
4/6	Just William (Ep.32)	20gns
	Prod. Alick Hayes, LP	
11/6	Just William (Ep.33)	20gns
	Prod. Alick Hayes, LP	
18/6	Just William (Ep.34)	20gns
	Prod. Alick Hayes, LP	
25/6	Just William (Ep.35)	20gns
	Prod. Alick Hayes, LP	
8/8	Dear Appointment	20gns
	Prod. Gordon Crier, HS	
25/9	Mystery of Moulton's Farm (NB)	18gns
	Prod. Josephine Plummer, CH	
6/10	This English – 1	20gns
	Prod. Jennifer Wayne, HS	
8/10	The Robinson Family (Ep.1431 RX)	6gns
	Prod. Mr. Milroy, PS	
14/10	The Wishing Apple	20gns
	Prod. Tom Ronald, HS	
16/10	The Robinson Family (Ep.1440 RX)	6gns
	Prod. Mr. Milroy, PS	
21/10	The Robinson Family (Ep.1447 RX)	6gns
	Prod. Mr. Milroy, PS	
26/10	They Went Singing	22gns
	(Role of Alfred Mortimer)	
	Prod. Howard Rose, HS	
30/10	The Trunk Without A Key (NB)	20gns
	Prod. Josephine Plummer, CH	
11/11	The Robinson Family (Ep.1458)	6gns
	Prod. Mr. Milroy, PS	
14/11	Harriet Mellon (?)	20gns
	Prod. Vernon Harris, HS	
27/11	Stolen Plans (NB)	20gns
	Prod. Josephine Plummer, CH	
24/12	Full Circle	20gns
	Prod. Michael North, HS	
25/12	Pied Piper	20gns
	Prod. Henry Reed, HS	
31/12	The Mystery of Brookside School (NB)	
	20gns Prod. Josephine Plummer, CH	

1947

5/1	The Story of David (Part 1)	20gns
	(Role of David, boy)	
	Prod. Derek McCulloch, CH	
16/1	No Sentiment in Business	20gns
	Prod. Tom Ronald, HS	
29/1	Secret Headquarters (NB)	20gns
	Prod. Josephine Plummer, CH	
14/2	Revue Programme	20gns
	Prod. Mr. Livesay, MHS **	
25/2	Dr. Sprat	20gns
	Prod. Mr. Livesay, MHS **	
9/3	General Booth	20gns
	(Roles of Jim and Albert)	
	Prod. Josephine Plummer, CH	
14/3	Don't Switch Off Prod. Philip Garston-Jones, MHS	
21/3	Treasure Island – How It Was Written	
	22gns Prod. John Keir Cross ***	
25/3	The Giant's Head (NB)	20gns
	Prod. Josephine Plummer, CH	
26/3	Robinson Family (Ep.1547 RX)	6gns
	Prod. Archie Campbell, PS	
3/4	Up and Doing	10gns
	LP	
7/4	Robinson Family (Ep.1555 RX)	6gns
	Prod. Archie Campbell, PS	
29/4	The Missing Show-Dog (NB)	20gns
	Prod. Josephine Plummer, CH	
3/5	Three Men in the Snow	22gns
	Prod. Gordon Geldard, SHS ****	
10/6	Deadly Nightshade (NB)	20gns
	Prod. Josephine Plummer, CH	
1/7	Secret Headquarters (NB)	20gns
	Prod. Josephine Plummer, CH	
12/11	The Curse of the Camdens (NB)	20gns
	Prod. Josephine Plummer, CH	
8/12	The Mysterious Lodger (NB)	20gns
	Prod. Josephine Plummer, CH	
9/12	The Eddystone Light(Role of Harry) Prod. David Davis, CH	

1948

7/3	Barnaby Rudge (Part 9)	20gns
	(Role of Simon Tappertit)	
	Prod. Hugh Stewart, HS	
28/3	Barnaby Rudge (Part 12)	20gns
	Prod. Hugh Stewart, HS (Part cut)	
9/4	The Giant's Head	20gns
	Prod. Josephine Plummer, CH	
19/4	A New Heaven and A New Earth (P.2)	
	20gns Prod. Josephine Plummer, CH	

27/4	Fallada! Fallada! Prod. Derek McCulloch, CH	20gns
7/5	The Ship in a Bottle Prod. Josephine Plummer, CH	20gns
30/5	May Calendar Prod. Derek McCulloch, CH	20gns
26/6	Tom Lord's Cricket Ground Prod. Derek McCulloch, CH	15gns
7/7	The Mark of the Adder Prod. Josephine Plummer, CH	15gns
8/8	The Old Wives Tale (Ep.7) Prod. Peter Watts, HS	15gns
13/8	Demson's Dummies Prod. Josephine Plummer, CH	15gns
15/8	The Old Wives Tale (Ep.8) Prod. Peter Watts, HS	20gns
22/8	The Old Wives Tale (Ep.9) Prod. Peter Watts, HS	20gns
29/8	The Old Wives Tale (Ep.10) Prod. Peter Watts, HS	20gns
5/9	The Old Wives Tale (Ep.11) Prod. Peter Watts, HS	20gns
12/9	The Old Wives Tale (Ep.12) Prod. Peter Watts, HS	20gns
18/9	Mystery Tour Prod. Josephine Plummer, CH	15gns
4/10	Major Rigby's Secret Prod. Josephine Plummer, CH	15gns
8/10	Biggles Flies West Prod. Josephine Plummer, CH ******	15gns
1/12	The Midnight Visitor Prod. Josephine Plummer, CH	15gns
9/12	The Box of Delights, Part 3 Prod. Josephine Plummer, CH	15gns

1949

5/1	State Secrets Prod. Josephine Plummer, CH	15gns
14/1	Golden Pavements (Part 1) Prod. Josephine Plummer, CH	15gns
21/1	Golden Pavements (Part 2) Prod. Josephine Plummer, CH	15gns
28/1	Golden Pavements (Part 3) Prod. Josephine Plummer, CH	15gns
1/2	The Phantom Telephone Prod. Josephine Plummer, CH	15gns
5/3	Surprise Packet Prod. Josephine Plummer, CH	15gns
28/3	Cottage On the Corner Prod. Alick Hayes, LP	20gns
9/4	Mystery Tour Prod. Josephine Plummer, CH	15gns

14/5	The Secrets of Lagdon Fell Prod. Josephine Plummer, CH	15gns
18/6	Golden Pride Prod. Josephine Plummer, CH	15gns
13/9	Hullo Children: Back To School Prod. Lionel Gamlin, CH	12gns
5/10	October Revue Prod. Pat Dixon, HS	15gns
15/10	The Missing Manuscript (NB) Prod. Josephine Plummer, CH	15gns
11/11	Request Week (NB) Prod. Josephine Plummer, CH	15gns
21/11	P.C. 49 Prod. Vernon Harris, LP	20gns
25/12	A Christmas Carol Prod. Derek McCulloch, HS	15gns
31/12	Goodbye Mr. Gibson (NB) Prod. Josephine Plummer, CH	15gns

1950

28/1	Lights Out At Nine (NB) Prod. Josephine Plummer, CH	15gns
25/2	Secret Society (NB) Prod. Josephine Plummer, CH	15gns
12/4	Pincer's Progress (Wednesday Matinee) 21gns Prod. David H. Godfrey, HS	
27/4	Success Story: Steve Donoghue Prod. Peter Eton, LP	15gns
6/5	Secret Society (NB) Prod. Josephine Plummer, CH	15gns
22/7	The Cry of the Curlew Prod. Josephine Plummer, CH	15gns
26/8	A Hand Unseen (NB) Prod. Josephine Plummer, CH	15gns
15/9	Hullo There Prod. Lionel Gamlin, LP	20gns
14/10	Autumn Holiday Prod. Josephine Plummer, CH	15gns
18/11	The Cry of the Curlew Prod. Josephine Plummer, CH	15gns

1951

17/2	The Great Attraction Prod. Josephine Plummer, CH	15gns
20/2	The North Wind Doth Blow (NB) Prod. Josephine Plummer, CH	15gns
6/4	Request Week: A Hand Unseen Prod. Josephine Plummer, CH	15gns
2/6	Norman and Henry Bones Prod. Josephine Plummer, CH	15gns
30/7	A House To Let Prod. May E. Jenkin, CH	15gns

6/8	A House To Let Prod. May E. Jenkin, CH	15gns	26/2	Ray's A Laugh Prod. George Inns, HS	18gns
			5/3	Ray's A Laugh Prod. George Inns, HS	18gns
20/8	A House To Let Prod. May E. Jenkin, CH	15gns	12/3	Ray's A Laugh Prod. George Inns, HS	18gns
27/8	A House To Let Prod. May E. Jenkin, CH	15gns	19/3	Ray's A Laugh Prod. George Inns, HS	18gns
3/9	A House To Let Prod. May E. Jenkin, CH	15gns	26/3	Ray's A Laugh Prod. George Inns, HS	18gns
13/10	The House of Shadows Prod. Josephine Plummer, CH	15gns	28/3	Pictures in the Fire Prod. Josephine Plummer, CH	18gns
10/11	The Secret of the Black Box Prod. Josephine Plummer, CH	15gns	2/4	Ray's A Laugh Prod. George Inns, HS	18gns
			9/4	Ray's A Laugh Prod. George Inns, HS	18gns
1952			16/4	Ray's A Laugh Prod. George Inns, HS	18gns
26/1	The King John Goblet Prod. Josephine Plummer, CH	15gns	23/4	Ray's A Laugh Prod. George Inns, HS	18gns
22/3	The Pick of the Bunch Prod. Josephine Plummer, CH	15gns	30/4	Ray's A Laugh Prod. George Inns, HS	18gns
30/3	Oliver Twist (Ep.12) Prod. Charles Lefeaux, HS	15gns	7/5	Ray's A Laugh Prod. George Inns, HS	18gns
31/3	The Secret of the Black Box Prod. Josephine Plummer, CH	15gns	9/5	The Sealed Package Prod. Josephine Plummer, CH	19gns
10/5	Good Morning Mr. Valentine Prod. Josephine Plummer, CH	15gns	14/5	Ray's A Laugh Prod. George Inns, HS	18gns
13/11	Ray's A Laugh (Trial Recording for HS) Prod. George Inns	18gns	21/5	Ray's A Laugh Prod. George Inns, HS	18gns
29/11	Lost Property (NB) Prod. Josephine Plummer, CH	15gns	28/5	Ray's A Laugh Prod. George Inns, HS	18gns
20/12	Henry of Navarre (SNT) Prod. Hugh Stewart, HS	25gns	4/6	Ray's A Laugh Prod. George Inns, HS	18gns
			11/6	Ray's A Laugh Prod. George Inns, HS	18gns
1953			18/6	Ray's A Laugh Prod. George Inns, HS	18gns
1/1	Ray's A Laugh Prod. George Inns, HS	18gns	20/6	Strange Departure (NB) Prod. Josephine Plummer, CH	18gns
8/1	Ray's A Laugh Prod. George Inns, HS	18gns	25/6	Ray's A Laugh Prod. George Inns, HS	18gns
10/1	The Flying Flash (NB) Prod. Josephine Plummer, CH	18gns	20/7	Fables of the Fifties Prod. Peter Eton, HS	20gns
15/1	Ray's A Laugh Prod. George Inns, HS	18gns	3/9	Ray's A Laugh (RX) Prod. George Inns, HS	20gns
22/1	Ray's A Laugh Prod. George Inns, HS	18gns	1/10	Ray's A Laugh Prod. George Inns, HS	18gns
29/1	Ray's A Laugh Prod. George Inns, HS	18gns	8/10	Ray's A Laugh Prod. George Inns, HS	18gns
5/2	Ray's A Laugh Prod. George Inns, HS	18gns	15/10	Ray's A Laugh Prod. George Inns, HS	18gns
12/2	Ray's A Laugh Prod. George Inns, HS	18gns			
19/2	Ray's A Laugh Prod. George Inns, HS	18gns			

22/10	Ray's A Laugh Prod. George Inns, HS	18gns
29/10	Ray's A Laugh Prod. George Inns, HS	18gns
5/11	Ray's A Laugh Prod. George Inns, HS	18gns
12/11	Ray's A Laugh Prod. George Inns, HS	18gns
19/11	Ray's A Laugh Prod. George Inns, HS	18gns
21/11	The Temple Vase (NB) Prod. Josephine Plummer, CH	18gns
26/11	Ray's A Laugh Prod. George Inns, HS	18gns
3/12	Ray's A Laugh Prod. George Inns, HS	18gns
10/12	Ray's A Laugh Prod. George Inns, HS	18gns
17/12	Ray's A Laugh Prod. George Inns, HS	18gns
19/12	The Devil's Pool Prod. Josephine Plummer, CH	18gns
24/12	Ray's A Laugh Prod. George Inns, HS	18gns
31/12	Ray's A Laugh Prod. George Inns, HS	18gns

1954

4/1	Ray's A Laugh Prod. George Inns, HS	18gns
11/1	Ray's A Laugh Prod. George Inns, HS	18gns
18/1	Ray's A Laugh Prod. George Inns, HS	18gns
25/1	Ray's A Laugh Prod. George Inns, HS	18gns
4/2	Ray's A Laugh Prod. George Inns, HS	18gns
11/2	Ray's A Laugh Prod. George Inns, HS	18gns
13/2	The High & Mighty (SNT) Prod. Hugh Stewart, HS	20gns
18/2	Ray's A Laugh Prod. George Inns, HS	18gns
25/2	Ray's A Laugh Prod. George Inns, HS	18gns
1/3	Ray's A Laugh Prod. George Inns, HS	18gns
8/3	Ray's A Laugh Prod. George Inns, HS	18gns
15/3	Ray's A Laugh Prod. George Inns, HS	18gns

22/3	Ray's A Laugh Prod. George Inns, HS	18gns
25/3	Storm Over the Fell (NB) Prod. Josephine Plummer, CH	18gns
25/3	Line of Fire (NB) Prod. Josephine Plummer, CH	18gns
31/3	Little Pig Robinson Prod. R.D. Smith, TS	10gns
22/4	The Blue Envelope (NB) Prod. Josephine Plummer, CH	18gns
13/6	Melville's Choice Prod. Eileen Molony, LP	14gns
17/6	The Chinese Dragon (NB) Prod. Josephine Plummer, CH	18gns
7/11	Arthur Marshall Chooses Prod. Eileen Molony, LP	14gns
13/11	When the Bough Breaks Prod. Josephine Plummer, CH	18gns
11/12	The Five Pines Problem Prod. Josephine Plummer, CH	18gns

1955

6/1	Life With the Lyons Prod. Tom Ronald, LP	20gns
13/1	Life With the Lyons Prod. Tom Ronald, LP	20gns
27/1	Life With the Lyons Prod. Tom Ronald, LP	20gns
10/2	Life With the Lyons Prod. Tom Ronald, LP	20gns
24/2	Life With the Lyons Prod. Tom Ronald, LP	20gns
10/3	Life With the Lyons Prod. Tom Ronald, LP	20gns
17/3	Life With the Lyons Prod. Tom Ronald, LP	20gns
29/3	The Ugly Duckling Prod. Francis Dillon, HS	20gns
14/4	Life With the Lyons Prod. Tom Ronald, LP	20gns
22/4	Strange Departure (NB) Prod. Josephine Plummer, CH	18gns
19/5	Life With the Lyons Prod. Tom Ronald, LP	20gns
25/5	The Feast of Lanterns Prod. Josephine Plummer, CH	18gns
2/6	Life With the Lyons Prod. Tom Ronald, LP	20gns
4/8	The Tale of Johnny Town Mouse Prod. R.D. Smith, TS	9gns
12/9	Tomorrow Mr. Tompion Prod. Charles Lefeaux, HS	20gns

5/11	The White Cube (NB)	18gns
	Prod. Josephine Plummer, CH	
1/12	Life With the Lyons	20gns
	Prod. Tom Ronald, LP	
2/12	The Box of Delights	18gns
	Prod. Josephine Plummer, CH	
8/12	Life With the Lyons	20gns
	Prod. Tom Ronald, LP	
21/12	Life With the Lyons (RX)	20gns
	Prod. Tom Ronald, LP	

1956

5/1	Life With the Lyons	20gns
	Prod. Tom Ronald, LP	
21/1	Minstrel's Gallery (NB)	18gns
	Prod. Josephine Plummer, CH	
26/1	Life With the Lyons	20gns
	Prod. Tom Ronald, LP	
28/1	The Siege of Mocking Hill (SNT)	20gns
	Prod. Archie Campbell, HS	
9/2	Life With the Lyons	20gns
	Prod. Tom Ronald, LP	
24/2	Henry Hall's Guest Night	14gns
	Prod. John Simmonds, HS	
17/3	The Mystery of Cragford	
	Heights (NB)	18gns
	Prod. Josephine Plummer, CH	
5/5	The Witch's Elbow (NB)	18gns
	Prod. Josephine Plummer, CH	
2/6	The Riddle of the Rocks (NB)	18gns
	Prod. Josephine Plummer, CH	
18/9	Dreaming Bandsmen (WFS)	20gns
	Prod. David Thomson, HS	
8/12	The Rainbow Ray (NB)	22gns
	Prod. Josephine Plummer, CH	
9/12	Life With the Lyons	22gns
	Prod. Tom Ronald, LP	
16/12	Life With the Lyons	22gns
	Prod. Tom Ronald, LP	

1957

20/1	Life With the Lyons	22gns
	Prod. Tom Ronald, LP	
24/2	Life With the Lyons	22gns
	Prod. Tom Ronald, LP	
28/2	Ray's A Laugh	22gns
	Prod. Leslie Bridgmont, LP	
17/3	Life With the Lyons	22gns
	Prod. Tom Ronald, LP	
30/3	The Secret of Pengrythmyr (NB)	22gns
	Prod. Josephine Plummer, CH	
31/3	Life With the Lyons	22gns
	Prod. Tom Ronald, LP	

28/4	Life With the Lyons	22gns
	Prod. Tom Ronald, LP	
31/8	The Mystery of Grimsdyke Hollow	
	22gns Prod. Josephine Plummer, CH	
28/9	The Passage Under the Lake	22gns
	Prod. Josephine Plummer, CH	
25/10	Ray's A Laugh	22gns
	Prod. Leslie Bridgmont, LP	
21/12	The Mystery of the Tyford Towers	22gns
	Prod. Josephine Plummer, CH	

1958

25/1	The Forest Cat	22gns
	Prod. Josephine Plummer, CH	
16/2	Life With the Lyons	22gns
	Prod. Tom Ronald, LP	
22/2	Line of Fire	22gns
	Prod. Josephine Plummer, CH	
22/3	A Case of Forgeries	22gns
	Prod. Josephine Plummer, CH	
25/4	Oak Before Ash	22gns
	Prod. Josephine Plummer, CH	
23/8	The Road To York	22gns
	Prod. Josephine Plummer, CH	
27/9	The Ruttledge Inheritance	22gns
	Prod. Josephine Plummer, CH	
25/10	The Legend of Marcus Mere	22gns
	Prod. Josephine Plummer, CH	
29/11	Norman and Henry Bones play	22gns
	Prod. Josephine Plummer, CH	

1959

10/1	Norman and Henry Bones play	22gns
	Prod. Josephine Plummer, CH	
14/2	Norman and Henry Bones play	22gns
	Prod. Josephine Plummer, CH	
14/3	Norman and Henry Bones play	22gns
	Prod. Josephine Plummer, CH	
8/10	The Case of the Missing Pianist	22gns
	Prod. Josephine Plummer, CH	
12/11	The Langdon Legacy	22gns
	Prod. Josephine Plummer, CH	
10/12	The Nelson Letter	22gns
	Prod. Josephine Plummer, CH	

1960

9/1	A Case of Coins	22gns
	Prod. Josephine Plummer, CH	
11/2	Red Light Warning	22gns
	Prod. Josephine Plummer, CH	
10/3	Forced Landing (NB)	25gns
	Prod. Josephine Plummer, CH	

29/4	Exit Edward Eastman	25gns
	Prod. Josephine Plummer, CH	

1965

15/10	Not For Children	30gns
	Prod. Trafford Whitelock, HS	
22/10	Not For Children	30gns
	Prod. Trafford Whitelock, HS	
29/10	Not For Children	30gns
	Prod. Trafford Whitelock, HS	
5/11	Not For Children	30gns
	Prod. Trafford Whitelock, HS	
12/11	Not For Children	30gns
	Prod. Trafford Whitelock, HS	
19/11	Not For Children	30gns
	Prod. Trafford Whitelock, HS	

1967

13/8	Sounds Familiar	10gns
	Prod. Bill Worsley, HS *	
3/9	Sounds Familiar	10gns
	Prod. Bill Worsley, HS *	

1972

24/12	Pete Myers interviews CH and Kenneth Williams	£30
	Prod. Veronica Manoukian, AS	

1975

11/4	The 78 Show (RX) (Panellist)	£28
	Prod. John Dyas, Radio 2	

1979

15/12	Burglar's Bargains	£93
	Prod. Martin Jenkins, Radio 4	

1980

28/11	The Late Show (Interview)	£18
	Prod. Barry Knight, Radio 2	

1981

19/5	Funny You Should Ask (Panellist)	£45
	Prod. Paul Mayhew-Archer, Radio 2	

1982

22/2	A Right Royal Robbery (SNT, RX)	
		£126.50
	Prod. Martin Jenkins, BBC Radio 4	
23/2	A Right Royal Robbery (SNT, RX)	
		£126.50
	Prod. Martin Jenkins, BBC Radio 4	
24/2	A Right Royal Robbery (SNT, RX)	
		£126.50
	Prod. Martin Jenkins, BBC Radio 4	
25/2	A Right Royal Robbery (SNT, RX)	
		£126.50
	Prod. Martin Jenkins, BBC Radio 4	

1985

3/8	The Bigger They Are	£151.50
	Prod. Martin Jenkins, BBC Radio 4	

BBC Television

1947

16/8	New Faces	30gns
	Prod. Henry Caldwell	
20/9	New Faces	22gns
	Prod. Henry Caldwell	

1948

12/6	Tell Her The Truth	
	(Role of Bobby Howes)	50gns
	Prod. Michael Mills	
18/6	Tell Her The Truth	
	(Role of Bobby Howes)	50gns
	Prod. Michael Mills	
4/12	Chain Male	
	(Role of Mr.Wellington)	35gns
	Prod. John Glyn-Jones	
7/12	Chain Male	
	(Role of Mr.Wellington)	35gns
	Prod. John Glyn-Jones	

1953

7/6	All On A Summer's Day	
	(Role of Arty)	65 gns
	Prod. Cambell Logan	
11/6	All On A Summer's Day	
	(Role of Arty)	65 gns
	Prod. Cambell Logan	
30/6	Who Dotes Yet Doubts	
	(Role of Dickie Dodson)	35gns
	Prod. Tatiana Lieven	

1954

15/5	Music Hall	18gns
	Prod. Richard Afton	
7/6	Fred Emney Show	
	(Role of Office Boy)	32gns
	Prod. Bill Ward	
26/7	Limelight	22gns
	Prod. Henry Caldwell	

1955

| 29/6 | Life With the Lyons | 38gns |
| | Prod. Bryan Sears | |

1956

1/1	Alice in Wonderland (Role of The	
	Caterpillar)	43gns
	Producer Peter Newington	
27/10	Tess and Jim	42gns
	Prod. George Inns	
24/11	Tess and Jim	42gns
	Prod. George Inns	

1957

| 3/1 | Laughter in Store | 39gns |
| | Prod. George Inns | |

1965

10/2	Hugh and I (Role of Pilot at	
	Gatwick Airport)	£78 15s
	Producer David Croft	
21/5	Memoirs of a Chaise Longue (CP) (Role	
	of the Voice of the Chaise Longue.)	
	135 guineas, cancelled.	

1969

6/5	Line Up (Reading poetry)	£26 5s
	Prod. Steve Roberts	
5/11	Line Up (Interview re.	
	Carry On Jungle Boy)	10gns
	Prod. Barry Brown	

Independent Television

1957

The Army Game
(Series 1)

19/6	Episode 1
3/7	Episode 2
17/7	Episode 3
31/7	Episode 4
14/8	Episode 5
28/8	Episode 6
11/9	Episode 7
25/9	Episode 8
9/10	Episode 9
23/10	Episode 10
6/11	Episode 11
20/11	Episode 12
4/12	Episode 13

The Army Game
(Series 2)

| 20/12 | Episode 1 |
| 27/12 | Episode 2 |

1958

3/1	Episode 3
10/1	Episode 4
17/1	Episode 5
24/1	Episode 6
31/1	Episode 7
7/2	Episode 8
14/2	Episode 9
21/2	Episode 10
28/2	Episode 11
7/3	Episode 12
14/3	Episode 13
21/3	Episode 14
28/3	Episode 15
4/4	Episode 16
11/4	Episode 17
18/4	Episode 18
25/4	Episode 19
2/5	Episode 20
9/5	Episode 21
16/5	Episode 22
23/5	Episode 23
30/5	Episode 24
6/6	Episode 25
13/6	Episode 26

1960
Our House
(Series 1)

11/9	Moving In
18/9	Simply Simon
25/9	A Thin Tim
2/10	The Man Who Knew Nothing
9/10	Annie Does Live Here
16/10	Surprise For Stephen
23/10	All In A Good Cause
30/10	To Please Louise
6/11	Speechless
13/11	Day-Time
20/11	Love To Georgina
27/11	Things of the Past
4/12	And Then There Was One

1961
Our House (Series 2)

16/9	Not For Sale
30/9	Vote For Georgina
14/10	A Quiet Time

28/10 ....Revolution In Walthamstow
11/11 ....Best Man
25/11 ....Battle of the Borough
9/12 ....Knocko
16/12 ....Willow the Winger
23/12 ....Complications of the Season
30/12......................................Treble Mischance

1962
Our House (Series 3)
6/1 ....Where Is Everybody?
13/1 ....Riviera Incident
20/1 ....Georgina Goes To Press
27/1...............................Simon Comes To Stay
3/2...Hobbies Galore
10/2 ....There's No Business like ...
17/2..Off the Rails
24/2..............................The Tooth Will Out!
3/3..Economy Wave
10/3 ....Horse Power
17/3 ....Uncle Silas
24/3 ....The Den of Vice
31/3 ....First Night
7/4...Safari
14/4...Oh, Julie!
21/4...Talking Shop

1963
6/1 ....Best of Friends
(every Sunday for thirteen weeks)

1969

24/12 ....Carry On Christmas

1970
? ....Stop Exchange
(Panorama Films for South African television,
directed by Howard Rennie)
24/12 ....Carry On Again Christmas
(AKA: Carry On Long John)

1971
17/9 ....Grasshopper Island (Escape)
24/9 ....Grasshopper Island (The Elderly Boy)

1972
1/3......................This is Your Life Hylda Baker
19/4 ....This is Your Life Patricia Hayes

1976
21/9 ....This is Your Life ITV
31/10 ....Runaround

1979
17/12 ....The Plank

1980
12/12 ....Movie Memories (RX)

1981
7/1..........................This is Your Life Bill Owen
6/11 ....Live From Two

1987
12/4 ....Supergran and the State Visit

Bibliography

Bourne, Stephen, *Brief Encounters, Lesbians and Gays in British Films 1930-1971* (Cassell, 1996)

Brooker, John, *Movie Memories* (Haynes Publishing, 1982)

Butters, Wes and Russell Davies, *Kenneth Williams Unseen* (HarperCollins, 2008)

Coward, Noël, *Present Indicative* (William Heineman, 1937)

Dyer, Richard, *The Culture of Queers* (Routledge, 2002)

Eastaugh, Kenneth, *The Carry-On Book* (David and Charles, 1978)

Ellmann, Richard, *Oscar Wilde* (Hamish Hamilton, 1987)

Foster, Andy and Steve Furst, *Radio Comedy 1938-1968* (Virgin Publishing, 1996)

Freud, Sigmund, *The Interpretation of Dreams* (Macmillan, New York, 1913)

Gifford, Denis, *The British Film Catalogue, Volume 1, Fiction Film 1895 – 1994* (Fitzroy Dearborn Publishers, 2001)

Goddard, Simon, *Mozipedia, The Encyclopedia of Morrissey and The Smiths* (Ebury Press, 2009)

Hawtrey, Sir Charles, *The Truth At Last from Charles Hawtrey*, ed. W.Somerset Maugham (Thornton Butterworth, 1924)

Hibbin, Sally and Nina, *What a Carry On: The Official Story of the Carry On Film Series* (Hamlyn, 1988)

Hounslow Library, *Collection of Middlesex County Directories (Kelly's, 1913-1928), Town Directories (Thomason's 1936-1937), Rate Book and Electoral Registers (1926-1935)*

Howerd, Frankie, *On the Way I Lost It* (W.H. Allen, 1976)

Hudis, Norman, *No Laughing Matter: How I Carried On* (Apex Publishing, 2008)

Lewis, Roger, *The Man Who Was Private Widdle* (Faber and Faber, 2001)

Morley, Sheridan, *Noël Coward* (Haus Publishing, 2005)

O'Connor, Garry, *Ralph Richardson, An Actor's Life* (Hodder and Stoughton, 1982)

Park, John D.D. *Who's Who in the Theatre, 11th Edition* (London, 1952)

Rinaldi, Graham, *Will Hay* (Tomahawk Press, 2009)

Ross, Robert, *The Carry On Companion* (B.T. Batsford, 1996)

Seaton, Ray and Roy Martin, Good Morning Boys: Will Hay, Master of Comedy (London Barrie and Jenkins Ltd., 1978)

Selby-Lowndes, Joan, *The Conti Story* (Collins, 1954)

Sims, Joan, *High Spirits* (Transworld, 2000)

Upton, Julian, *Fallen Stars, Tragic Lives and Lost Careers* (Headpress, 2004)

Williams, Kenneth;

—— *The Kenneth Williams Diaries* and *The Kenneth Williams Letters*, ed. Russell Davies (HarperCollins, 1993 and 1994)

—— *Back Drops* (Dent, 1983)

—— *Just Williams* (Dent, 1985)

Windsor, Barbara;

—— *All of Me: My Extraordinary Life* (Headline, 2001)

—— *Barbara: The Laughter and Tears of a Cockney Sparrow* (Century Hutchinson, 1990)

Newspapers & Magazines

ABC Film Review, interview with Vincent Frith (1961)

Attitude, *Idols: Charles Hawtrey* (Richard Dyer, May 1994)

Bournemouth Times and Directory, review of *The Windmill Man* (25 December 1926)

Brixton Free Press, review of *Counterfeit* (1 September 1939)

Cor! *Magazine Number 8, Charles Hawtrey Special* (Robert Ross, 1995)

Dancing Times (c.1940)

Daily Express, *Before Make-Up, After Make-Up* (16 August 1939)

Daily Mail, *Carry On Hawtrey Dies at 72* (28 October 1988)

Daily Mirror, *Carry-On Star Hawtrey Dies* (28 October 1988)

Daily Sketch, review of *Counterfeit* (16 August 1939)

Evening News, (24 May 1969)

Evening Standard, *Carry On star left £163,165 but no will* (25 January 1989)

Film Review, *This Carry On Phenomenon* (September 1972)

Film Weekly, *Jack Payne Says it With Music* (1 July 1932)

Kinematograph Weekly;

—— review of *This Freedom* (26 April 1923)

—— reviews of *Dumb Dora Discovers Tobacco* and *What Do We Do Now?* (17 January 1946)

New Statesman, *The Possibility of Happiness* (Peter Bradshaw, 1 October 2001)

News of the World, *Carry On Star in Hospital* (7 June 1981)

Nottingham Journal, review of *Counterfeit* (26 August 1939)

NME;

—— *Stop Me if You've Heard This One Before* (February 1988)

—— *Headful Of Heroes* (September 1989)

Middlesex Chronicle;

— review of *Theodore* (27 May 1933)

—— *Charles Hawtrey in Film With Will Fyffe* (14 November 1937)

—— *Famous actor is bereaved —- Fall in lounge led to mother's death* (19 March 1965)

Monthly Film Bulletin;

—— review of *Well Done Henry* (c.1937)

—— review of *Jailbirds* (Vol. 6 No. 72, 31 December 1939)

—— review of *Dumb Dora Discovers Tobacco* (Vol. 13 No. 145, 31 January 1946)

—— review of *Fag End* (Vol. 14 No. 165, 30 September 1947)

—— review of *Carry On Sergeant* (Vo1. 25 1958)

Southern Evening Echo, *It Will Be Carry On Carnival*, 18 June 1965

Sporting Life, review of *Counterfeit* (18 August 1939)

That Funny Fella With the Glasses (Wes Butters, November 1998)

The Cinema Booking Guide, review of *Marry Me* (Vol. 2 No. 7, January 1933).

The Daily Telegraph;

—— *Celebrities in Peter Pan* (c. December 1936)

—— *'Counterfeit' in West End* (16 August 1939)

—— *TV Actor Taken Ill in Sketch* (8 April 1957)

—— *2 Drink Cases in 8 Days, Actor Fined and Banned* (13 September 1963)

—— *Charles Hawtrey Obituary* (28 October 1988)

The Doncaster Star, *Charles Hawtrey Obituary* (29 October 1988)

The East Kent Mercury;

—— *Carry On Star Saved From Blaze* (Steve Langley, 8 August 1984)

—— *Carry On Star is Dead* (2 November 1988)

—— *The 'Eccentric' in the Fur Coat* (Peter Krinks, 18 September 1997)

—— *Lasting Tribute to the Man Who Brought Laughter* (Sue Briggs, 19 November 1998)

The Guardian, *Carry On Camping At the Piano* (Peter Cotes, 28 October 1988)

The Mail on Sunday, Peter Rogers on the *Carry Ons* (c.2000)

The Observer, review of *Counterfeit* (20 August 1939)

The People, *Shunned, the star who gets no laughs as a sad drunk* (Phil Hall and Chris Murphy, 29 May 1988)

The Pink Paper, *Charles Hawtrey Obituary* (Patrick Newley, November 1988)

The Play Pictorial, *Where the Rainbow Ends* (Vol. 62 No. 370, January 1933)

The Radio Times;

—— (c.1952)

—— *A right carry-on by Charles* (25-31 August 1973)

The Stage;

—— review of *The Windmill Man* (20 January 1927)

—— review of *Babes in the Wood* (2 January 1930)

—— review of *Loves Labour's Lost* (20 March 1930)

—— review of *Member's Only* (23 December 1937)

—— review of *Strange Family* (17 November 1938)

—— review of *Counterfeit* (17 August 1939)

—— review of *New Faces* (18 April 1940)

—— review of *New Faces* (2 January 1941)

—— review of *Old Chelsea* (25 February 1943)

—— review of *Merrie England* (26 October 1944)

—— review of *Temporary Ladies* (24 May 1945)

—— review of *Oflag 3* (28 June 1945)

—— review of *The Blue Lamp* (11 June 1953)

—— *Our House* (15 September 1960)

—— *Summer's Coming* (27 January 1961)

—— *Best of Friends series* (3 January 1963)

—— *Night of 100 Stars* (30 July 1964)

—— review of *Jack and the Beastalk* (4 January 1968)

—— review of *Jack and the Beanstalk* (8 January 1970)

—— review of *Carry On Holiday Startime* (13 August 1970)

—— *review of Stop it Nurse!* (17 August 1972)

—— *review of Snow White and the Seven Dwarfs* (10 January 1974)

—— *Michael Sullivan Obituary* (15 June 1995)

The Star, *review of Counterfeit* (16 August 1939)

The Sun;

—— *Carry On, what's his name!* (Fergus Cashin, 16 August 1972)

—— *What a Carry On* (Tom Merrin and Alastair Campbell, 6 August 1984)
—— *Naked ordeal for Hawtrey, 68* (Tim Wapshott, 6 August 1984)
—— *What Became of the Carry On Crowd?* (Tim Ewbank, 15 August 1987)
—— *Carry On Star Must Lose Both Legs or Die* and *Carry On Boozing* (Paul Hooper, Tracey Kandohla and Alan Watkins, 29 September 1988)
—— *It's So Sad!* (Mandy Allott and Angela Davies, 30 September 1988)
—— *Carry On Star Charles Hawtrey is Dead* (Tracey Kandohla and Alan Watkins, 28 October 1988)
—— *Sad Star Who Kept All of Us Laughing* (Dave Jarvis, Ruki Sayid and Mark Solomons, 28 October 1988)
—— *Carry-On Charles is Buried in Secret* (3 November 1988)
The Times;
—— review of *Counterfeit* (16 August 1939)
—— *Charles Hawtrey Obituary* (Gilbert Adair, 8 November 1988)
—— *Cor, What a Lovely Pair of Fireplaces* (John Naish, 23 September 2000)
Today's Cinema;
—— review of *Jailbirds*, (6 December 1939)
—— review of *Dumb Dora Discovers Tobacco* (15 January 1946)
—— review of *Fag End* (15 August 1947)
West Sussex County Times (c.1973)

Television

Movie Memories, Anglia, 1980
An Audience with Kenneth Williams, LWT, 1983
Carry On Darkly, Channel 4, 1999

Radio

Charles Hawtrey interview with Brian Matthew, BBC Radio 2, 28 November 1980 (BBC Archive number: LP 39566 f61–3)
Funny You Should Ask, BBC Radio 2, 19 May 1981
The Carry On Clan, BBC Radio 2, 8 April 1996
Carry On Carrying On, BBC Radio 2, 1993

Lecture

Carry On Regardless: The Genius of Charles Hawtrey, by Richard Dyer at the National Film Theatre (as part of the fourth London Lesbian and Gay Festival), 24 October 1989

INDEX

Entries shown in **Bold** indicate illustrations

117 Middle Street 33, 34, 42, **43**, 207, 218, 222, 225, 231, **242**
66 Mortlake Road 178, 181, 207

Alice in Wonderland 128
All On A Summer's Day 127
Allister, Claud 107, 113
Andrews, Eamonn **196**
Army Game, The 129, 130, 131, **132**, 133, 134, 135, 139, 140, 141, 156, 187
Ashton, Brad xvii, 153, 154, 160
Ashwell, Ann 242-243

Babes in the Wood **70**, 207
Baddeley, Hermione 117, 118
Bainbridge, Elisabeth 218
Baker, Hylda 148, 153, 154
Banks, Monty 77
Barnes, Barry K. 113
Barron, Marcus **91**
Bass, Alfie **132**, **134**, **140**
Bats in the Belfry 90
BBC's Written Archive 103, 104
Best of Friends 131, 148, 153, 154, 183
Block, Bob 153
Blue Lamp, The 107
Booker, John 56
Bowker, Judi 212
Boyd, Don xvii, 212, 213
Brandreth, Gyles 24
Brandy For the Parson 125
Bresslaw, Bernard 131, **132**, 133, **140**, 155, 156, **180**, 233
Bright, Roger 207
British Film Institute 77, 112, 113
Broad, Tim 239
Brown, Burton 112
Brown, Janet 207
Brown Wallet, The 77
Bullock, Barry 28, **226**, 228-229

Burdon, Albert **97**
Burrows, Chris 235
Burton, Josephine 115, 121, 122
Butterworth, Peter **176**, 177, **180**, 181, 207
Byrne, Peter xvii, 62, 66, 81, 84, 85, 86, 213, 214

Caldwell, Henry 114-115
Campbell, Judy xvii, 98-99
Campion, Gerald **136**
Canterbury Tale, A 105
Carney, Terry 145

Carry On film series:
   fee 27, 170
   team 26, 28, 38, 155
   dislike of the series 24, 29-30, 73, 155, 156, 160-161, 173, 193, 245
   liking for the series 27, 159
   popularity in the series xiii, 26, 170, 173-**174**
   proposed return to the series 42, 195

Carry On … Up the Khyber 178, **179**, **180**, 181
Carry On Abroad 30, 188, **192**, 202, 203, 204, 212, 239
Carry On Again Doctor 93, **94**, 185, 206
Carry On Again Nurse 42
Carry On At Your Convenience **190**, **191**, 202, 204
Carry On Cabby 161, 213
Carry On Camping xv-xvi, 28, 30, 178, 185, 201, 204
Carry On Christmas 193
Carry On Cleo **172**, 173, 188, 202, 239
Carry On Columbus 26, 44
Carry On Constable 56, **58**, 93, **94**, **95**, 148, 187, **240**
Carry On Cowboy, 171, 178
Carry On Cruising 160
Carry On Doctor 177, 178
Carry On Don't Lose Your Head **175**

Carry On England 26
Carry On Follow That Camel **176**, 177
Carry On Henry 88, **189**, 204, **205**
Carry On Holiday Startime **199**, 201
Carry On Jack **162**, **164**, 165
Carry On London 26
Carry On Loving **186**, 187
Carry On Matron **192**
Carry On Nurse **138**, 139, 177
Carry On Regardless 157, 158-159, 165
Carry On Screaming 173, **174**, 175
Carry On Sergeant 131, 135, **136**, 137, 209
Carry On Spying 165, **166**
Carry On Teacher 68, 93, **143**
Carry On Up the Jungle 30, 187, **201**, 202

Carry On Companion, The (book) 157
Carry-On Book, The (book) 42, 167, 169, 195
Carry On Regardless: The Genius of Charles
    Hawtrey (lecture) 101, 201
Castle, Roy xvii, 181
Chain Male 119, 120-121
Chinese Bungalow 107
Cinema Museum 112
Clare, Mary 107
Clark, John 85
Clarke, Nigel **100**
Claudius the Bee **100**
Clear, Chris 32
Cleo, Camping, Emmanuelle, Dick 48
Colin, Sid 130
Comedy Playhouse 170
Compton, Fay 59
Connor, Kenneth 31, 56, 104, 139, **143**, 153,
    156-157, 159, **161**, **192**, 209
Conti, Bianca 66, 67
Conti, Italia 42, 46, 62, **63**, 65, 66, 67, 68, 71,
    73, 77, 213
Cor Blimey 48
Corbett, Harry H. 212
Corbett, Ronnie 125
Cotes, Peter 69
Counterfeit 91-93, 98, 101
Coward, Noël 46, 61, 66, 67, 88
Coyles, Ronnè xvii, 182, 183, 184, 219
Cribbins, Bernard **166**
Crisp, Donald 57
Crisp, Quentin 188
Croft, David 170
Culture of Queers, The (book), 204
Cummins, Peggy xvii, 106
Czechmate 107

Dale, Jim **176**, 177, 206
Darlington, W.A. 90, 91
Dawson, Nancy 218
Dennis, Ray 224, 218, 225
Denver, Paul xvii, 199, 200, 201, 206, 220, 222
Diary of a Schoolmaster 81
Dickie Henderson Show, The 130
Douglas, Jack xviii, 156, 165, 173, 183
Dumb Dora Discovers Tobacco 107, 112, 113
Dyer, Richard xviii, 101, 139, 201, 204

East Kent Mercury, The 33, 38, 229
Eastaugh, Kenneth 167, 169
Eaton, Shirley 139
Ellison, Carole xviii, 39, 41, 46
End of the River 117
Errol Flynn 24, **74**, 77
Evans, Maurice 77

Fairbanks Junior, Douglas 77
Farr, Derek **89**
Field, Sid 200
Filbrey, Sid 55
Flanagan and Allen 90
For the Children 115
Formby, George 105
Frankau, Ronald 112
Fraser, Liz xiv, 31, **102**, 158
Fred Emney Show, The 128
Fry, Stephen 87
Funny Thing Happened On the Way To the Forum,
    A 178
Fyffe, Will 78, 79

Gerrard, Gene 113
Ghost of St. Michael's, The 81, **82**, **83**, 84
Gibbons, Spencer K. xviii, 214, 215
Gidman, Marcus xviii, 228, 231
Gielgud, John 70, 168
Gigi 237
Gilbert, Lewis 105
Gilbraith, Barney 130
Gingold, Hermione 90
Glyn-Jones, John 119-121
Good Morning Boys (book) 85
Good Morning, Boys! (film) 81, 84
Goose Steps Out, The 81, **83**, 85
Gould, Graham 144-145, 146
Grant, Ronald 112-113
Grasshopper Island 187, 188
Greenwood, Joan 107
Griffiths, Evelyn xviii, 41, 71, **72**

Hancock, Tony 238
Hanson, Joan 55
Happy Birthday 107
Happy Returns 90
Hargrave, Marlene 167
Harris, Anita **176**
Hartnell, William 131, **132**, **137**, 142
Hartree , George (boy) 46, **54**, 55, **57**, 60, 63,
    198
Hartree, Alice (mother):
    35, 46, 47, **48**, 49, 50, 51, 53, **54**, 55, 60,
        62, 65, 93, 106, 150, 163, 167, 168,
        178, 197, 199, 233
    death of 170-171, 178, 197, 199, 219,
        220, 223
    mental health 47-48, 93, 150, 167-168,
        171, 199

Hartree, Jack (brother) 35, 41, 46, 49, 51, 52,
    53, **54**, 163, 168, 198
Hartree, John (nephew) xviii, 41, 47, 52, **54**,
    163, 165, 168, 198
Hartree, Maureen (niece in law) 51, 171
Hartree, Rosina (sister in law) **54**
Hartree, William (father) 35, 46, 47, **48**, 49,
    50, 51, 53
Hawkins, Bryn 234

Hawtrey, Charles:
    alcoholism xii-xiv, **25**, **27**, 32, 36, 56-57,
        141, 150, 152, 155, 165, 167, 168,
        170, 171, 175, 183, 187, 188, 195,
        197, 199, 206, 207, 208, 211, 213,
        214, 218, 223, 224, 231, 234, 235,
        245
    amateur dramatics 59
    baptism 50, **52**
    birth of 50
    blue plaque **vi**, xiii
    boy soprano **64**, 71-**72**, 73, 81
    catchphrases 104, 170

    characters:

    Big Heap 241
    Charlie Muggins xv-xvi, 178, 185, 241
    Clarence, Duke of Claridge **235**, 236
    Dan Dann 173, **174**
    Dr Goode **192**
    Dr Stoppidge 187, 206
    Duke de Pomfrit **175**, 241
    Eustace Tuttle **x**, 188, **192**, **203**, 239, 241,

Golightly 135-**136**, 209
James Bedsop **186**, 187
Le Pice 177
Mr. Barron 177, 241
Mr. Hinton **138**, 139, 177
Pint-Pot 161, 213, 241
Private Widdle 178, **179**, **180**, 236
Sir Roger de Lodgerley **189**, 204, **205**
The Elderly Boy 187
The Professor 131, **133**, 134, 236
Tonka the Great 187, **201**
Walter Sweetley **162**

    character's sexuality 200-202, 204, 206
    death of **35**, 36, **37**, 239
    director/producer ambitions 106, 107, 112,
        113
    dislike of family members 41, 53, 65, 80
    drink driving 163-164, 165
    drunken behaviour 28, 125-126, 163-164,
        165, 167, 171, 177, 183, 188, 199,
        208, 214, 218, 224
    dubious claims 51, 53, 65, 90, 118, 139-
        140, 177-178, 194
    early theatrical career 55, 60, 66, 68
    family background 46, 47
    family roots 46-47
    female impersonation 92, 93, **94**, **95**, 98,
        99, 100, 101, **151**
    fire at 117 Middle Street 28, 225, **226**,
        227, 228-229, **230**, 231
    frugality 113-114, 206-207, 243
    funeral **38**, 39-40
    gambling 165, 167, 169
    heart attack 25
    ill health 25, 29, 32, 130, 154, 165, 167,
        243-244
    insecurities and anxieties 104, 114, 119,
        122, 156, 158, 185, 233, 234, 235,
        236, 241
    interaction with other people 28, 34, 157,
        209, 214, 217, 218, 224, 225
    knitting 134, 141
    last will and testament 34, 42
    love for cat 37, 177, 223
    love of music 30, 41
    mental health 184-185, 197, 199, 223-
        224, 233-234
    move to Deal 33, 207
    move to Mortlake 178, 181
    obsession with billing 85-86, 119, 120-
        121, 140, 144-146, 149, 157, 160,
        187, 193-194, 198

physical look 24, 25, 53, 55, 56, 67, 71,
   81, 84, 87, 90, 98, 105, 106, 154-155,
   173, 188, 193, **210**, 221, 235, 238,
   241, 243, 245
piano playing 24, 59, 69, 88, 106, 118,
   123, 169
professionalism, 55, 85, 106, 141, 150,
   152, 154, 156, 160, 169, 171-172,
   175, 182-183, 245
proposed amputation of legs 24-25, **28**,
   29, **31**, 33, 44
proposed autobiography 32, 233-234, 243-
   244
proposed TV series 141-144
pseudonym (Alice Dunne) **232**, 233, 238,
   243-244
relationship with mother 51, 52-53, 150,
   171, 198
religious beliefs 35, 175
rumours of illegitimacy 51-52, 53
schooling 46
sexuality 65, 98, 101, 147, 183, 219, 225,
   230
toupee 56, 131-132, 229
typecasting 104, 105, 106, 149-150, 170,
   193, 212, 236
use of language 132
voice 24, 104

Hawtrey, Sir Charles 23, 26, **46**, 62, 63, 65,
   67, 68, 69-70
Hay, Will 79-**80**, 81, 82, **83**, 84, 85, 86, 169,
   182, 207, 213
Hayes, Cynthia xviii, 59, 63, 66, 67, 68, 69
Hayes, Patricia **102**, 104, 144, 145, 153, 154,
   196
Helpmann, Robert 91
High and I 170
Hills, Courtney 225, 228
Hitchcock, Alfred 57, 78, 107, 213
Holloway, Stanley 118
Hordern, Michael 212
Houston, Renée 202, **204**
Howerd, Frankie 30, 37, 177, 178, 238
Hudd, Roy xviii, 56, **57**
Hudis, Norman xix, 135, 143, 148, 150, 152,
   157, 236, 241-242
Humphries, Violet 53, 55, 170
Hunter, Ian 77
Husbands Don't Count **124**, 125

I Only Arsked! **134**, **140**, 156
Inman, John 101
Inn For Trouble 160, 185

Jack and the Beanstalk (1967) 181, 183, 184,
   188
Jack and the Beanstalk (1979) 213-215
Jacques, Hattie 131, 142, **143**, 148, 149, 150,
   156, **161**, 167, **192**, 193, 194, 204, 220-
   221
Jailbirds 93, **96**, **97**, 101
James, Sid 31, 56, 155, 158, 160, 185, **186**,
   190, 193, 202
Jenkins, Martin xix, 65, 233
Johnson, Bryan xix, 32, 199, 209
Jumping For Joy 178
Just William 104

Kendall, Henry 107, 113
Kidd, Basil xix, 225, 227, 229
Kimber, William 233
Kinnear, Roy 212, 213
L'Epine Smith, Eric 141-142, 144, 145, 160

La Plante, Laura 77
Lanchester, Elsa 88, 182
Landau, David **70**
Lansiaux, Derek **100**
Last Day of Term, The 85, 86
Laughton, Charles 24, 88, 90, 113, 182
Laurel and Hardy 84
Leigh, Vivien 33, 90, **91**
Leon, Valerie **201**
Leonard, Fr. 35, 36
Leonard, Joy **vi**, xix, 44, 51, 53, 154, 157, 175,
   220-221, 223, 225, 234, 235, 243
Let the People Sing 105
Lewis, Roger 70, 224
Life With the Lyons 128
Love, Bessie 107
Loves Labour Lost 71
Lumley, Joanna 212

Maddison, Leigh 241
Man of the Moment (1935) 77
Manderson, David 122
March, Iris **79**
Marr, Johnny 239
Marry Me 77, 81
Marx, Groucho 169
Maschwitz, Eric 141-144
Matthew, Brian xix, 53, 88, 90, 194
Matthews, Francis xix, 131, 132, 215

Maxin, Ernest xix, 131, 148, 150, 152, 153, 154-155, 156, 159, 183, 215, 241
Maxin, Gerry 153
McLellan, Gary 228
McNaughton, Gus 107
Medwin, Michael xx, **132**, **134**, **140**, 141
Meet Me At Dawn 117
Members Only 90
Memoirs of a Chaise Longue 170, 171
Merry England 105
Miller, Max 78
Milligan, Spike 30
Moffatt, Graham 84
Moon, George 112
Morrissey 238, 239-241
Mother of Men 107
Mount, Peggy xx, 170, 185
Much Too Shy 105
Muller, Renate 77
Murder At Monte Carlo **74**, 77
Mutiny On the Bounty 90

Neagle, Anna 170
Nesbitt, Cathleen **79**
New Ambassador's Revue, The 98, **99**
New Faces (theatre) 98
New Faces (TV) 114, 214
Newley, Patrick xx, 32, 80, 117, 185, 188, 193, 219, 233
Nicholls, Billy 85
Nixon, David 188
Norman and Henry Bones 103, 104, 115, 123, 144, 145, 154, **196**

O'Callaghan, Richard xx, 76, 101, 104, 105, 163
Oflag 3 106-107
Old Chelsea 106, 118
Olivier, Laurence 24, 33, 193
Our House 148, **149**, **151**, 152, 153, 183

Pagliacci (opera) 238
Parry, Harry 112
Passport To Pimlico 117, 118, **119**, 182
Patch, Wally 107
Percival, Lance 160
Pertwee, Jon 156
Pertwee, Michael 120
Peter Pan 24, 46, 88, 198

Phillips, Aubrey xx, 35, 36, 42, 113, 139, 155, 156, 168, 177, 178, 181-182, 184, 188, 195, 197, 199, 200, 201, 206-207, 208, **209**, 211, 214, 219, 220, 222-223, 229, 234, 244
Phillips, Leslie 56, **143**
Plank, The 212
Please Turn Over 160
Plummer, Josephine 105
Pocock, Doris xx, 53, **54**, 55
Portman, Eric 93
Powell, Michael 77, 105, 213
Pressburger, Emeric 105
Princess and the Pea, The 212, **213**

Quality Street 68

Rawlinson, A. R. 120
Ray, Ted **102**, 104, **143**
Ray's A Laugh **102**, 104, 130
Reid, David 229
Richardson, Ralph 69, 167
Riggs, Geoffrey, E. O. 125
Robertson Justice, James **184**, 185
Robinson, Smokey 30
Robson, Flora 113
Rogers, Eric 173
Rogers, Peter xx, 26, 42, 134, 135, 136, 137, 150, 155, 157, 160, 163, 167, 169, 173, 177, 178, 184, 187, 193, 195, 198, 223, 245
Ronson, Mark 239
Ros, Edmundo 188
Ross, Robert 130, 173
Rossington, Norman 131, **132**, **140**, 141, **149**
Rothwell, Talbot 130, 161, 188
Rowlands, Patsy **190**
Royal, Anthony 220-221, 223

Sabotage 78, 107
Sabu 117
Scoop 98, **99**
Scott, Terry 36
Sellers, Peter 104
Senior, Dennis 218, 225
Servoss, Mary **70**
Shaw, Sandie 238
Sheridan, Dinah 88, **89**
Silvers, Phil **176**
Sim, Alastair 105
Sims, Joan xxi, 33, 93, **143**, 148, 155, 156, 157, 167, 175, 177, **180**, **190**, **191**, 204, 221, 234

Smiths, The 238, **239**
Snow White and the Seven Dwarfs xii, 42, 208, **209**, 211
Stephens, Barbara 42
Stephens, Peter 42, 225
Stirling, Pamela 113
Stone, Marianne **190**
Stop Exchange 185
Stop It Nurse! 156-**157**
Story of Shirley Yorke, The 88, **89**
Street Scene **70**, 71
Sullivan, Michael 170, 181
Summerfield, Eleanor **89**, 158
Summers, Jill 112
Supergran **235**, 236
Sykes, Eric 212

Taming of the Shrew, The 91
Tauber, Richard 105-106, 118, 156
Tell Her the Truth 116, 117
Tell Your Children 56, **57**, 59
Temporary Ladies 106
Ten Year Plan, The 105
Tesler, Brian 130
Thesiger, Ernest 99
This Freedom 59
This is Your Life **196**
Thomas, Gerald xxi, 26, 40, 76, 136, 160, 165, 169, 177, 178, 193, 194
Trouble in the House 107
Truth At Last, The 23, 63
Twelfth Night (play) 238

Uncle Harry 107

Vice Versa 114

Walsh, Bernard xxi, 28, 33, 39, 41, 42, 65, **176**, 207, 220, 244
Ward, Bill 116
Wareing, Lesley **91**
Warren, Betty 118
Well Done Henry 78-**79**
What a Carry On (book) 65
What Do We Do Now? 107, **108-111**, 112
Where the Rainbow Ends 46, 62, 63, **66**, 68
Where's That Fire? 81, **83**
Whitfield, June **192**
Williams, Brock 142
Williams, Frank xxi, 131, 132, 134
Williams, Kenneth xiv, 24, 26, 30, 37, 38, 56, 84, 90, 93, 137, 139, **143**, 155, 156, 157, 159, 163, 165, **166**, 169, **172**, 175, **176**, 177, 181, 183, 185, 187, 188, **190**, 193, 200, 204, 206, 209, 221-222, 230, 238
Will Hay Programme, The 86
Willis, Michael 116, 117, 118
Willis, Peter xxi, 40
Wilson, Anthony C. 104
Windsor, Barbara xxi, 26, 30, 31, 37, 38, 155, 156, 165, **166**, 167, 168, 204, 209
Windsor, Lucy 231
Winston, Bruce **100**
Woodley, Joan xxi, 59
Wright, Denis 72-73

You Can't Take It With You 107
You're Only Young Twice 125, **126**

Zeta One **184**, 185

HOSPICES GIFT AID ITEM
PRICE.
No. 14730